Entrepreneurial Ecosystems

Based on extensive fieldwork, this book demonstrates how gender is an organizing principle of entrepreneurial ecosystems and makes a difference in how ecosystem resources are assembled and how they can be accessed. By bringing visibility to how ecosystem actors are heterogeneous across identities, interactions and experiences, the book highlights the role and complexity of individual, organizational, and institutional factors working in concert to create and maintain gendered inequities. *Entrepreneurial Ecosystems* provides research-driven insights around effective organizational practices and policies aimed at remedying gendered and intersectional inequalities associated with entrepreneurship activities and economic growth. Proposing a typology of four ecosystem identities, it highlights how some might be more amenable and organized towards gender inclusion and change, while others may be much more difficult to change, reorganize and restructure. It offers scholars, students, practitioners and policymakers insights about gender in relation to analyzing entrepreneurial ecosystems and for fostering inclusive economic development policies.

BANU OZKAZANC-PAN, Ph.D. is Professor of Practice in Engineering and Founder and Director of the Venture Capital Inclusion Lab at Brown University. Banu is co-editor-in-chief of Gender, Work & Organization. Her research on entrepreneurial ecosystems has been awarded grants from The Ewing Marion Kauffman Foundation and INBIA/JP Morgan Chase. Recently, she testified at the US Senate Committee on Small Business & Entrepreneurship to speak about the importance of women and minority investors and entrepreneurs. She is a member of CNBC's Disruptor fifty Advisory Council, a global group of fifty-five leading thinkers in the field of innovation and entrepreneurship.

SUSAN CLARK MUNTEAN, Ph.D. is Associate Professor of Management at the University of North Carolina, Asheville. Her research strives to improve our understanding of entrepreneurial support organizations, entrepreneurial ecosystems, and corporate and family business, particularly with respect to governance, inclusion, politics and gender equality. Recognitions for this research include a grant award from The Kauffman Foundation, the United States Association for Small Business and Entrepreneurship's ('USASBE') best paper in entrepreneurship and ethics award in 2017, USASBE's best paper in family business honorable mention in 2014, and best paper in women's entrepreneurship at the International Council for Small Business in 2011.

Entrepreneurial Ecosystems

A Gender Perspective

BANU OZKAZANC-PAN
Brown University

SUSAN CLARK MUNTEAN
University of North Carolina, Asheville

CAMBRIDGE
UNIVERSITY PRESS

CAMBRIDGE
UNIVERSITY PRESS

Shaftesbury Road, Cambridge CB2 8EA, United Kingdom

One Liberty Plaza, 20th Floor, New York, NY 10006, USA

477 Williamstown Road, Port Melbourne, VIC 3207, Australia

314–321, 3rd Floor, Plot 3, Splendor Forum, Jasola District Centre, New Delhi – 110025, India

103 Penang Road, #05–06/07, Visioncrest Commercial, Singapore 238467

Cambridge University Press is part of Cambridge University Press & Assessment, a department of the University of Cambridge.

We share the University's mission to contribute to society through the pursuit of education, learning and research at the highest international levels of excellence.

www.cambridge.org
Information on this title: www.cambridge.org/9781009010498

DOI: 10.1017/9781009023641

First published 2022
First paperback edition 2024

A catalogue record for this publication is available from the British Library

Library of Congress Cataloging-in-Publication data
Names: Ozkazanc-Pan, Banu, 1975– author. | Clark Muntean, Susan, 1971– author.
Title: Entrepreneurial ecosystems : a gender perspective / Banu Ozkazanc-Pan, Brown University, Rhode Island, Susan Clark Muntean, University of North Carolina, Asheville.
Description: Cambridge, United Kingdom; New York, NY : Cambridge University Press, 2022. | Includes bibliographical references and index.
Identifiers: LCCN 2021025377 (print) | LCCN 2021025378 (ebook) | ISBN 9781316519431 (hardback) | ISBN 9781009010498 (paperback) | ISBN 9781009023641 (epub)
Subjects: LCSH: Entrepreneurship. | Businesswomen.
Classification: LCC HB615 .O95 2022 (print) | LCC HB615 (ebook) | DDC 658.4/21082–dc23
LC record available at https://lccn.loc.gov/2021025377
LC ebook record available at https://lccn.loc.gov/2021025378

ISBN   978-1-316-51943-1   Hardback
ISBN   978-1-009-01049-8   Paperback

Cambridge University Press & Assessment has no responsibility for the persistence or accuracy of URLs for external or third-party internet websites referred to in this publication and does not guarantee that any content on such websites is, or will remain, accurate or appropriate.

Contents

Tables

Preface

This book is the result of many years of fieldwork, spanning multiple cities in the United States, with the aim of understanding the drivers and mechanisms of gender inclusion (and exclusion) in entrepreneurial ecosystems. Our approach has been multifaceted, deriving insights from feminist scholarship in entrepreneurship, sociology, and economics to highlight assumptions in entrepreneurial ecosystems research and frameworks. It has taken many iterations and years of writing on this topic to provide a holistic framework that not only brings together different disciplines but does so in a manner that pushes forward research and thinking in entrepreneurship studies. We have found much support for our research but have also been forced to answer ongoing questions about why gender matters. It seems that the scholarly community in entrepreneurship still considers gender as a variable or an identity dimension rather than an organizing principle of society and the economy – something we explicitly address and debunk in our book.

With these considerations, our goal is to critically examine underlying assumptions about the homogenous nature of ecosystem actors to highlight how identities, interactions, and institutions impact how and why certain entrepreneurs may find themselves distanced from the resources existing to support entrepreneurship activities. Rather than relying only on one dimension or level of analysis to explain the marginalization of women with respect to accessing networks, resources, and funding in ecosystems, our research points to a multilevel and complex system of individual actions, organizational practices, and institutional factors working concurrently. Taken together, these attributes contribute to the production and replication of entrepreneurial ecosystem dynamics that are gendered and racialized. In other words, economic activities in the form of entrepreneurship are always embedded within power dynamics of social structures, giving way to gendered social relations that impact how and why women, particularly women of color, continue to face organizational and institutional barriers.

In outlining these factors, we contribute to a much more complex understanding of entrepreneurial ecosystems as sites where gendered reproduction of social relations takes shape in the context of economic exchanges. By doing so, we provide insights about different types of entrepreneurial ecosystems through our concept of "ecosystem identity." This provides guidance about the complexity of simultaneous factors that define an ecosystem's ability to engage in social change, namely that of gender inclusion. We hope that our research findings and recommendations for policymakers and leaders in ecosystems provide much-needed insights about why gender inclusion remains elusive even in contemporary times and despite its value in promoting economic growth. Moreover, our research changes the conversations around the ways in which we understand how "gender makes a difference" in our lives and in our scholarship.

Banu would like to thank her family for their unwavering support during the writing of this book, including during the pandemic. And a special thank you to Lila and Noah for helping pick the design cover and Jeff for supplying coffee!

Both the authors thank the Ewing Marion Kauffman Foundation for supporting much of the research through grants.

1 Introduction

In recent years, entrepreneurs and entrepreneurship have become an important topic of conversation in established organizations, academia, policy circles, and popular media. The seemingly exponential growth and success of startups (despite evidence that the rate of startups has gone down) coupled with the importance of entrepreneurship for job creation have fueled the rise of scholarly research as well as public and private support for entrepreneurs. Influential foundations, think tanks, and institutions, such as the Ewing Marion Kauffman Foundation, the Bill and Melinda Gates Foundation, and the World Bank among others, have put up millions of dollars to support entrepreneurship in terms of scholarly work, practical solutions, and startup training in the United States (US) and around the world. Over the same time period, the popularity of US-based shows featuring entrepreneurial activity, such as *Shark Tank*, growing social media attention toward (and notoriety of) founders (e.g. Elon Musk, Elizabeth Holmes, Adam Neumann, etc.), and celebrity-founded companies (such as Goop by Gwyneth Paltrow and Fenty Beauty by Rihanna) have allowed entrepreneurs and startups to capture social imaginaries across the globe. Books by well-known and respected entrepreneurs, such as Brad Feld's (2012) *Startup Community*, have become popular in creating a sense of hope, optimism, and opportunity through intentional efforts to create entrepreneurial communities. In this sense, entrepreneurs have come to occupy a central place in people's imaginations as individuals who have achieved success through their business ventures as much as through their personalities and personal antics.

Such individuals have become "influencers" in their ability to shape conversations around business and related topics and to influence behaviors in society. This has been possible through their online platforms and the social media attention related to their ventures, often garnering millions of followers through a combination of their celebrity status, their companies, and their personal behaviors. While celebrities may live more public lives – to the extent that they are used to media and fan attention, both in its positive and negative iterations – the scrutiny and attention that has been bestowed on business founders and leaders is unique in its blending of the personal, social, and political in the context of business. As Davis and White (2015) suggest, this could be seen as a new era of corporate activism whereby business leaders are expected to take political stances and engage in activist behavior on social and other issues. These expectations and behaviors stand in stark contrast to previous decades, when such behavior was considered outside the domain of business and organizational boundaries. Entrepreneurs are also taking on more activist positions related to social, environmental, and political issues through their platforms and engaged audiences. It seems that in times of economic difficulty, entrepreneurs and the practice of entrepreneurship have been called on to engage conversations around individual success "despite the odds" and, at times, seem to embody an individualistic hero narrative (Hamilton et al., 2009). As Anderson and Warren (2011) suggest, the spectacle of entrepreneurship and the ways in which entrepreneurial identity takes shape in public spaces plays an important part in bringing together the rational and the emotional to create strategic advantages for entrepreneurs.

I.I THE GROWTH OF ENTREPRENEURSHIP

Importantly, these trends have ignited discussions around the infinite possibilities for success that can come about from one's business ventures. Popular publications, such as *Entrepreneur* magazine, coupled with mainstream books by entrepreneurs, academics, and celebrities aimed at providing guidance for entrepreneurs and those aspiring to have their own startups have helped fuel an entrepreneur revolution. In this context, extensive social media rhetoric has come to associate entrepreneurs, entrepreneurial action, and entrepreneurship with success, and being entrepreneurial has now become a badge of empowerment, agency, and innovation. A cursory search on LinkedIn, a professional networking platform, yields many individuals who now self-identify as "entrepreneur," "founder," "thought leader," "influencer," and so forth. This way of presenting oneself on a professional platform has emerged only recently as a way of identifying and differentiating individuals, contrasting with traditional occupational descriptors such as "manager" or "business leader."

Within the domain of established organizations, entrepreneurial thinking, innovation, and creativity are now seen as valuable ways of ensuring competitive success and differentiating one's brand and company from others. In the last two decades, intrapreneurship has become an important asset within established organizations (Antoncic & Hisrich, 2001). Generally understood as the practice of adopting "innovative activities and orientations such as development of new products, services, technologies, administrative techniques, strategies, and competitive postures" (Antoncic & Hisrich, 2003: 9) in established businesses guided generally by hierarchy and coordinating and control mechanisms, intrapreneurship provides new ideas and directions for organizations operating in a global context.

Entrepreneurial aspirations have also grown in the context of academic institutions. Classes on subjects such as "design thinking," "creativity," "entrepreneurship," and "starting your business" are now readily available in the curriculums of many schools, ranging from middle schools to postgraduate programs in higher education. Many university students now aspire to be entrepreneurs rather than managers, an emergent trend based on the seeming opportunities reflected in entrepreneurship as a practice and as a way of thinking. To address this new wave of professional aspiration and, at the same time, fuel it, entrepreneurship centers have been established across universities in the US and in many other countries around the world, with the idea that entrepreneurship can be taught (see Rideout & Gray, 2013; Winkel et al., 2013). In particular, entrepreneurial education and training has become an important area of investment in universities (Henry, Hill, & Leitch, 2005a, b). These new additions to educational curricula reflect the changing times, as the role of entrepreneurs and their ability to think beyond existing resources have developed into an aspiration, something that students want to emulate. As such, the growth of student-centric entrepreneurship activities across institutes of higher learning has created a new dynamism around jobs and the potential for making one's own decisions about careers rather than being beholden to bosses, corporations, or organizations. Yet within academia, entrepreneurial thinking isn't reserved only for students.

Administrators, generally seen as adhering to bureaucracy, are now aiming to do more with less as they pivot their ways of addressing resource constraints in creative ways. While certainly associated with cost-cutting measures, entrepreneurial thinking is seen as an important skill set to possess even at administrative levels. There have also been increased calls to create better and more synergies between universities and industry through technology transfer centers, research and industry collaborations on innovation projects, and commercialization of faculty research and work (Markman et al., 2005) while, at the same, questioning the role and effectiveness of intermediaries between industry and university research (Villani, Rasmussen, & Grimaldi, 2017). Fueled by a sense of choice, economic opportunity, and authenticity to live a meaningful and purposeful life, entrepreneurial dreams are now supported by many different stakeholders, ranging from educational institutions to nonprofit organizations to entrepreneur support organizations (ESOs) to government actors. Even supranational organizations such as the United Nations (UN) and the World Bank have come to recognize the ways in which entrepreneurship can provide good job options when governments and the private sector are unable or unwilling to provide living wage opportunities. Thus, beyond the individual hero-mythology associated with entrepreneurs, there are economic narratives that dominate conversations around the value and role of entrepreneurship for economies.

I.2 ENTREPRENEURSHIP AND ECONOMIC GROWTH

There is long-standing research that points to the ways entrepreneurs and startups are important contributors to economic growth and development (Acs & Storey, 2004; Acs & Szerb, 2007; Wennekers & Thurik, 1999; Wong, Ho & Autio, 2005), a discussion that is now being taken seriously by policymakers (Thurik, 2009). The relevance of entrepreneurship and startups for the economy has resulted in increased focus on them through national policy initiatives undertaken by private sector organizations and the public sector as well as global institutions. For example, in the US, Venture for America is an organization that offers paid fellowships for recent college graduates to work in startups across the nation. The aim is for individuals to gain a set of business and leadership skills that can be used to start their own companies, thereby creating opportunities for economic growth and employment. In the European Union (EU), the European Commission has an explicit goal of supporting entrepreneurship as a key driver of growth across member countries. Their mission on this front is stated as:

> The European Commission's objective is to encourage more people to become entrepreneurs, set up their own companies and create jobs in the EU. To help them do so, the Commission runs an exchange programme Erasmus for Young Entrepreneurs and supports [the] introduction of entrepreneurship education in schools in all EU countries.
>
> *European Commission (2020)*

Globally, the World Bank[1] recognizes the ways in which innovation and entrepreneurship can drive economic growth and has created a division focusing specifically on these issues across regions and countries. This division advises on and provides insights on policies that can be beneficial to individual countries as well as

---

[1] See www.worldbank.org/en/topic/innovation-entrepreneurship

regions aiming to create jobs for millions of citizens. Across the globe, the Global Entrepreneurship Monitor[2] (GEM) provides insights into different policies, support mechanisms, attitudes, and cultural/social norms among other dimensions, creating a broad overview of how different nations are engaging with and supporting entrepreneurship efforts among their citizens. To this end, data-driven approaches to entrepreneurship policies are gaining traction across many nations (see GEM, 2020).

1.3   ENTREPRENEURSHIP MEETS PANDEMIC MEETS BLACKS LIVES MATTER

The growing attention toward entrepreneurship across a range of domains has come at a time when, globally, economic and political uncertainty have impacted job opportunities in many nations. Most recently, a global pandemic caused by the COVID-19 virus has upended business as usual across the globe, as interconnected and interdependent supply chains, human labor, and financial markets have come to the brink of collapse. While the long-term impact on economies and societies around the world is yet to be known, what has become clear in the short term is the fragility of various economic, sociocultural, and political structures in addressing the associated challenges of the pandemic. During this time, businesses across all industries, sectors, and geographies, and those of all sizes, are being impacted financially and socially. As the scale and scope of the impact unfolds, it is likely that business owners, particularly of small businesses and startups, will face additional struggles related to financial solvency, hiring, and workforce availability due to health concerns and cash flow among many other challenges.[3]

---

[2] www.gemconsortium.org
[3] See www.nytimes.com/2020/04/01/technology/virus-start-ups-pummeled-layoffs-unwinding.html

At the same time, the pandemic has shown that massive disruptions in economies and societies have gendered consequences,[4] often exacerbating gendered inequities in the domains of health, economics, education, and society, as many white-collar workers have started to work from home. The brunt of childcare, eldercare, and pastoral care still continues to be taken up by women in the global context despite the new ways in which work is being reorganized to address health concerns related to the pandemic (Care.org, 2020). Already, research shows a gender gap in working hours of between 20 percent and 50 percent as women have reduced their work hours due to home demands, likely resulting in decreased opportunities for advancement and promotion post-pandemic (Collins et al., 2021). As organizations move to contain further outbreaks related to the virus, remote working, learning, and teaching have become the new normal in many sectors, but only for the privileged workers who are not considered essential workers or who have jobs that can be done remotely. Within this context, social distancing is a privilege exercised predominantly by the wealthy or those with teleworking-amenable jobs in developed nations (Ayyub, 2020).

While some governments struggle to mitigate the economic consequences of the pandemic as best they can, others have been quicker to provide relief for small businesses and, specifically, women entrepreneurs. For example, Canada's Women Entrepreneur Knowledge Hub has already assembled a list of resources for women entrepreneurs, which are now available through national and regional governments as well as public and private organizations.[5] In the US, the national response has been much slower and has generally taken shape piecemeal at the state and even city levels. While a historic $2 trillion stimulus package was passed on March 25, 2020, the ability of women-led businesses to sustain themselves during this time is being tested. The new Coronavirus Aid, Relief and Economic Security

---

[4] www.care.org/sites/default/files/gendered_implications_of_covid-19_-_full_paper.pdf
[5] See https://wekh.ca/covid-19-resources-for-women-entrepreneurs/

Act is part of the massive relief bill.[6] The bill provides financial support for various sectors and industries, including around $44 billion for education, around $154 billion for hospitals and public health groups, around $340 billion for local and state governments, $377 billion for small businesses, $500 billion for large corporations, and around $560 billion for individuals. For small businesses, where the majority of startups would likely go under, there are various programs, including emergency grants up to $10,000 to cover costs associated with running the business (operation costs), forgivable loans of up to $10 million per business, and six months of relief for businesses who already have Small Business Administration (SBA) loans. Yet despite these initial measures, the allocation for SBA loans for small businesses had already been depleted as of April 16, 2020, triggering conversations about additional support and funding for small businesses struggling to survive in the midst of the pandemic – conversations and bipartisan wrangling that is currently taking place (midsummer 2020). In all likelihood, many small businesses, including those owned by women, will not survive the economic impact associated with the measures taken to mitigate public health considerations.

Already, emerging data suggest the devastating effects on the economy and specifically on businesses that are owned by women or minorities. Fairlie finds that

> the number of active business owners in the United States
> plummeted by 3.3 million or 22 percent over the crucial two-month
> window from February to April 2020. The drop in business owners
> was the largest on record, and losses were felt across nearly all
> industries and even for incorporated businesses. African-American
> businesses were hit especially hard experiencing a 41 percent drop.
> Latinx business owners fell by 32 percent, and Asian business

---

[6] See https://assets.documentcloud.org/documents/6819239/FINAL-FINAL-CARES-ACT .pdf

owners dropped by 26 percent. Simulations indicate that industry compositions partly placed these groups at a higher risk of losses. Immigrant business owners experienced substantial losses of 36 percent. Female-owned businesses were also disproportionately hit by 25 percent.

(2020: 1)

While some businesses have rebounded, more recent research finds that the decline in Black business ownership is three times that of other groups and that Black women-owned businesses have had the biggest losses.[7] These findings suggest that recovery from the pandemic will be much more difficult for businesses owned by minority and immigrant women over the long run. Such considerations are quite important in the context of the pandemic but also the ongoing social unrest and the movement against racial injustice, including through Black Lives Matter.

As historic racial inequities continue to plague US society in the domains of housing, health, education, government/political representation, and labor markets/employment among other areas, Black Lives Matter has become a large social movement highlighting these ongoing racial injustices that are evident across all manners of organization and institution. As such, understanding these inequalities as they are manifest in entrepreneurship and opportunities for business success requires a dedicated analysis – a point raised in our discussion in Chapter 7, where we take an intersectional approach to understanding the ways identities, interactions, and institutions intersect to create opportunities for some but not other entrepreneurs. In all, we recognize that the pandemic and Black Lives Matter are defining moments of our time and relevant for our analyses moving forward, particularly in relation to gender and business ownership.

---

[7] https://cdn.advocacy.sba.gov/wp-content/uploads/2020/08/31083212/Black-Business-Owners-Hit-Hard-By-Pandemic.pdf

I.4   ON GENDER AND ENTREPRENEURSHIP

To this end, at the state level, some cautious optimism is warranted, as governors are putting together resources to support small business owners, including specific funds for women business owners. For example, in the state of Connecticut, the lieutenant governor is providing information and resources for women-owned businesses. Across the US, private, public, and nonprofit groups are each providing different resources for women-owned/led businesses.[8] Despite the array of attention being given to female entrepreneurs, sectoral effects of stay-at-home orders, contracting global demand, and lack of available childcare and in-person schooling options are threatening to reverse the past decades' progress by aggravating the gender gap in entrepreneurship (Clark Muntean, 2021).

Weaknesses in governance structures that have resulted in chronic unemployment or underemployment have also provided incentive for individuals to engage in entrepreneurship, particularly in the context of developing nations. Coupled with growing concerns over environmental degradation, climate change, and sustainability, entrepreneurship has become a solution to the many ills plaguing societies and businesses globally. Ranging from microfinance to urban farming, from fintech accelerators to drones for predicting weather patterns impacting crops in developing nations, entrepreneurs and entrepreneurship have become the de facto focus in conversations around creative solutions, innovation, and jobs.

Within this context, the ways in which gender, race, and other relations of difference impact who can become a successful entrepreneur and, equally importantly, how entrepreneurship gets studied have yet to be examined fully. Moreover, the opportunities and resources that are available toward entrepreneurship are not necessarily readily accessible by everyone who aspires toward starting their own business. From a scholarly perspective, understanding the

---

[8] See www.thehelm.co/emergency-funding-female-founders/

assumptions driving research on entrepreneurship and the policies supporting entrepreneurship can offer novel insights into blind spots, in particular for those groups who may have traditionally been marginalized in academic research and in policy considerations. For example, based on research by the International Labour Organization (ILO, 2020a), around 72 percent of all chief executives and senior officials and legislators around the world are men. Given that women are not represented in senior positions, these numbers indicate that decision-making and resource allocation toward entrepreneurial activities in organizations and by governments can potentially be biased against women. Further to this consideration, the gender gap in labor force participation globally is 43 percent: 95 percent of men between the ages of 25 and 54 participate in the labor force compared to just 52 percent of women (ILO, 2020b). The main explanation for this gap is childcare responsibilities, which, globally, still fall disproportionately on women. As a consequence, women in general and mothers in particular face additional challenges related to entrepreneurship in the form of decreased mentorship and networking opportunities, access to capital, and biases related to their ability to be successful (Krause & Fetsch, 2016).

Toward this end, a growing number of scholars have called attention to and critiqued the foundational assumptions of mainstream entrepreneurship research, including its epistemological and methodological approaches rooted in positivism (Essers et al., 2017; Tedmanson et al., 2012). Generally under the umbrella of critical entrepreneurship studies, such work has focused on conversations and approaches generally not examined within the broader domain of entrepreneurship. These critical works join others from feminist traditions that question the underlying male-centric foundation of entrepreneurship research and reorient existing frameworks by making central the role of gender in theorizing entrepreneurship (Calás, Smircich, & Bourne, 2009; Greer & Greene, 2003). Currently, the study of women in the context of entrepreneurship is often guided by gender binary notions of male versus female (Brush, de

Bruin, & Welter, 2009) rather than gender relations and gendering of entrepreneurship practices and activities (see, for example, the work of Ahl, 2002; also Bruni, Gherardi, & Poggio, 2004a, b). More recently, scholars have focused on the impact of gender nonconforming behavior in entrepreneurship leadership, exposing how binary notions of gender do not reflect the complexity of lived experiences (Patterson, Mavin, & Turner, 2012). In fact, new research highlighting liminal gender, or the ways in which individuals can be between or "betwixt" stereotypical male and female normative frameworks, in the context of entrepreneurship based on STEM (science, technology, engineering, and math) sheds much needed light on the complexity of lived gender experiences (Birkner, 2020). In highlighting and expanding on these existing frameworks, our approach is to deploy gender as a multidimensional concept and understand it as an organizing principle of societies globally. To understand the ways in which gender can be brought to bear on entrepreneurship as a field of academic inquiry, as a field of practice, and as an economic policy, we focus explicitly on the arena of entrepreneurial ecosystems.

1.5   ENTREPRENEURIAL ECOSYSTEMS: BRIEF OVERVIEW AND GENDER-LENS APPROACH

Using entrepreneurial ecosystems as a framework allows examination and consideration of the multiple actors and stakeholders involved in entrepreneurship. In general, these ecosystems can be defined as a community of entrepreneurs engaged in reciprocal social and economic exchanges in the context of intermediary organizations, other actors, and institutions. As an emergent theoretical framework within the broader entrepreneurship field, entrepreneurial ecosystems have gained traction for conceptualizing the various networked actors engaged in entrepreneurship in and across different contexts. The entrepreneurial ecosystem framework provides insights into the networked, relational, and processual elements of entrepreneurial activities, focusing explicitly on the ways actors engage with each other, with organizations, and with institutions. The dynamic examination of actors within the context of entrepreneurship has proved to be quite popular with academics, as it has brought focus to the agentic ways individuals engage with, access, and navigate the various resources required for successful startups. Similarly, entrepreneurial ecosystems have also found resonance with policymakers; and given that entrepreneurship is often heralded as a path of economic development and job creation (Harper, 2003), creating robust entrepreneurial ecosystems through institutions has become an important policy tool (Acs, Desai, & Hessels, 2008).

With the development and popularity of this approach to the study of entrepreneurship, there has also been a robust and critical perspective questioning the boundaries and spatial focus of the concept and a concern over the lack of clarity on exactly which actors are connected to each other, how, and why (see Alvedalen & Boschma, 2017). Moreover, questions about the boundaries of ecosystems vis-à-vis cities and other geographic considerations have also grown – where are the boundaries of ecosystems and who decides what they are? These and many other questions remain to be debated and researched within the entrepreneurship field. At the same time, emerging scholarship within the entrepreneurial ecosystem framework has emphasized that ecosystem diversity and coherence are important considerations, particularly in explaining resilience of some entrepreneurial ecosystems over others, suggesting that differentiation between ecosystems is a key element that should be examined (Roundy, Brockman, & Bradshaw, 2017). Thus, while the concept remains popular, it has also come under scrutiny for its lack of precision and focus on providing clarity in relation to the dynamics of entrepreneurial relationships, activities, and actors (Brown & Mason, 2017). In fact, some scholarship seems to include just about every actor and institution possible when considering the ways entrepreneurial ecosystems take shape and function (Spigel, 2017), making it difficult to understand how and why certain relationships form, how particular actors may occupy different power positions in relation to others, and why certain institutional factors matter more than others.

1.6 OVERVIEW OF BOOK AND CONTRIBUTIONS TO ENTREPRENEURIAL ECOSYSTEM SCHOLARSHIP

We contribute to these conversations in the entrepreneurial ecosystem literature through a critical gender perspective and provide insights as to the ways in which gender makes a difference for the conceptualization and study of entrepreneurial ecosystems. In doing so, our aim is to highlight that rather than being a binary formation or a variable, gender is a complex lived experience drawing from a range of male, female, and nonconforming dimensions that are manifest in obvious as well as more subtle ways. That is, gender is not necessarily just about categories of women and men, but rather a set of socially constructed relationships and differences that manifest in visible and invisible ways in social interactions, activities, and practices. In the case of entrepreneurship, gender makes a difference in terms of how activities are defined, how resources assembled and accessed, and how success and identity factors come into play in the course of engaging in business ventures (see Clark Muntean & Ozkazanc-Pan, 2015). These dimensions of gender are relevant for understanding and analyzing ecosystem identity, a concept we create and examine to underscore the ways ecosystems are organized and function based on informal and formal institutional factors, highlighting, in particular, how different identities may be more open to gender inclusion.

Our goal is to demonstrate, through the concept of ecosystem identity, the multifaceted, various ways gender contributes to a richer understanding of entrepreneurial ecosystems and in doing so, show that by bringing gender in only as a variable to compare male and female entrepreneurs, much nuance and complexity is missed in the ways gender becomes enacted in entrepreneurship and ecosystems. Based on institutional factors, we provide a typology of four ecosystem identities by categorizing informal and formal systems as strong or weak and/or emergent or established. We label these identities as "nascent" (weak informal and emergent formal institutional factors), "communal" (strong informal and emergent formal institutional factors), "bureaucratic" (weak informal and established formal institutional factors), and "stable" (strong informal and established formal institutional factors). Based on these identities, our approach is to categorize entrepreneurial ecosystems, highlighting how some might be more amenable and organized toward gender inclusion and change in general, while others may be much more difficult to change and/or reorganize and restructure. In other words, gender is not simply a property of an individual, but an important organizing principle of society which is reflected in institutions, both in terms of formal economic, political, and legal systems as well as informal ones comprising belief systems, norms, and values.

The institutional consideration is important because in many metrics, scales, and questionnaires, women are seen as a type of entrepreneur without consideration of how the very institutions of society are gendered. For example, one of the most widely used data sets comes from GEM, which considers women entrepreneurs as a "special topic" in the broader entrepreneurship research they undertake globally.[9] While this in itself is not necessarily unhelpful, it does signify that the category of women is seen as distinct from entrepreneurs, which are assumed to be male. Without voicing or uncovering these assumptions, conversations around inclusion in scholarship attending to entrepreneurship and entrepreneurial ecosystems generally focus on what women can be doing differently; for example, telling women to pitch differently in the face of gendered questions (Kanze et al., 2018). This "fix the women" approach focuses on individual behavior changes women should enact, rather than examining the related and interconnected ways individuals factors, organizational practices, and institutionalized sociocultural norms are gendered. It also leaves out ecosystem identity as an important aspect for understanding the context in which many of these lived

---

[9] See www.gemconsortium.org/report

experiences and relationships take shape – some ecosystems are simply better suited to adapt and change toward gender inclusion.

In many ways, when research is guided by the assumption that gender can be equated with biological sex and, thus, treated as a variable, comparisons between male and female entrepreneurs are then assumed to yield insights about differences in behavior, attitudes, practices, and so forth that are based on gender. This tautological approach confounds the socially constructed and relational aspects of differences with those that are biological or genetics-based – a consideration that is probably best left to biological sciences than social science scholarship. Our approach is to highlight further the ways in which gender gets done and the ways in which gender organizes activities and possibilities for action and connection in entrepreneurial ecosystems. Without a multidimensional analysis that considers individuals, interactions, and institutions, gender inclusion cannot come about only by changing behaviors. Ecosystem identity allows us to provide a set of institutional concepts and language to understand how these elements may play out and, in turn, may influence how gender gets done (Bruni, Gherardi, & Poggio, 2004b) and how changes toward gender equality might take shape.

Yet there is much more work to be done to realize how gender underscores the ways in which entrepreneurial ecosystems are organized and replicated through social interactions, economic exchanges, and community building. Looking at the existing literature at the intersections of gender and entrepreneurship (Jennings & Brush, 2013) or gender and entrepreneurial ecosystems (Brush et al., 2019; McAdam, Harrison, & Leitch, 2019; Manolova et al., 2017), we find that critical and feminist iterations are still quite rare, with some notable exceptions (Calás, Smircich, & Bourne, 2007, 2009; Henry, Foss, & Ahl, 2016; Ozkazanc-Pan, 2015). Based on feminist insights, we build a new understanding of entrepreneurial ecosystems as a gendered phenomenon with implications for concerns around inclusion and inclusive economic growth. By considering the centrality of gender as an organizing principle of entrepreneurial ecosystems, we highlight shortcomings of existing approaches and also expand on them to demonstrate the role and complexity of individual, organizational, and institutional factors working in concert to create and maintain gendered inequities. But beyond this, we also highlight ways to expand current entrepreneurship scholarship to recognize the role of gender as a dimension of theory and theorizing, an epistemological concern around how we know and theorize ecosystems, rather than gender being viewed as a static variable based on biology or even genetics. We offer insights around effective organizational practices and policies aimed at remedying gendered inequalities associated with entrepreneurship and economic growth, a hallmark consideration for many ESOs, supranational institutions, government leaders, and policymakers across the globe. In all, this book provides insights into the relevance of gender for understanding entrepreneurial ecosystems and for supporting inclusive economic development.

In order to accomplish these aims, the book brings together insights from fieldwork carried out by the authors between 2014 and 2019 across multiple cities in the US, including Boston, St. Louis, and Asheville. Beyond this introductory chapter, the book is organized as follows. Chapter 2 provides a foundation for the different streams of research and concepts in entrepreneurial ecosystem literature. Chapter 3 then provides a gender perspective arriving from different theoretical traditions, thus expanding our understanding of gender beyond sex and making relevant how inclusion can be understood from these various perspectives in relation to entrepreneurial ecosystem research. Chapter 3 focuses on aspects of gender inclusion in entrepreneurial ecosystems and includes insights and key ideas from feminist scholarship in the domain of gender and gender relations. Chapters 4–6 each provide insights focusing on a single level of the multidimensional and interrelated elements that simultaneously can yield inclusion or, conversely, continued exclusion of particular groups from entrepreneurial ecosystems. These include, respectively, the level of individuals, organizations, and institutions, and the chapters provide insights from each of the three cities when applicable. Chapter 7 provides an intersectionality analysis, focusing on Boston as a case study, to underscore the multiple and intersecting ways gender, race, and immigrant status impact identities, interactions, and institutions in entrepreneurial ecosystems. Chapter 8, the final chapter, provides a holistic framework for moving forward with inclusive entrepreneurial ecosystems and economic growth policies. Below, additional details about each chapter provide more nuanced insights for readers who may be interested in understanding the structure and organization of the book.

1.6.1 Chapter 1: Introduction

The first chapter provides an overview of the rise and popularity of entrepreneurship as a practice and as a scholarly field of research. It notes how entrepreneurship has been shown to contribute positively to economic development and indicates that scholarship related to promoting and supporting entrepreneurs through building robust entrepreneurial ecosystems is on the rise. In general, entrepreneurial ecosystems can be defined as a community of entrepreneurs engaged in reciprocal social and economic exchanges in the context of intermediary organizations, other actors, and institutions. The popularity of the entrepreneurial ecosystems concept is evident in the growth of research dedicated to the topic in the last decade across several academic disciplines. Such research has focused on theory refinement as well as the development of metrics and "playbooks" for communities that want to foster entrepreneurship. At the same time, policymakers are increasingly supporting the building of successful entrepreneurial ecosystems in their cities and states through public funding. Despite the greater attention to entrepreneurial ecosystems in both the academic and policy world, there continues to be a dearth of research that addresses the relevance of gender for understanding and supporting entrepreneurial ecosystems. This chapter emphasizes the relevance and importance of a gender perspective for understanding how and why entrepreneurial ecosystems may not benefit female entrepreneurs in the same ways that they benefit male entrepreneurs.

It provides insights into the ways a gender perspective can contribute to a new conceptual model of entrepreneurial ecosystems and eventually lead to effective policies for inclusive economic development.

1.6.2   Chapter 2: Entrepreneurial Ecosystems: An Overview

The second chapter concentrates on the concept of entrepreneurial ecosystems (Auerswald, 2015; Bosma & Holvoet, 2015; Spigel, 2017), providing various ways to conceptualize and define it and then moving on to discuss its importance for supporting economic development. Given the growing body of work on entrepreneurial ecosystems, the chapter first outlines how the field of entrepreneurial ecosystems evolved from existing work on clusters (Motoyama, 2008) and carries much of its assumptions around homogeneity of actors while being firmly rooted in place-based analysis (see O'Connor et al., 2017). In contrast to these assumptions, we demonstrate that actors are not homogenous but heterogeneous and that existing concepts of entrepreneurial ecosystems do not differentiate among entrepreneurs as actors within ecosystems. These arguments are further elaborated on with evidence in the chapters that follow.

1.6.3   Chapter 3: Understanding Gender and Inclusion in Entrepreneurial Ecosystems

The third chapter focuses explicitly on the relevance of gender for entrepreneurial ecosystems. The chapter first discusses the differences between sex, gender, and gender relations to lay the foundation for a dynamic understanding of actors and entrepreneurial ecosystems. Guided by feminist perspectives in entrepreneurship (Ahl & Marlow, 2012; Calás, Smircich, & Bourne, 2007, 2009; Clark Muntean & Ozkazanc-Pan, 2016) and sociology (Acker, 1992, 2006), the chapter provides theoretical insights, derived from the various ways in which gender is studied, on how gender can be conceptualized and how inclusion is a multifaceted concept and practice. The chapter then offers a guiding definition of gender inclusion in relation to entrepreneurial ecosystems and moves on to provide insights about how to study it in relation to individuals, organizations, and sociocultural norms at the same time. In doing so, this chapter provides a multifactor and multilevel gender framework for understanding economic inclusion in relation to entrepreneurial ecosystems.

1.6.4 Chapter 4: Individual-Level Dynamics: Beyond Motivation, Identity, and Networks

This chapter focuses on individual-level aspects of inclusion in entrepreneurial ecosystems, using examples from gender-focused ecosystems research in Boston, Massachusetts, as part of broader research carried out by the authors between 2014 and 2017 (Knowlton et al., 2015; Ozkazanc-Pan, Knowlton, & Clark Muntean, 2017). Using data from fieldwork carried out in Boston, we outline how individual-level gender biases operate in entrepreneurial ecosystems and how they impact women entrepreneurs differently than male entrepreneurs. Our focus is explicitly on the gendering of social capital and trust within entrepreneurial ecosystems, as we highlight their gendered dimensions which lead to exclusion for women, even if "unintentionally."

1.6.5 Chapter 5: Organization-Level Dynamics: Practices and Policies

This chapter shares examples of organization-level barriers to full participation of women in entrepreneurial ecosystems by way of the three cities that were the sites of our fieldwork – Boston, Massachusetts, St. Louis, Missouri, and Asheville, North Carolina. Here, the focus is on the ways in which intermediary organizations, such as incubators, accelerators, coworking spaces, and investors among others, can act as gatekeepers to the resources of the ecosystem. The chapter focuses specifically on access to networks, outreach, selection, support mechanisms (ESOs) available in the ecosystem, and ecosystem culture. In speaking to these issues, the chapter focuses on the role of meso-level organizational actors and how their norms, values, and practices differentially impact entrepreneurs and lead to inclusion or exclusion from the ecosystem.

1.6.6   Chapter 6: Institution-Level Dynamics: Institutions and Sociocultural Gender Norms

This chapter outlines the importance and role of institutional factors in the analysis of entrepreneurial ecosystems, particularly in relation to gender. We focus explicitly on informal and formal factors – that is, belief systems as well as economic, political, and legal systems – as important considerations in how entrepreneurial ecosystems are organized and replicated. We conclude this chapter by introducing the concept of "ecosystem identity" as a framework that offers a typology of ecosystems and thereby expands how scholarship attending to entrepreneurial ecosystems can conceptualize and categorize different types of ecosystem. Our goal here is to offer suggestions as to how the institutional organization and identity of an ecosystem can offer different mechanisms and drivers of change toward gender inclusion. We point out that ecosystem identity impacts the possibilities for change, and, on this basis, we offer insights as to challenges as well as opportunities for institutional shifts.

1.6.7   Chapter 7: Intersectional Analysis

This chapter focuses on the city of Boston and delves into how intersectional differences (Acker, 2012) among women entrepreneurs result in additional and different biasing forces for women of color and immigrant women entrepreneurs compared to White women engaging in entrepreneurship. As such, the chapter provides a holistic consideration of how gender, race, and other relations of difference may play out in experiences of entrepreneurship within entrepreneurial ecosystems. The chapter aims to provide a complex and holistic picture of how entrepreneurial ecosystems essentially provide very different experiences, interactions, and institutional support for actors in ecosystems, thereby supporting our argument that actors, even if in the same category, are indeed heterogeneous and not homogeneous.

1.6.8   Chapter 8: Inclusive Entrepreneurial Ecosystems and Economic Development

This chapter examines all three levels to present a holistic framework for understanding gender in relation to entrepreneurial ecosystems and policies for supporting inclusive economic development. It builds off the authors' previous research in this area within the technology startup sector (Ozkazanc-Pan & Clark Muntean, 2018). The chapter provides effective approaches for building inclusive entrepreneurial ecosystems that range from individual approaches to organizational ones and, finally, to approaches by policymakers at local, state, and country levels. The chapter also outlines how gender should be an important dimension of policy efforts aimed at helping cities, states, and nations combat rising economic inequality in the midst of economic development efforts. More urgently, the impact of the ongoing pandemic is also examined given the gendered outcomes it will likely have on entrepreneurial success.

Readers will find that the book offers a combination of new theoretical insights derived from critical epistemological traditions, such as feminist work and intersectionality, and empirical research to push existing approaches and ideas within the entrepreneurship field, specifically in relation to entrepreneurial ecosystem scholarship. By doing so, our goal is to make gender relevant to theorizing of entrepreneurial ecosystems such that we call into question taken-for-granted assumptions about the homogeneity and identity of ecosystem actors, the relationships among them, and the institutionalized norms and values associated with supporting entrepreneurial success. We believe that this approach will make scholarship on and about entrepreneurial ecosystems richer in addressing concerns around inclusion, equity, and economic growth – considerations that are being addressed by cities, states, and supranational organizations globally. By providing the field with a new set of conceptual tools that are explicitly based on gender and what is essentially a new concept, ecosystem identity, to speak about inclusion through a gender lens, we hope to move entrepreneurship scholarship beyond its current state. We believe this will provide important new directions for research that aspires to create equitable entrepreneurship opportunities. As scholars, we know that research can bring important insights and influence organizations and policymakers by demonstrating the value of inclusion and the cost of exclusion for economic growth. Thus, we see our efforts as yielding positive contributions not only to academic research but also to new conversations that can impact practice as well as popular media opinions about gender, inclusion, and success in entrepreneurship – an equally important aspect of influencing the influencers and decision makers through rigorous research and scholarship.

REFERENCES

Acker, J. (1992). From sex roles to gendered institutions. *Contemporary Sociology*, *21*(5): 565–569.

Acker, J. (2006). Inequality regimes gender, class, and race in organizations. *Gender & Society*, *20*(4): 441–464.

Acker, J. (2012). Gendered organizations and intersectionality: Problems and possibilities. *Equality, Diversity and Inclusion: An International Journal*, *31*(3): 214–224.

Acs, Z. J., Desai, S., & Hessels, J. (2008). Entrepreneurship, economic development and institutions. *Small Business Economics*, *31*(3): 219–234.

Acs, Z. J., & Storey, D. (2004). Introduction: Entrepreneurship and economic development. *Regional Studies*, *38*(8): 871–876.

Acs, Z. J., & Szerb, L. (2007). Entrepreneurship, economic growth and public policy. *Small Business Economics*, *28*(2–3): 109–122.

Ahl, H. J. (2002). *The making of the female entrepreneur: A discourse analysis of research texts on women's entrepreneurship* (Doctoral dissertation). Internationella Handelshögskolan. Available at www.diva-portal.org/smash/record.jsf?pid=diva2%3A3890&dswid=7897 (accessed January 15, 2021).

Ahl, H. J., & Marlow, S. (2012). Exploring the dynamics of gender, feminism and entrepreneurship: Advancing debate to escape a dead end? *Organization*, *19*: 543–562.

Alvedalen, J., & Boschma, R. (2017). A critical review of entrepreneurial ecosystems research: Towards a future research agenda. *European Planning Studies, 25*(6): 887–903.

Anderson, A. R., & Warren, L. (2011). The entrepreneur as hero and jester: Enacting the entrepreneurial discourse. *International Small Business Journal, 29*(6): 589–609.

Antoncic, B., & Hisrich, R. D. (2001). Intrapreneurship: Construct refinement and cross-cultural validation. *Journal of Business Venturing, 16*(5): 495–527.

Antoncic, B., & Hisrich, R. D. (2003). Clarifying the intrapreneurship concept. *Journal of Small Business and Enterprise Development, 10*(1): 7–24.

Auerswald, P. E. (2015). Enabling entrepreneurial ecosystems. Kauffman Foundation Research Series on City, Metro and Regional Entrepreneurship. Available at www.kauffman.org/~/media/kauffman_org/research%20reports%20and%20covers/2015/10/enabling_entrepreneurial_ecosystems.pdf (accessed January 15, 2020).

Ayyub, R. (2020). Social distancing is a privilege. Foreign Policy. Available at https://foreignpolicy.com/2020/03/28/social-distancing-is-a-privilege/ (accessed June 2, 2020).

Birkner, S. (2020). To belong or not to belong, that is the question?! Explorative insights on liminal gender states within women's STEMpreneurship. *International Entrepreneurship and Management Journal, 16*: 1–22.

Bosma, N., & Holvoet, T. (2015). The role of culture in entrepreneurial ecosystems: An investigation for European regions. Presented at *6th Annual George Washington University (GWU)-International Council for Small Business (ICSB) Global Entrepreneurship Research and Policy Conference*. Available at http://dx.doi.org/10.2139/ssrn.2700798 (accessed September 30, 2020).

Brown, R., & Mason, C. (2017). Looking inside the spiky bits: A critical review and conceptualisation of entrepreneurial ecosystems. *Small Business Economics, 49*(1): 11–30.

Bruni, A., Gherardi, S., & Poggio, B. (2004a). Entrepreneur-mentality, gender and the study of women entrepreneurs. *Journal of Organizational Change Management, 17*(3): 256–268.

Bruni, A., Gherardi, S., & Poggio, B. (2004b). Doing gender, doing entrepreneurship: An ethnographic account of intertwined practices. *Gender, Work & Organization, 11*(4): 406–429.

Brush, C. G., De Bruin, A., & Welter, F. (2009). A gender-aware framework for women's entrepreneurship. *International Journal of Gender and Entrepreneurship, 1*(1): 8–24.

Brush, C. G., Edelman, L. F., Manolova, T., & Welter, F. (2019). A gendered look at entrepreneurship ecosystems. *Small Business Economics, 53*(2): 393–408.

Calás, M. B., Smircich, L., & Bourne, K. A. (2007). Knowing Lisa? Feminist analyses of "gender and entrepreneurship." In D. Bilimoria & S. K. Piderit (Eds.), *Handbook on women in business and management* (pp. 78–105). Northampton, MA: Edward Elgar, ,.

Calás, M. B., Smircich, L., & Bourne, K. A. (2009). Extending the boundaries: Reframing "entrepreneurship as social change" through feminist perspectives. *Academy of Management Review, 34*(3): 552–569.

Care.org (2020). New Covid-19 global rapid gender analysis addresses concerns of women and girls in pandemic. Care.org. Available at www.care.org/sites/default/files/global_rga_covid_rdm_3.31.20_final.pdf (accessed June 30, 2020).

Clark Muntean, S. (2021). Contextualizing the experiences of women entrepreneurs and comparative responses to challenges during a global pandemic. In M. McAdam & J. Cunningham (Eds.), *Women and global entrepreneurship: Contextualizing everyday experiences* (chapter 20). New York: Routledge.

Clark Muntean, S., & Ozkazanc-Pan, B. (2015). A gender integrative conceptualization of entrepreneurship. *New England Journal of Entrepreneurship, 18*(1): 27–40.

Clark Muntean, S., & Ozkazanc-Pan, B. (2016). Feminist perspectives on social entrepreneurship: Critique and new directions. *International Journal of Gender and Entrepreneurship, 8*(3): 221–241.

Collins, C., Landivar, L. C., Ruppanner, L., & Scarborough, W. J. (2021). COVID-19 and the gender gap in work hours. *Gender, Work & Organization, 28*(S1): 101–112.

Davis, G. F., & White, C. J. (2015). The new face of corporate activism. *Stanford Social Innovation Review, 2015*(Fall): 40–45.

Essers, C., Dey, P., Tedmanson, D., & Verduyn, K. (2017). Critical entrepreneurship studies: A manifesto. In C. Essers, P. Dey, D. Tedmanson, & K. Verduyn (Eds.), *Critical perspectives on entrepreneurship* (pp. 1–14). New York: Routledge.

European Commission (2020). Internal market, industry, entrepreneurship and innovation. Available at https://ec.europa.eu/growth/smes/promoting-entrepreneurship/support_en (accessed June 30, 2020).

Fairlie, R. (2020). The impact of Covid-19 on small business owners: Evidence of early-stage losses from the April 2020 current population survey. National Bureau of Economic Research, Working Paper 27309. Available at www.nber.org/papers/w27309.pdf (accessed June 30, 2020).

Feld, B. (2012). *Startup communities: Building an entrepreneurial ecosystem in your city.* Hoboken, NJ: John Wiley & Sons.

GEM (Global Entrepreneurship Monitor). (2020). The influence of GEM on policy. Available at www.gemconsortium.org/report/the-influence-of-gem-on-policy-2017-2018 (accessed March 20, 2020).

Greer, M. J., & Greene, P. G. (2003). Feminist theory and the study of entrepreneurship. In J. E. Butler (Ed.), *New perspectives on women entrepreneurs* (pp. 1–24). Greenwich, CT: Information Age Publishing.

Hamilton, D., Atkinson, G., Dugger, W. M., & Waller Jr, W. T. (2009). The entrepreneur as a cultural hero. In D. Hamilton, G. Atkinson, W. M. Dugger, & W. T. Waller Jr. (Eds), *Cultural economics and theory* (pp. 78–86). New York: Routledge.

Harper, D. A. (2003). *Foundations of entrepreneurship and economic development.* New York: Routledge.

Henry, C., Foss, L., & Ahl, H. (2016). Gender and entrepreneurship research: A review of methodological approaches. *International Small Business Journal,* 34(3): 217–241.

Henry, C., Hill, F., & Leitch, C. (2005a). Entrepreneurship education and training: Can entrepreneurship be taught? Part I. *Education + Training,* 47(2): 98–111.

Henry, C., Hill, F., & Leitch, C. (2005b). Entrepreneurship education and training: Can entrepreneurship be taught? Part II. *Education + Training,* 47(3), 158–169.

ILO (2020a). These occupations are dominated by women. Available at https://ilostat.ilo.org/2020/03/06/these-occupations-are-dominated-by-women/ (accessed June 30, 2020).

ILO (2020b). Having kids sets women's labour force participation more so than getting married. Available at https://ilostat.ilo.org/2020/03/03/having-kids-sets-back-womens-labour-force-participation-more-so-than-getting-married/ (accessed June 30, 2020).

Jennings, J. E., & Brush, C. G. (2013). Research on women entrepreneurs: Challenges to (and from) the broader entrepreneurship literature?. *The Academy of Management Annals,* 7(1): 663–715.

Kanze, D., Huang, L., Conley, M. A., & Higgins, E. T. (2018). We ask men to win and women not to lose: Closing the gender gap in startup funding. *Academy of Management Journal,* 61(2): 586–614.

Knowlton, K., Özkazanç-Pan, B., Clark Muntean, S., & Motoyama, Y. (2015). Support organizations and remediating the gender gap in entrepreneurial ecosystems: A case study of St. Louis. SSRN. Available at http://ssrn.com/abstract=2685116

Krause, A., & Fetsch, E. (2016). Labor after Labor. Kauffman Foundation Research Series on Entrepreneurship and Motherhood Report 1. SSRN. Available at https://ssrn.com/abstract=2776680 (accessed September 20, 2020).

Manolova, T., Brush, C. G., Edelman, L. F., Robb, A., & Welter, F. (2017). *Entrepreneurial ecosystems and the growth of women entrepreneurship: A comparative analysis.* Northampton, MA: Edward Elgar Publishing.

Markman, G. D., Phan, P. H., Balkin, D. B., & Gianiodis, P. T. (2005). Entrepreneurship and university-based technology transfer. *Journal of Business Venturing, 20*(2): 241–263.

McAdam, M., Harrison, R. T., & Leitch, C. M. (2019). Stories from the field: Women's networking as gender capital in entrepreneurial ecosystems. *Small Business Economics, 53*(2): 459–474.

Motoyama, Y. (2008). What was new about the cluster theory? What could it answer and what could it not answer?. *Economic Development Quarterly, 22*(4): 353–363.

O'Connor, A., Stam, E., Sussan, F., & Audretsch, D. B. (2017). *Entrepreneurial ecosystems: Place-based transformations and transitions.* Cham: Springer International Publishing AG.

Ozkazanc-Pan, B. (2015). Secular and Islamic feminist entrepreneurship in Turkey. *International Journal of Gender and Entrepreneurship, 7*(1): 45–65.

Ozkazanc-Pan, B., & Clark Muntean, S. (2018). Networking towards (in)equality: Women entrepreneurs in technology. *Gender, Work & Organization, 25*(4): 379–400.

Ozkazanc-Pan, B., Knowlton, K., & Clark Muntean, S., (2017). Gender inclusion activities in entrepreneurship ecosystems: The case of St. Louis, MO and Boston, MA. SSRN. Available at https://ssrn.com/abstract=2982414 (accessed September 20, 2020).

Patterson, N., Mavin, S., & Turner, J. (2012). Unsettling the gender binary: Experiences of gender in entrepreneurial leadership and implications for HRD. *European Journal of Training and Development, 36*(7): 687–711.

Rideout, E. C., & Gray, D. O. (2013). Does entrepreneurship education really work? A review and methodological critique of the empirical literature on the effects of university-based entrepreneurship education. *Journal of Small Business Management, 51*(3): 329–351.

Roundy, P. T., Brockman, B. K., & Bradshaw, M. (2017). The resilience of entrepreneurial ecosystems. *Journal of Business Venturing Insights, 8*: 99–104.

Spigel, B. (2017). The relational organization of entrepreneurial ecosystems. *Entrepreneurship Theory and Practice, 41*(1): 49–72.

Tedmanson, D., Verduyn, K., Essers, C., & Gartner, W. B. (2012). Critical perspectives in entrepreneurship research. *Organization, 19*(5): 531–541.

Thurik, A. R. (2009). Entreprenomics: Entrepreneurship, economic growth and policy. In D. B. Audretsch & R. Strom (Eds.), *Entrepreneurship, growth and public policy* (pp. 219–249). Cambridge: Cambridge University Press.

Villani, E., Rasmussen, E., & Grimaldi, R. (2017). How intermediary organizations facilitate university–industry technology transfer: A proximity approach. *Technological Forecasting and Social Change, 114*: 86–102.

Wennekers, S., & Thurik, R. (1999). Linking entrepreneurship and economic growth. *Small Business Economics, 13*(1): 27–56.

Winkel, D., Vanevenhoven, J., Drago, W. A., & Clements, C. (2013). The structure and scope of entrepreneurship programs in higher education around the world. *Journal of Entrepreneurship Education, 16*: 15–30.

Wong, P. K., Ho, Y. P., & Autio, E. (2005). Entrepreneurship, innovation and economic growth: Evidence from GEM data. *Small Business Economics, 24*(3): 335–350.

2 Entrepreneurial Ecosystems
An Overview

2.1 INTRODUCTION

This chapter introduces the concept of *entrepreneurial ecosystems* (Auerswald, 2015; Bosma & Holvoet, 2015; Spigel, 2015), provides various ways to consider and define the concept, and then moves on to discuss its importance for supporting economic development. Given the growing body of work on entrepreneurial ecosystems, we first outline how the field of entrepreneurial ecosystems recently evolved from existing work on clusters (Motoyama, 2008) and carries much of its assumptions around homogeneity of actors. We build on this argument by suggesting that clusters are a specific form of institutional arrangement which impact governance and resource allocation. Our contention is that while clusters offer economies of scale and reduction in transaction costs to firms and can be supportive of collaborations between firms, they do not challenge the formal "rules of the game" (North, 1991) or the assumptions of property rights that guide how firms "play the game" (i.e. contracts and governance). Within this domain, not all actors have the same property rights, and hence not all actors are the same in their ability to participate in contracting. In the case of entrepreneurship, not all actors have the same access to or ownership of capital, the same rights to ideas (i.e. patents), or the same opportunities to benefit from resources. Further, informal institutions, such as customs, values, and norms, that impact the institutional environment or the formal rules of the game are not singular but are, in fact, different for different groups of people.

In the domain of entrepreneurship, we use the term "institutional environment" to examine the ways in which ecosystems are formalized, organized, and operationalized through actors and relationships. Our contention is that entrepreneurial ecosystems are a networked type of governance mechanism, relying on trust, relationships, and loose coordination, but that their form and function are gendered. We demonstrate that *informal institutions* (values, norms), the *institutional environment* (formal rules of the game), *governance* (how the game is played), and *resource allocation* (see Williamson, 1993, 1998, 2008) are heterogeneous to the extent that they can be manifest differently in different contexts. And, specifically, existing concepts of entrepreneurial ecosystems, derived from cluster theory, do not provide conceptual differentiation beyond categories or types (i.e. entrepreneurs, intermediary support organizations, investors, etc.) among the different actors that "play the game" within ecosystems. To demonstrate that, in fact, there is differentiation rather than homogeneity, we rely on gender as a conceptual framework to guide our reimagining of entrepreneurial ecosystems. Gender offers a lens through which to launch arguments about the ways in which informal institutions are gendered, that there are gendered rules of the game, and that there are gender differences in how actors (can) play the game and participate in resource allocation. In all, this chapter explains the foundation of the entrepreneurial ecosystem concept as derived from institutional economics and sociology as well as cluster theory, but expands on this through a gender framework.

The emergence of entrepreneurial ecosystems as an analytic lens through which to understand entrepreneurs and entrepreneurship activity has grown rapidly in the last decade. This new approach has garnered much attention in the entrepreneurship field as well as in urban planning, economic geography, and other disciplines. While there is not an agreed-on definition, for the purposes of this book, *entrepreneurial ecosystems can be broadly defined as communities of entrepreneurs who are in exchange relationships with each other and various entrepreneur support organizations in the context of institutions and institutionalized sociocultural norms.* This definition acknowledges three important tenets of ecosystems: relational dynamics, such as exchanges and relationships between and among actors; the role of entrepreneur communities; and the role of institutions and norms as factors impacting how and why particular relationships among/between actors may take place.

First, while the term *relational dynamics* may be broad, it allows consideration of exchanges and relationships within entrepreneurial ecosystems. That is, the social components of how individuals and groups relate to each other and interact among themselves provide an added dimension to purely economic perspectives that do not acknowledge or focus on the social dynamics of entrepreneurship activities. Moreover, the relational focus ensures an understanding not only of how ecosystems take shape but also of how they continue to be maintained through exchanges and relationships. Without this focus, which is distinguished from that of cluster theory, understanding of entrepreneurial activities is based on multiple transactions between parties with an emphasis on the economic dimensions of such exchanges. In other words, an ecosystem approach expands the understanding of entrepreneurship as simply a number of mostly economic transactions (a transactional approach) between different actors to a relational understanding of the dynamics between and among actors. This exchange and relationship building takes place between and among entrepreneurs but also includes other actors, such as university programs, incubators, accelerators, coworking spaces, among others, under the umbrella of ESOs.

Second, the idea of communities is an important aspect of entrepreneurship in that exchanges, such as those related to information, resources, and knowledge as well as relationships, take shape in a particular context (rather than in a vacuum). Understanding the role and value of communities in ecosystems can provide important insights as to who is part of a community and who is potentially left out, either intentionally or as an unintended consequence. Communities can foster a sense of belonging, facilitate information exchange, and provide support and resources to entrepreneurs. Communities are also a form of governance through which the relationships and norms of the ecosystem are reinforced and replicated.

Thus, understanding how they contribute to the formation and maintenance of ecosystems is important, but so is clarity around how gender and other relations of difference may impact the ways in which entrepreneurial communities form and connect. In this sense, gendered governance mechanisms that manifest through community-building efforts need to be uncovered and examined for their role in creating a gender gap in entrepreneurship activities and opportunities. As we will point out, gender plays an important role in how entrepreneur communities may come to understand themselves and whether to grant access to those considered outside of the community.

Finally, institutionalization and institutions play a pivotal role in providing the context and norms for ecosystems, where a plethora of entrepreneurship activities take place. Here, both formal and informal institutions, such as economic development policies and unspoken but acted-on sociocultural norms, can be a significant influence on the acceptable practices and values of an ecosystem. In Chapter 1, we pointed out that gender is an important organizing principle of society and, hence, plays an important role in how we come to understand and define those who participate in entrepreneurship through the concept of ecosystems. In this chapter, we point out that ecosystem resources are not necessarily accessible to or known by *all* entrepreneurs in a context of institutional environments and arrangements. Our analytic focus on gender provides the missing but necessary framework to outline why certain actors do not or cannot connect to each other or to ecosystem resources, despite the existence of such resources. We suggest that factors at individual, organizational, and institutional levels are at play, and we show, at the individual level, how issues of identity and relationality impact access; at the level of organizations, how particular organizational practices create community for some but not others; and finally, at the institutional level, how policies and sociocultural norms can potentially hinder unfettered access to resources and opportunities for entrepreneurship.

In addition to insufficient consideration of the various embodied and relational identity dimensions of actors in entrepreneurial ecosystems, theories and frameworks tend to assume that economic actors are homogenous. Thus, the ways in which gender, race, and other intersectional dimensions of difference impact one's experiences and opportunities are not considered part of theorizing on entrepreneurial ecosystems. Moreover, there is little consideration of how the very ideas driving entrepreneurial ecosystems replicate problematic assumptions of earlier cluster theory research. Such work readily recognized the importance of firms and locational advantage in relation to competition but did little to further understanding of the role of heterogeneous actors in economic development.

In response to these observations, we show that recognizing heterogeneity rather than homogeneity of actors makes a difference for how we theorize, study, and understand entrepreneurial ecosystems, and how economic development efforts should take shape in an inclusive fashion. However, rather than focusing on all the different ways "difference makes a difference," the focus in this book is explicitly on gender, gender relations, and gendering processes as important considerations in relation to how entrepreneurial ecosystems are theorized and studied. Research demonstrates that it matters what kind of entrepreneur you are and whether or not you have access to the networks, resources, and information that are seemingly "readily" available in any given entrepreneurial ecosystem (Ozkazanc-Pan & Clark Muntean, 2018).

In the entrepreneurship field, the relationship between gender and entrepreneurial ecosystems has become an important consideration only in the last five to ten years. Prior to that, either the majority of research was on women entrepreneurs, and this stream still continues today (Jennings & Brush, 2013; Ozkazanc-Pan, 2018), or entrepreneurial ecosystems were not theorized by attending to the ways in which gender makes a difference in the informal institutions, the institutional environment, governance, and resource allocation. Currently, when ecosystems research attends to difference, it does so by keeping intact the theoretical framework of entrepreneurial ecosystems but adding in a dimension of difference, such as gender or race. More explicitly, research tends to focus on women entrepreneurs in entrepreneurial ecosystems rather than offering critique or new directions on the very ways in which entrepreneurial ecosystems have been conceptualized and studied. Rather than relying on identity categories to expand on these claims, our goal is to demonstrate that entrepreneurial ecosystems are in fact gendered, embodied, and relational governance systems for conducting entrepreneurship and are, in fact, the product of gendered institutional environments and arrangements.

As such, this chapter focuses on laying the foundation for our argument that gender is a missing theoretical component of research on entrepreneurial ecosystems, and our analysis contributes to a nuanced understanding of actors. Given the growing importance and relevance of entrepreneurial ecosystems for entrepreneurship research and economic development policies, understanding how policies may impact gendered institutional environments and governance mechanisms in relation to entrepreneurship activities is quite important. In addition, understanding how policies may impact women entrepreneurs when they are implemented without consideration of differences in how entrepreneurial actors participate in ecosystems may pose significant challenges for women-owned businesses. Policymakers who want to support entrepreneurship activities as a means for economic development must acknowledge that policies can have unintended consequences when differences between and among actors are not considered. By focusing on gender as a relevant theoretical framework for rethinking entrepreneurial ecosystems as inclusive of its actors, organizations, and institutions, this book sets the stage for new directions in scholarship research and policymaking at the intersections of entrepreneurship, ecosystems, and economic development.

Guided by these insights and to provide new directions in research on entrepreneurial ecosystems, this chapter provides an overview of entrepreneurial ecosystems research, including definitions, key concepts, and debates that have emerged, focusing explicitly on their ontological and epistemological assumptions. This overview is done for the purpose of reconsidering the main tenets and assumptions of the field specifically through the lens of gender. The focus in this book is on gender and how gender as an organizing principle of society, a set of relations, and a set of cultural and social norms impacts entrepreneurial experiences and the very formation of entrepreneurial ecosystems. To move toward a gender-integrative framework (Clark Muntean & Ozkazanc-Pan, 2015) for theorizing entrepreneurial ecosystems, this chapter offers three sections.

The first section focuses on how the ecosystems concept has been theorized, inclusive of its various definitions, elements, and nature, expanding on the values and ideas it has borrowed and continues to borrow from institutional economics and sociology. The second discusses the relevance of gender for (re)theorizing the assumed neutral nature of entrepreneurial ecosystems, including recent work that has aimed to introduce a "gender" perspective. The final section provides an overview of the holistic framework that will be utilized in the book – individual, organizational, and societal – as reflecting new conversations on how to rethink entrepreneurial ecosystems in the context of gendered informal institutions, gendered institutional environment, gendered governance, and gendered resource allocation. This framework is derived from conceptualization of gender from disciplines outside of entrepreneurship, including gender studies, feminist work, sociology, and management. In all, the goal of this chapter is to lay the foundation for new directions on how entrepreneurial ecosystems are theorized and studied in the broader entrepreneurship field by making gender a relevant conceptual tool for future work. In all, this chapter demonstrates why ecosystem actors are different from each other and how they may experience, and act in, ecosystems.

2.2   AN OVERVIEW OF ENTREPRENEURIAL ECOSYSTEMS: FROM TRANSACTION COST ECONOMICS TO CLUSTERS

To understand how the current analytic framework of entrepreneurial ecosystems was derived and continues to develop, it's important to understand the ways in which previous analytic frameworks around entrepreneurship and economic development have contributed to contemporary conversations. Moreover, to understand how new theories and policies related to entrepreneurial ecosystems can be developed, it is important to understand the guiding assumptions of the existing entrepreneurial ecosystems literature. As this chapter will demonstrate, analysis of entrepreneurial ecosystems still tends to replicate and borrow from institutional economics and sociology as well as economic cluster analysis, particularly in relation to underlying assumptions about actors in the ecosystem. Specifically, entrepreneurial ecosystem analysis adopted economic cluster analysis' disembodied understanding of actors, an approach that has historical precedent in the ways the fields of institutional economics and sociology have theorized informal institutions, the institutional environment, governance, and resource allocation. This understanding is based on engagement with institutional economics and sociology, and specifically conversations around transaction cost economics as the main contributor to cluster theory, a precursor to entrepreneurial ecosystem frameworks. We then expand on cluster theory and the various assumptions embedded in its analytic framework. Finally, we focus on entrepreneurial ecosystems, inclusive of the various elements that are contained within its analytic perspective.

2.2.1 New Institutional Economics and Economic Sociology: Brief Overview

While a historical overview of the development of institutional economics is not within the purview of this book, our focus in this section is on new institutional economics as the starting conversation for contemporary conversations on entrepreneurial ecosystems. Williamson (1993, 1998) succinctly suggests that the main tenets of new institutional economics are that institutions matter and that they can be analyzed with respect to understanding the functioning of the economy and the role of organizations (also see Ménard & Shirley, 2005, for an overview). Within this context, he contends that the fields of economics and sociology each bring different concepts to the analysis of institutions, albeit at times with very different assumptions around human behavior and organizations. These conversations revolve around the works of Coase (1937/1995, 1998), Alchian & Demsetz (1972), Davis & North (1971), Schumpeter (1943), and others as harbingers of new institutional economics that brings to bear two focal areas: institutional environment and institutional arrangements. Here, environment refers to the "set of fundamental political, social and legal ground rules that establishes the basis for production, exchange and distribution," while arrangements refer to the "arrangement between economic units that governs the ways in which these units can cooperate and/or compete" (Davis & North, 1971: 5–6). In general, transaction cost economics can be understood as a field of inquiry into the governance mechanisms of contractual relations as actors try to minimize costs associated with doing business (Williamson, 1993), and it is considered one of the main focal points of institutional arrangements.

Yet to understand transaction cost economics and how it contributed to cluster theory development, it is important to understand the broader context of institutional analysis in which it sits. To this end, Williamson (1998) further expands on the economics of institutions, establishing four levels of analysis. The first level refers to embeddedness (Granovetter, 1985) or the informal institutions, customs, norms, and traditions that are generally examined within the domain of social theory. For Williamson (1998), this level is not intentional or planned per se but rather spontaneous in its manifestation, making it more likely to be analyzed through the concepts of social theory than those of economics. The second level refers to the institutional environment or the formal rules of the game, with particular attention to property rights and generally studied under the economics of property rights. Here, Williamson (1998) suggests that it is possible to create particular institutional environments that can lead to economizing of transaction costs. The third level of analysis is that of governance, or how the game is played, with particular attention to contracts and the alignment of governance structures with transactions. Here, the right governance structure can contribute to economizing of transaction costs undertaken by actors, and is the main focus of transaction cost economics. Finally, the fourth level of analysis refers to resource allocation and employment, examined through pricing and quantities and alignment of incentives. Here, transaction costs can be minimized by getting the right marginal conditions in place, and these considerations are generally examined under the umbrella of agency theory/neoclassical economics (Eisenhardt, 1989).

Within this context, it's important to note that individual rights, property rights, and considerations over ownership are quite relevant to how institutions are formed as well as to how institutional change happens – in other words, how institutional environments take form and the various arrangements that arise in order to govern economic relationships. And as Williamson (1993) points out, transaction cost economics focuses on the study of contract laws and posits various theories about how actors try to minimize transaction costs through particular governance mechanisms and contracts. Yet in these theories about economic institutions, there is little consideration of the fact that political, social, and legal rights are gendered and that, globally, many women cannot enter into employment (or other) contracts, own property, exercise ownership, or engage in transactions without the approval of male family members or, in some cases, without breaking the law – a reality that continues even today. Thus, fundamentally, the field of institutional economics and economic sociology, as it developed, arrived from the particular set of experiences, vantage points, and perspectives of White male theorists and their views of the economic, sociological, and organizational domains. Historically, the institutional economics did not acknowledge or consider how its fundamental assumptions about human behavior, rights, and institutions were gendered, and it is only in recent years that the field has been expanded to include considerations around gender (Fernandez, 2018).

That is, gender plays a formative role in embeddedness or the emergence of informal institutions, in the formalization of institutional environments, in the governance of economic relationships, and in how resources can be allocated in light of agency problems and differences in risk sharing and risk tolerance. Norms, values, and traditions passed down from generation to generation in society include ideas about the "proper" roles of women in society, assumptions about their competence in matters outside the domestic domain, and ideas about their suitability for certain professions. As demonstrated by the history, across the globe, of women's rights in political, economic, and social domains, gender plays an important role in how the formal rules of the game (institutional environment) were developed and by whom – it certainly was not predominantly women deciding the polity and structuring the legal system or bureaucracy. And most certainly, governance considerations (i.e. playing the game) have different rules for different players or, in this case, economic actors.

For example, as the US was established through colonization and enslavement, the rights of married White women were not separate from those of their husbands, such that a married woman did not exist legally beyond her marriage. White married women got the right to own property in New York in 1848 through the Married Woman's Property Act, and other states followed suit such that by 1900 all states had ratified their version of this act. In 1862 the US Homestead Act allowed single, divorced, or widowed White women to own land in their own name. The UK passed the Married Woman's Property Act in 1870. In 1880 the first stock exchange for women in the US allowed them to use their own money to purchase/speculate on railroad stocks. In 1881 France allowed women to open bank accounts, and in 1886 married women were able to open a bank account without requiring the consent of their husbands. This did not happen in the US until the 1960s and in the UK until the 1970s. Beyond land rights, patent ownership was not available to women in the US until 1845 when New York state allowed married women to secure patents for their own invention as if they were not married (see Khan, 2005, for an overview of patents and copyrights in the US). It was 1965 before affirmative action covered women, 1968 when "help wanted" ads could no longer specify gender, and 1972 when the Fortune 500 saw its first woman CEO, Katherine Graham.

Today, there is a continued and large gender gap in patenting (Frietsch et al., 2009; Whittington & Smith-Doerr, 2005) and across many industries, such as finance (Bertrand, Goldin, & Katz, 2010). Moreover, in order to affect change, women need to be in decision-making structures and positions. In the US, women did not have the right to vote until 1920, through the Nineteenth Amendment, and Black women still continue to face discrimination while trying to exercise their right to vote. Institutional change related to voting came in part due to existing male political figures and decision-makers finding that alignment with suffragists was beneficial to their own chances of being re-elected. Sociologists point out that

> shifting gender relations produced a gendered opportunity for women's suffrage by altering attitudes among political decision-makers about the appropriate roles of women in society. That is, changing gender relations altered expectations about women's participation in the polity, and these changes in gendered expectations increased the willingness of political decision-makers to support suffrage.
>
> *McCammon et al. (2001: 51)*

Across the world, there are only eleven women heads of state and twelve serving as heads of government.[1] This large disparity in women's representation in the polity arising from gendered norms about the role of women in society has a significant impact on the creation of rules and regulations related to the economy and society. Globally, the rights of women in political, economic, social, and

---

[1] www.unwomen.org/en/what-we-do/leadership-and-political-participation/facts-and-figures#notes

cultural domains vary dramatically. Despite the passing of the Convention on the Elimination of All Forms of Discrimination against Women (CEDAW) by the UN General Assembly in 1979,[2] women around the world continue to face discrimination and violence, and lack equal opportunities for education, health, and political representation. These gender gaps arise from lack of robust governance mechanisms, social and cultural norms, gender stereotypes, and the enactment of laws and policies that perpetuate – intentionally or not – unequal opportunities for women. A 2020 report[3] by the UN focusing on gender, business, and law finds that legal differences in eight areas related to working life transitions impact men and women differently. Specifically, these areas are: *mobility* – laws affecting women's freedom of movement; *workplace* – laws affecting the decision to work; *pay* – laws and regulations affecting women's pay; *marriage* – legal constraints associated with marriage; *parenthood* – laws affecting women's work after having children; *entrepreneurship* – constraints on women's starting and running a business; *assets* – gender differences in property and inheritance; and *pensions* – laws affecting the size of a women's pension. Additionally,

> Of [the] 189 economies assessed in 2018, 104 economies still have laws preventing women from working in specific jobs,
> 59 economies have no laws on sexual harassment in the workplace, and in 18 economies, husbands can legally prevent their wives from working.[4]

Within this context, given that any change is likely to alter authority and displace existing male power structures, any changes that bring about gender equality for the sake of doing so may not be met with enthusiasm. This is despite evidence that women's economic participation is good for economic growth and has positive

---

[2] See www.ohchr.org/en/hrbodies/cedaw/pages/cedawindex.aspx
[3] https://openknowledge.worldbank.org/bitstream/handle/10986/32639/9781464815324.pdf
[4] www.unwomen.org/en/what-we-do/economic-empowerment/facts-and-figures

returns for organizational performance.[5] Thus, to speak about institutional environments and arrangements by referring only to disembodied actors in terms of decision-making, governance, transactions, or other elements of economic, sociological, or organizational theory simply does not represent or reflect the lived experiences of women globally.

To this end, understanding how institutional environments and arrangements, broadly defined but also at the four levels defined by Williamson (1998), are gendered is necessary for a full understanding of the complexities of economic institutions and institutional change. Notably, feminist scholarship in political economy (Luxton & Bezanson, 2006; Rai & Waylen, 2013) and economics (Ferber & Nelson, 2009; Waring & Steinem, 1988) have also addressed some of these concerns in their respective disciplines, while feminist sociologists have examined the social world by reimagining "classic" questions of sociology through feminist lenses (Ingraham, 1994; Smith, 1987; Stacey & Thorne, 1985). These efforts notwithstanding, our focus here is on how the contemporary field of entrepreneurial ecosystems has carried with it the same gender-blind assumptions of institutional economics by way of cluster theory.

2.2.2   Cluster Theory

To understand the relationship between institutional economics and cluster theory, we start by outlining the main assumptions and guiding concepts in cluster theory. In general, cluster theory continues to be a popular mode of analysis in deciphering how and why certain industries and sectors emerge. The idea of a cluster focuses on the geography or place of an organization, expanding on earlier notions of transaction cost economics to include geography as an important consideration on how firms can reduce costs associated with forging relationships and contracts to conduct business (Williamson, 1979, 1998). The notion of a cluster has been pivotal to

---

[5] Ibid.

theorizing about competition, innovation, and economic development in a geographic context (Castells, 1989; Rosenfeld, 1997; Scott & Storper, 2003). In his seminal work, Porter defines clusters as "geographic concentrations of interconnected companies and institutions in a particular field. Clusters encompass an array of linked industries and other entities important to competition ... often extend downstream ... and laterally ... [and] include governmental and other institutions" (1998: 78). His focus on co-location and interdependencies through the concept of "cluster" is an important contribution to our understanding of competition and economic development. The main takeaways are the relevance and importance of co-located industries for economic growth and even revival. Thus, clusters enable scholars to consider geography as an important factor in the governance of economic relationships, and the arising cooperation/competition dynamics as new considerations in minimizing transaction costs and agency problems.

Following this work, a large stream of research has focused on ways in which clusters can develop to provide competitive advantage to regions and nations, a broad perspective that focuses on geographic location, government regulatory actions and policies, and relationships between various actors and organizations across supply chains (Bradshaw & Blakely, 1999; Feser & Bergman, 2000; Ketels & Memedovic, 2008; Porter, 2000; Puga & Venables, 1996; Romanelli & Khessina, 2005; Waits, 2000). Despite these analyses, much research remains descriptive rather than predictive in outlining why certain industries were able to successfully grow while others did not. Moreover, there was little ability in the theories to provide parameters for what could be done: what could policymakers and others interested in economic development do to encourage the growth of industries in particular locations? These questions remain today and are now forming similarly in the context of entrepreneurship as policymakers strive to bring more investors and startups to their cities.

A number of research studies inspired by cluster theory have focused on finding appropriate business strategies for organizations

(Doeringer & Terkla, 1995) and enabling targeted occupations (Currid & Stolarick, 2009; Markusen, 2004) to remain innovative in the context of increased global competition around labor and resource costs, available tax and other incentives, and talent. One of the most relevant conversations has been around the role of clusters in relation to entrepreneurship. Given that entrepreneurship and clusters are each positively linked to economic growth, understanding the way clusters may impact entrepreneurship has engaged a number of scholars. To this end, they suggest that the stage of cluster coupled with advantages in cultural, relational, and institutional dimensions may contribute positively to entrepreneurship activities (Rocha, 2004; Rocha & Sternberg, 2005). Delgado, Porter, & Stern (2010, 2014) find clusters allow for the realization of location-based complementarities and thereby reduce barriers to new business creation.

Yet most studies theorizing this relationship have derived from population ecology, focusing only on density of firms within an industry rather than organizational characteristics or entrepreneurial activities, two important elements of the entrepreneurial process. Specifically, Motoyama (2008) suggests that network elements of clusters have not been sufficiently examined and much more needs to be done in order to understand exchange relationships between and among individuals and firms, and to gain a fuller picture of how clusters function as a system. At the same time, the major focus in the economic geography literature has been on aggregate factors, such as industry, region, and development, with little attention devoted to the nature and behavior of firms as well as the specific connections between them (Taylor & Asheim, 2001; Maskell, 2001).

In all, co-location (place), competitive advantage, and industry have been the hallmark elements of cluster theory and analysis. Yet these elements do little to provide an understanding of actors involved in economic development via organizations or startups. They derive from a location-place analysis of the firm as an extension of transaction cost economics, aimed at minimizing transaction costs while accruing benefits from economies of scale (particularly for small- and medium-sized firms). The focus on industry and location obscures any focus on people, agency, and action even more so than disembodied conversations about decision-making, behavior, and agency problems within institutional economics.

Recently, scholars have suggested that perhaps three key disciplines continue their reliance on cluster theory: strategic management, operations management, and economic geography (Manzini & Di Serio, 2017). Meanwhile, the growth of entrepreneurship as a field in its own right (see Javadian et al., 2018, for an overview of foundations in this field) has allowed for new theories and approaches to come into favor. In this regard, the growth of entrepreneurial ecosystems has emerged but not without carrying over some of the guiding assumptions of cluster theory (and, hence, institutional economics and economic sociology). In the next section, we suggest that some of the tenets of the entrepreneurial ecosystem concept are guided by previous ideas that emerged in cluster theory.

2.3   CORE CONCEPTS IN ENTREPRENEURIAL ECOSYSTEMS RESEARCH

While cluster approaches have proliferated, particularly in relation to competition and economic development in the industrial context, in recent years, a focus on "ecosystems" has emerged as a more holistic approach that includes a wider variety of actors in the innovation- and entrepreneurship-related settings including local design (see Collins, 2015). First used by Moore, the notion of ecosystem was used to describe how "companies co-evolve capabilities around a new innovation: they work cooperatively and competitively to support new products, satisfy customer needs, and eventually incorporate the next round of innovations" (1993: 76). As such, firms were considered to be part of the broader system rather than members of an industry, allowing for consideration of the diverse and different sets of actors that impacted organizations. Since then, scholars have deployed this concept to examine the ways in which innovation takes shape under the umbrella concept of "innovation ecosystems," focusing on interactions and networks at the firm level. In general, this research stream has examined the role of central/anchor firms and the various actors on the production and use sides (Autio & Thomas, 2014).

Further research has focused on establishing the boundaries of ecosystems and understanding value-creation innovation activities (Adner & Kapoor, 2010a, b). Others have focused on business strategies relevant for building innovation ecosystems (Adner, 2006) as well as strategic couplings (Brusoni & Prencipe, 2013). Finally, a stream of research has emerged comparing and outlining innovation ecosystems across different nations (Mercan & Goktas, 2011; Rubens et al., 2011). Overall, the notion of an ecosystem has been used in a wide variety of ways to understand innovation, business, and entrepreneurship (see Pilinkiene & Mačiulis, 2014, for an overview) without much differentiation among concepts such as entrepreneurial versus innovation ecosystems, which, while not the focus of this book, represents emergent discussions within the broader field of entrepreneurship studies.

With respect to entrepreneurial ecosystems, early research focused on identifying major constitutive elements, essentially trying to create a concept that allows for the study of a phenomenon. In this regard, in one of the earliest engagements with what would later be termed "ecosystems" research, Van de Ven (1993) identifies engaged actors and a human competence pool under the concept of "social system framework." Tan et al. (1997) focus on "entrepreneurial infrastructure", which they define as "facilities and services present within a given geographic area which encourage the birth of new ventures and the growth and development of small and medium-sized businesses" (p. 117). Moving towards a more-entrepreneur oriented framework, Feldman (2001) examines the ways in which a successful entrepreneurial culture emerged in the US Capital out of the interactions of entrepreneurs who had supportive social capital, access to investors and venture capital, intermediary organizations, and research universities. Nijkemp (2003) brings forth the idea of a networked society as foundational to entrepreneurship research, positing that networking or connecting is key to entrepreneurial success.

In the decade following Van de Ven (1993), research into ecosystems flourishes as more research and researchers engage in this domain of study. Neck et al. (2004) focus on the emergence of high-tech firms in Boulder County, Colorado and posit that success can be attributed to regional entrepreneurial culture, formal and informal networks, incubator organizations, spin-offs, and physical infrastructure. To this end, Cohen (2006) suggests that ecosystems research needs to focus on communities, formal and informal networks, and physical infrastructure and culture in order to create a "sustainable valley" for entrepreneurship. Meanwhile, Isenberg (2013) brings together markets, human capital, supports, culture, finance, and policy to create a conceptual framework for the study of entrepreneurial ecosystems. In many ways, the elements posited under the umbrella of ecosystems research are quite similar to those that were already studied as part of cluster analyses: risk capital (such as venture capitalists), specialized support services, research universities and corporate research labs, core customers, and a labor force (see Porter, 1998), a point made by Motoyama and Knowlton (2016).

In recent years, there has been a proliferation of approaches including more dynamic models focusing on various aspects of entrepreneurial ecosystems. For example, while Auerswald (2015) does not define an entrepreneurial ecosystem, he differentiates neoclassical approaches from ecological ecosystem approaches to the study of firms and economic development. By doing so, he offers policy prescriptions for growing entrepreneurial ecosystems – an area that we also consider in this book but from a gender lens. And while Mason & Brown (2014) suggest that the locality and temporal elements of ecosystems are under-theorized, their work does not address the nature of relationships between and among ecosystems actors, thereby assuming that all actors can be differentiated by type rather than other characteristics (i.e., demography). Mack & Mayer (2016) focus on the entrepreneurial ecosystems in Phoenix, Arizona to understand perceptions of ecosystem growth while more contemporary work examines the processual nature of ecosystems (Spigel & Harrison, 2018) include focusing on the ways in which ecosystems emerge through complex, inter-related network activities (Roundy et al., 2018).

To date, we find that there is little consideration of the nature of relationships between actors in entrepreneurial ecosystems with some exceptions (Motoyama et al., 2021), despite growing interest. In their recent overview piece, Acs et al. suggest the following in their introduction to the special issue of *Small Business Economics* on entrepreneurial ecosystems:

> The entrepreneurial ecosystem approach has the promise to correct these shortcomings. Its two dominant lineages are the regional development literature and the strategy literature. Both lineages share common roots in ecological systems thinking, providing fresh insights into the interdependence of actors in a particular community to create new value.
>
> *(2017, 1)*

Even in this most recent examination of entrepreneurial ecosystems, there is little attention to the actors beyond the fact that they exist and are engaged in some relationships or exchange activities. In other words, the focus is on the existence of actors and the connections these actors have to each other and resources. In that sense, the actor and connection aspect is a differentiator between cluster theory and entrepreneurial ecosystems approach. However, as we further suggest, the acknowledgement of actors does not suffice in differentiation between different kinds of actors and the kinds of relationships or exchanges they are engaged in: not all relationships, connections, and exchanges are available to all actors. Moreover, entrepreneurial ecosystems have a problem in terms of unit of analysis: it is not clear who or what is being studied under this umbrella concept. Given the various and emergent themes of research on this topic and their different focal areas, it seems likely that ecosystem research reaches a point where scholars are studying everything and nothing at the same time.

In fact, when scholars do examine the connections within an ecosystem, their scope expands extremely widely and becomes vague. For instance, Bloom and Dees (2008) differentiate their ecosystem approach from Michael Porter's economic cluster analysis by including political, cultural, economic, and physical dimensions as important to entrepreneurship activities, but they do not acknowledge the role of networks or connections between/among actors as relevant to this conversation. And while some scholars offer a much more expansive and broad approach to the study of ecosystems, these frameworks do not explicitly focus on who participates or how they participate, (Spigel 2015; Bosma & Holvoet, 2015). Others focus on institutions, but do not provide a refined discussion or differentiation between local and national entrepreneurship systems (Acs, Autio, & Szerb, 2014; Acs et al., 2016), thereby not addressing the fact that actors may or may not participate in the same ways across contexts.

Stangler and Bell-Masterson (2015) note the importance of connectivity in measuring entrepreneurial ecosystems but find that it is difficult to achieve empirically. Some studies examine the connection between a few specific actors within the ecosystem. Águeda (2016) suggests that connectivity between ecosystem founders and investors is relevant for the growth of entrepreneurial ecosystems. Mayer (2011) points out the importance of mentors for entrepreneurs but Scheidgen (2020) suggests that in certain ecosystems, fragmentation leads to certain entrepreneurs connecting to resources, such as mentors, while others are not able to do so. Feldman and Zoller (2012) suggest that dealmakers or intermediaries are important for firm creation, while Kemeny et al. (2016) focus on how local social capital fostered by such dealmakers can be extremely helpful towards new firm creation. Kwon et al. (2020) provide a robust summary of brokerage within entrepreneurship to highlight the value and role of such action. In more recent work, Stam and Van de Ven (2019) bring together a broad systems perspective with a measurement proposition to link ecosystem elements to successful entrepreneurial outcomes in hopes of impacting policies to support entrepreneurship.

In all, there is a robust and lively stream of research that has started to focus on entrepreneurial ecosystems despite the fact that there is no agreed-on definition or shared understanding of a phenomenon or clarity on the unit of analysis used to understand and research the topic. Thus, it seems that this field-formative stage, aiming to understand how gender is relevant to theorizing and research related to entrepreneurial ecosystems, is quite timely. In particular, world events related to the COVID-19 pandemic as well as those that have surfaced historical racial injustices have called attention to the ways in which rules are made, by whom, and for whose benefit. The discipline of entrepreneurship should be no different. If our theories cannot account for the complexity of the world in which we live, then we must take steps to expand, challenge, and redirect them. While the focus of this book is on theoretical engagement of gender with entrepreneurial ecosystem scholarship, we recognize that the arguments we formulate in this book around the ways gender has served as an organizing principle for many societies and economies in terms of institutions, rights, and governance can also be made for race and ethnicity as well as other relations of difference. Notwithstanding this recognition, we believe understanding gender is essential to producing research that has very real, material consequences for policy and practice – an ethical consideration that warrants our attention not at the expense of race/ethnicity and other differences but one that centers gender, gendering, and gendered formations as part of a broader dialogue of who is included in theory and who is left out. It is in this vein that we forge our understanding of gender, bringing an intersectional understanding arising out of antiracist feminist perspective to our work at the intersections of gender and entrepreneurship.

2.4 MAKING SPACE FOR GENDER IN ENTREPRENEURIAL ECOSYSTEMS

To date, only a few scholars have examined the nuanced complexities of connectivity or how entrepreneurs and ESOs connect and relate to each other (Motoyama & Knowlton, 2016; Motoyama et al., 2021) and who may be left out from such connections and networks (Knowlton et al., 2015). We address this gap by focusing explicitly on gender as an organizing principle of entrepreneurial ecosystems and as an important factor for differentiating between/among actors in ecosystems. Gender as an analytic lens allows us to consider the relational dimensions of ecosystems by providing a nuanced approach to understanding how and why certain actors connect to each other and to resources through ESOs. In this sense, we return to our earlier critique of institutional economics and economic sociology in their espousal of disembodied actors, but do so through a focused critique of entrepreneurial ecosystems research. Here, our contention is this: while entrepreneurial ecosystems recognize the social-relational aspects of actors beyond an economic imperative (thus moving the field beyond the idea of pure economic actors as central to ecosystem theory), there is little understanding of such actors as gendered. In other words, the uptake of gender in entrepreneurial ecosystems research relies on it as a category of difference rather than understanding how the very institutional environments and arrangements are themselves gendered and how this gendering is relevant for understanding any "gender differences" that might arise.

Consequently, in recent years, gender in relation to entrepreneurial ecosystems specifically has been of growing interest to scholars in the broad field of gender and entrepreneurship studies. While this growing interest is important and relevant, much of the recent literature in entrepreneurial ecosystems focuses on gender as categorical sex, comparing women and men. In other words, much of this recent work still understands gender as a binary sex category and focuses on women/female entrepreneurs. For example, Berger and

Kuckertz's (2016) qualitative research on why certain entrepreneurial ecosystems have a dearth of female founders identifies factors that may help explain the paucity. Their findings suggest that ecosystems with favorable markets, access to talent and capital, startup experience, as well as general gender equality make up the factors related to higher instances of female founders in the ecosystem. They suggest that policies aimed at fostering and supporting entrepreneurship in general may not necessarily translate into support for female entrepreneurs. This is due to the fact that women may associate government support for entrepreneurship as really benefiting males rather than females. Similarly, Simmons et al. (2018) focus on gender gaps in re-entry to entrepreneurship across different national contexts by examining institutions and stigmas associated with business failure. They suggest that ecosystem inefficiencies need to be addressed in order to mitigate such gaps.

Yet what is missing from these conversations is the paucity of women who control capital, not just of those who have tried to gain access to it or the ways in which existing institutions are already gendered. Policies aimed at remediating access to capital for women or those that focus on institutions as if they were gender-neutral do not necessarily recognize or remedy gendered ownership and control of capital in market-based economies; such a recognition would require a conversation about governance and resource allocation at the very least, but also about the creation of institutional environments that favor, maintain, and replicate majority male ownership of capital and control over governance structures.

Other recent work in this domain focuses on the ways women-only networking platforms create gender capital, enabling women to participate in entrepreneurial ecosystems (McAdam, Harrison, & Leitch, 2019). As a point of contrast, other findings suggest that such approaches create parallel and unequal opportunities in the context of tech-entrepreneurship (Ozkazanc-Pan & Clark Muntean, 2018) rather create additional or different opportunities for women to participate in entrepreneurial ecosystems. Additional work in this domain focuses on how males and females experience support for their start-ups in entrepreneurial ecosystems (Sperber & Linder, 2019) and exam-ines how race, ethnicity, and previous venture experience impact the ways social capital is distributed among women entrepreneurs in entrepreneurial ecosystems (Neumeyer et al., 2018). Or in some instances, scholars use terms like "gendered" without a full explan-ation or understanding of what gendered might mean in relation to entrepreneurial ecosystems (Brush et al., 2018), actors and ESOs.

In all, much of these recent publications and research on entrepreneurial ecosystems replicate the approach utilized in the women's entrepreneurship literature, which we review in the next chapter through feminist frameworks, whereby gender and sex are used interchangeably and comparisons between male and female entrepreneurs offered. As such, our book provides novel insights as to the ways gender "makes a difference" in how entrepreneurial ecosystems are theorized and studied in relation to individual actors/entrepreneurs, ESOs, and broader sociocultural norms by deriv-ing insights from gender studies and feminist perspectives. Our con-tention is that it's not only "differences" between the actors in entrepreneurial ecosystems that accounts for the ways women experi-ence and engage within ecosystems, but that the very ways in which entrepreneurial ecosystem are conceptualized and studied inclusive of the concepts available do not allow for an examination of gendered ideas, norms, and practices of entrepreneurship arising from gendered informal institution, environments, governance, and resource allocation.

Our approach is to bring in key concepts from gender studies to provide three important contributions to the study of entrepreneurial ecosystems. The first contribution emanates from an analysis and conceptualization of actors in entrepreneurial ecosystems as gendered and embodied rather than disembodied and homogenous. Fundamentally, this changes how entrepreneurial ecosystems are theorized and studied in relation to who participates, connects to each other, and connects to resources. Second, we focus on the ways gender, gender relations, and gendering take shape individually at different "levels" – the micro, meso, and macro – in ecosystems. At the micro level, we focus on individual entrepreneurs and biases, at the meso level, we focus on entrepreneurship support organizations and networks, and at the macro level, we focus on broader sociocultural norms and policies that impact gender, gender relations, and gendering. Our analysis at each level addresses the ways gender makes a difference for how we theorize and understand entrepreneurial ecosystems with respect to the concept/level in question. Our third and final contribution is to develop a holistic framework for studying gender at all three levels simultaneously and to provide novel insights for the rethinking entrepreneurial ecosystems as gendered, embodied, and relational systems for entrepreneurship activities. This framework allows us to provide recommendations for policymakers who want to support entrepreneurship and support inclusive economic development activities in their cities.

It further allows us to remark that the field of entrepreneurial ecosystems specifically and entrepreneurship broadly require urgent engagement with the complexities of the political, social, and cultural kind to carry out research and offer insights that do not replicate gendered inequalities in economic opportunities. If entrepreneurship is seen as a way for women to gain economic empowerment and autonomy across the globe, then our theories for understanding and studying the institutional systems that can allow this social change to take shape must be able to account for gender in the first place. We demonstrate this through our empirical work in the following three chapters, focusing explicitly on individual, organizational, and institutional level considerations arising from feminist critique and analysis. And at each level, we do so by highlighting those assumptions, practices, and policies that arise from gendered frameworks with the intention of shedding light on blind spots that continue to operate without challenge or remedy in contemporary society.

Witnessing the gendered and racialized outcomes of the ongoing pandemic coupled with social and civil unrest behooves us as scholars to understand and address the ways our theories about the social and the economic domains may contribute to continued blind spots. We believe that it is our duty as responsible scholars to expand our current approaches and theories to be able to account for the complexities, paradoxes, and lived experiences of groups traditionally marginalized from entrepreneurship scholars. We undertake this engagement through the frameworks and concepts derived from feminist perspectives and use them to provide an understanding of the various elements of entrepreneurial ecosystems and, ultimately, to make recommendations for a holistic approach to gender-inclusive economic development policies.

REFERENCES

Acs, Z. J., Audretsch, D. B., Lehmann, E. E., & Licht, G. (2016). National systems of innovation. *Small Business Economics*, *46*(4): 527–535.

Acs, Z. J., Autio, E., & Szerb, L. (2014). National systems of entrepreneurship: Measurement issues and policy implications. *Research Policy*, *43*(3): 476–494.

Acs, Z. J., Stam, E., Audretsch, D. B., & O'Connor, A. (2017). The lineages of the entrepreneurial ecosystem approach. *Small Business Economics*, *49*(1): 1–10.

Adner, R. (2006). Match your innovation strategy to your innovation ecosystem. *Harvard Business Review*, *84*(4): 98.

Adner, R., & Kapoor, R. (2010a). Value creation in innovation ecosystems: How the structure of technological interdependence affects firm performance in new technology generations. *Strategic Management Journal*, *31*(3): 306–333.

Adner, R., & Kapoor, R. (2010b). Innovation ecosystems and the pace of substitution: Re-examining technology S-curves. *Strategic Management Journal*, *37*: 625–648.

Águeda, A. F. P. (2016). *Interconnectivity between ecosystem builders and investor groups in European startup ecosystems* (Doctoral dissertation). Available at https://run.unl.pt/handle/10362/18268 (accessed July 18, 2019).

Alchian, A. A., & Demsetz, H. (1972). Production, information costs, and economic organization. *The American Economic Review*, *62*(5): 777–795.

Auerswald, P. E. (2015). Enabling entrepreneurial ecosystems. Kauffman Foundation Research Series on City, Metro and Regional Entrepreneurship. Available at www.kauffman.org/~/media/kauffman_org/research%20reports%20and%20covers/2015/10/enabling_entrepreneurial_ecosystems.pdf (accessed January 15, 2020).

Autio, E., & Thomas, L. (2014). Innovation ecosystems. In M. Dodgson, N. Phillips, & D. M. Gann (Eds.), *The Oxford handbook of innovation management* (pp. 204–288). Oxford: Oxford University Press.

Berger, E. S., & Kuckertz, A. (2016). Female entrepreneurship in startup ecosystems worldwide. *Journal of Business Research*, 69(11): 5163–5168.

Bertrand, M., Goldin, C., & Katz, L. F. (2010). Dynamics of the gender gap for young professionals in the financial and corporate sectors. *American Economic Journal: Applied Economics*, 2(3): 228–255.

Bloom, P. N., & Dees, G. (2008). Cultivate your ecosystem. *Stanford Social Innovation Review*, 6(1): 47–53.

Bosma, N., & Holvoet, T. (2015). The role of culture in entrepreneurial ecosystems: An investigation for European regions. Presented at the *6th Annual George Washington University (GWU)-International Council for Small Business (ICSB) Global Entrepreneurship Research and Policy Conference*. Available at http://dx.doi.org/10.2139/ssrn.2700798 (accessed September 30, 2020).

Bradshaw, T. K., & Blakely, E. J. (1999). What are "third-wave" state economic development efforts? From incentives to industrial policy. *Economic Development Quarterly*, 13(3): 229–244.

Brush, C., Edelman, L. F., Manolova, T., & Welter, F. (2018). A gendered look at entrepreneurship ecosystems. *Small Business Economics*, 53: 393–408.

Brusoni, S., & Prencipe, A. (2013). The organization of innovation in ecosystems: Problem framing, problem solving, and patterns of coupling. In R. Adner, J. E. Oxley, & B. S. Silverman (Eds.), *Collaboration and competition in business ecosystems* (pp. 167–194). Bingley: Emerald Group Publishing Limited.

Castells, M. (1989). *Informational city: Information technology, economic restructuring, and the urban-regional process*. Oxford: Blackwell.

Clark Muntean, S., & Ozkazanc-Pan, B. (2015). A gender integrative conceptualization of entrepreneurship. *New England Journal of Entrepreneurship*, 18(1): 27–40.

Coase, R. (1998). The new institutional economics. *The American Economic Review*, 88(2): 72–74.

Coase, R. H. (1937/1995). The nature of the firm. Reprinted in S. Estrin & A. Marin (Eds.), *Essential readings in economics* (pp. 37–54). London: Palgrave.

Cohen, B. (2006). Sustainable valley entrepreneurial ecosystems. *Business Strategy and the Environment*, 15(1): 1–14.

Collins, P. K. (2015). Building a local design and entrepreneurship ecosystem. *Procedia Technology*, 20: 258–262.

Currid, E., & Stolarick, K. (2009). The occupation–industry mismatch: New trajectories for regional cluster analysis and economic development. *Urban Studies*, 47(2): 337–362.

Davis, L. E., & North, D. C. (1971). *Institutional change and American economic growth*. Cambridge: Cambridge University Press.

Delgado, M., Porter, M. E., & Stern, S. (2010). Clusters and entrepreneurship. *Journal of Economic Geography*, 10(4): 495–518.

Delgado, M., Porter, M. E., & Stern, S. (2014). Clusters, convergence, and economic performance. *Research Policy*, 43(10): 1785–1799.

Doeringer, P. B., & Terkla, D. G. (1995). Business strategy and cross-industry clusters. *Economic Development Quarterly*, 9(3): 225–237.

Eisenhardt, K. M. (1989). Agency theory: An assessment and review. *Academy of Management Review*, 14(1): 57–74.

Feldman, M. P. (2001). The entrepreneurial event revisited: Firm formation in a regional context. *Industrial and Corporate Change*, 10(4): 861–891.

Feldman, M., & Zoller, T. D. (2012). Dealmakers in place: Social capital connections in regional entrepreneurial economies. *Regional Studies*, 46(1): 23–37.

Ferber, M. A., & Nelson, J. A. (Eds.). (2009). *Beyond economic man: Feminist theory and economics*. Chicago: University of Chicago Press.

Fernandez, R. (2018). Family and gender: Questions for the new institutional economics. In C. Menard & M. M. Shirley (Eds.), *A research agenda for new institutional economics* (pp. 189–195). Northampton, MA: Edward Elgar Publishing.

Feser, E. J., & Bergman, E. M. (2000). National industry cluster templates: A framework for applied regional cluster analysis. *Regional Studies*, 34(1): 1–19.

Frietsch, R., Haller, I., Funken-Vrohlings, M., & Grupp, H. (2009). Gender-specific patterns in patenting and publishing. *Research Policy*, 38: 590–599.

Granovetter, M. (1985). Economic action and social structure: The problem of embeddedness. *American Journal of Sociology*, 91(3): 481–510.

Ingraham, C. (1994). The heterosexual imaginary: Feminist sociology and theories of gender. *Sociological Theory*, 12(2): 203–219.

Javadian, G., Gupta, V. K., Dutta, D. K., Guo, G. C., Osorio, A. E., & Ozkazanc-Pan, B. (2018). *Foundational research in entrepreneurship studies*. Cham: Palgrave-MacMillan. doi: 10.1007/978-3-319-73528-3.

Jennings, J. E., & Brush, C. G. (2013). Research on women entrepreneurs: Challenges to (and from) the broader entrepreneurship literature?. *The Academy of Management Annals*, 7(1): 663–715.

Kemeny, T., Feldman, M., Ethridge, F., & Zoller, T. (2016). The economic value of local social networks. *Journal of Economic Geography*, 16(5): 1101–1122.

Ketels, C. H., & Memedovic, O. (2008). From clusters to cluster-based economic development. *International Journal of Technological Learning, Innovation and Development*, 1(3): 375–392.

Khan, B. Z. (2005). *The democratization of invention: Patents and copyrights in American economic development, 1790–1920*. New York: Cambridge University Press.

Knowlton, K., Ozkazanc-Pan, B., Clark Muntean, S., & Motoyama, Y. (2015). Support organizations and remediating the gender gap in entrepreneurial ecosystems: A case study of St. Louis. Available at http://dx.doi.org/10.2139/ssrn .2685116 (accessed May 15, 2019).

Kwon, S. W., Rondi, E., Levin, D. Z., De Massis, A., & Brass, D. J. (2020). Network brokerage: An integrative review and future research agenda. *Journal of Management*, 46(6): 1092–1120.

Luxton, M., & Bezanson, K. (Eds.). (2006). *Social reproduction: Feminist political economy challenges neo-liberalism*. Montreal, Canada: McGill-Queen's Press (MQUP).

Mack, E., & Mayer, H. (2016). The evolutionary dynamics of entrepreneurial ecosystems. *Urban Studies*, 53(10): 2118–2133.

Manzini, R. B., & Di Serio, L. C. (2017). Current thinking on cluster theory and its translation in economic geography and strategic and operations management: Is a reconciliation possible?. *Competitiveness Review: An International Business Journal*, 27(4): 366–389.

Markusen, A. (2004). Targeting occupations in regional and community economic development. *Journal of the American Planning Association*, 70(3): 253–268.

Maskell, P. (2001). Firm in economic gography. *Economic Geography*, 77(4): 329–343.

Mason, C., & Brown, R. (2014). Entrepreneurial ecosystems and growth oriented entrepreneurship. Final Report to OECD, Paris, 1–38.

Mayer, H. (2011). *Entrepreneurship and innovation in second tier regions*. Bingley: Edward Elgar Publishing.

McAdam, M., Harrison, R. T., & Leitch, C. M. (2019). Stories from the field: Women's networking as gender capital in entrepreneurial ecosystems. *Small Business Economics*, 53(2): 459–474.

McCammon, H. J., Campbell, K. E., Granberg, E. M., & Mowery, C. (2001). How movements win: Gendered opportunity structures and US women's suffrage movements, 1866 to 1919. *American Sociological Review*, 66(1): 49–70.

Ménard, C., & Shirley, M. M. (Eds.). (2005). *Handbook of new institutional economics* (Vol. 9). Dordrecht: Springer.

Mercan, B., & Goktas, D. (2011). Components of innovation ecosystems: A cross-country study. *International Research Journal of Finance and Economics*, 76: 102–112.

Moore, J. F. (1993). Predators and prey: A new ecology of competition. *Harvard Business Review*, 71(3): 75–83.

Motoyama, Y. (2008). What was new about the cluster theory? What could it answer and what could it not answer?. *Economic Development Quarterly*, 22(4): 353–363.

Motoyama, Y., & Knowlton, K. (2016). Examining the connections within the startup ecosystem: A case study of St. Louis. *Entrepreneurship Research Journal*, 7(1), online. doi: 10.1515/erj-2016-0011.

Motoyama, Y., Muntean, S. C., Knowlton, K., & Ozkazanc-Pan, B. (2021). Causes of the gender divide within entrepreneurship ecosystems. *Local Economy*. doi: 10.1177/0269094221995783.

Neck, H. M., Meyer, G. D., Cohen, B., & Corbett, A. C. (2004). An entrepreneurial system view of new venture creation. *Journal of Small Business Management*, 42(2): 190–208.

Neumeyer, X., Santos, S. C., Caetano, A., & Kalbfleisch, P. (2018). Entrepreneurship ecosystems and women entrepreneurs: A social capital and network approach. *Small Business Economics*, 1–15.

Nijkamp, P. (2003). Entrepreneurship in a modern network economy. *Regional Studies*, 37(4): 395–405.

North, D. C. (1991). Institutions. *Journal of Economic Perspectives*, 5(1): 97–112.

Ozkazanc-Pan, B. (2018). Bowen and Hisrich (1986) on the female entrepreneur: 30 years of research and new directions for gender and entrepreneurship scholarship. In G. Javadian, V. Gupta, D. Dutta, G. Guo, A. Osorio, & B. Ozkazanc-Pan (Eds.), *Foundational research in entrepreneurship studies: Insightful contributions and future pathways* (pp. 103–126). Cham, Switzerland: Palgrave Macmillan.

Ozkazanc-Pan, B., & Clark Muntean, S. (2018). Networking towards (in) equality: Women entrepreneurs in technology. *Gender, Work & Organization*, 25(4): 379–400.

Pilinkienė, V., & Mačiulis, P. (2014). Comparison of different ecosystem analogies: The main economic determinants and levels of impact. *Procedia-Social and Behavioral Sciences*, 156: 365–370.

Porter, M. E. (1998). Clusters and the new economics of competition. *Harvard Business Review*, 76(6): 77–90.

Porter, M. E. (2000). Location, competition, and economic development: Local clusters in a global economy. *Economic Development Quarterly*, 14(1): 15–34.

Puga, D., & Venables, A. J. (1996). The spread of industry: Spatial agglomeration in economic development. Available at http://eprints.lse.ac.uk/20683/1/The_Spread_of_Industry_Spatial_Agglomeration_in_Economic_Development.pdf

Rai, S. M., & Waylen, G. (Eds.). (2013). *New frontiers in feminist political economy.* New York: Routledge.

Rocha, H. O. (2004). Entrepreneurship and development: The role of clusters. *Small Business Economics, 23*(5): 363–400.

Rocha, H. O., & Sternberg, R. (2005). Entrepreneurship: The role of clusters theoretical perspectives and empirical evidence from Germany. *Small Business Economics, 24*(3): 267–292.

Romanelli, E., & Khessina, O. M. (2005). Regional industrial identity: Cluster configurations and economic development. *Organization Science, 16*(4): 344–358.

Rosenfeld, S. A. (1997). Bringing business clusters into the mainstream of economic development. *European Planning Studies, 5*(1): 3–23.

Roundy, P. T., Bradshaw, M., & Brockman, B. K. (2018). The emergence of entrepreneurial ecosystems: A complex adaptive systems approach. *Journal of Business Research,*86: 1–10.

Rubens, N., Still, K., Huhtamäki, J., & Russell, M. G. (2011). A network analysis of investment firms as resource routers in Chinese innovation ecosystem. *Journal of Software, 6*(9): 1737–1745.

Scheidgen, K. (2020). Degrees of integration: How a fragmented entrepreneurial ecosystem promotes different types of entrepreneurs. *Entrepreneurship & Regional Development, 33*: 1–26.

Schumpeter, J. (1943). *Capitalism, socialism & democracy.* New York: Routledge.

Scott, A. J., & Storper, M. (2003). Regions, globalization, development. *Regional Studies, 37*(6–7): 579–593.

Simmons, S. A., Wiklund, J., Levie, J., Bradley, S. W., & Sunny, S. A. (2018). Gender gaps and reentry into entrepreneurial ecosystems after business failure. *Small Business Economics, 57*: 517–531.

Small Business Economics (2017). Special issue on entrepreneurial ecosystems. Available at www.springer.com/cda/content/document/cda_downloaddocu ment/Entrepreneurial+Ecosystems+SBE+Call+for+Papers_13052015.pdf? SGWID=0-0-45-1508968-p35745940

Smith, D. E. (1987). *The everyday world as problematic: A feminist sociology.* Toronto: University of Toronto Press.

Sperber, S., & Linder, C. (2019). Gender-specifics in start-up strategies and the role of the entrepreneurial ecosystem. *Small Business Economics, 53*(2): 533–546.

Spigel, B. (2015). The relational organization of entrepreneurial ecosystems. *Entrepreneurship Theory and Practice, 41*(1): 49–72.

Spigel, B., & Harrison, R. (2018). Toward a process theory of entrepreneurial ecosystems. *Strategic Entrepreneurship Journal, 12*(1): 151–168.

Stacey, J., & Thorne, B. (1985). The missing feminist revolution in sociology. *Social Problems, 32*(4): 301–316.

Stam, E., & van de Ven, A. (2019). Entrepreneurial ecosystem elements. *Small Business Economics, 56*: 809–832.

Stangler, D., & Bell-Masterson, J. (2015). Measuring an entrepreneurial ecosystem. Kauffman Foundation Research Series on City, Metro, and Regional Entrepreneurship, 1–16. Available at http://dx.doi.org/10.2139/ssrn.2580336

Tan, T. M., Tan, W. L., & Young, J. E. (1997). The decision to participate in entrepreneurial networks: The case of Singapore. *Proceedings of the USASBE*, pp. 116–131.

Taylor, M., & Asheim, B. (2001). Concept of the firm in economic geography. *Economic Geography, 77*(4): 315–328.

Van de Ven, H. (1993). The development of an infrastructure for entrepreneurship. *Journal of Business Venturing, 8*(3): 211–230.

Waits, M. J. (2000). The added value of the industry cluster approach to economic analysis, strategy development, and service delivery. *Economic Development Quarterly, 14*(1): 35–50.

Waring, M., & Steinem, G. (1988). *If women counted: A new feminist economics.* San Francisco: Harper & Row.

Whittington, K., & Smith-Doerr, L. (2005). Gender and commercial science: Women's patenting in the life sciences. *Journal of Technology Transfer, 30*: 355–370.

Williamson, O. E. (1979). Transaction-cost economics: The governance of contractual relations. *The Journal of Law and Economics, 22*(2): 233–261.

Williamson, O. E. (1993). Transaction cost economics and organization theory. *Industrial and Corporate Change, 2*(2): 107–156.

Williamson, O. E. (1998). Transaction cost economics: How it works; where it is headed. *De economist, 146*(1): 23–58.

Williamson, O. E. (2008). Transaction cost economics. In C. Ménard & M. M. Shirley (Eds.), *Handbook of new institutional economics* (pp. 41–65). Berlin, Heidelberg: Springer.

3 Understanding Gender and Inclusion in Entrepreneurial Ecosystems

3.1 INTRODUCTION

By relying on insights from feminist scholarship in entrepreneurship (Ahl & Marlow, 2012; Calás, Smircich, & Bourne, 2007, 2009; Clark Muntean & Ozkazanc-Pan, 2016) and sociology (Acker, 1992, 2006; Ridgeway & Correll, 2004), this chapter provides key theoretical insights about the ways gender can be conceptualized and studied with respect to entrepreneurial ecosystems. Feminist work allows for differentiation among the concepts of sex, gender, and gender relations to lay the foundation for a dynamic understanding of human behavior in entrepreneurial ecosystems. Gender is revealed as an organizing principle in society that manifests itself in decision-making among entrepreneurial actors rather than simply a dimension of an individual's sense of self or identity. Further, this body of work presents inclusion as a multifaceted concept and practice. In all, feminist insights allow us to consider macro-level (i.e. institutional and structural) explanations for the gender gap in entrepreneurship as we locate individuals' experiences within broader societal constructs, relations, and structures. Beyond recommending interventions targeted to individual women or female entrepreneurs as a social group, this chapter provides recommendations on interventions targeted to changing male behaviors and the preference for the masculine in the system, while offering challenges to assumptions underlying the entrepreneurial ecosystem itself. To this end, a recent and relevant case study is presented to challenge the widespread belief that meritocracy and rationality are the primary bases for investment decisions. Lastly, this chapter provides insights about effective ways to study and promote gender inclusion in relation to individuals, organizations, and institutionalized sociocultural norms derived from feminist frameworks. In doing so, we provide a multifactor and multi-level gender framework for improving inclusion in entrepreneurship activities and entrepreneurial ecosystems.

According to Stangler and Bell-Masterson (2015), a healthy and inclusive entrepreneurial ecosystem requires density (high numbers and percentages of persons engaged in entrepreneurial activities), fluidity (immigration, flexible labor market, firm growth), connectivity (networks that promote deal flow and dealmaking), and diversity of opportunity. Yet for all four of these conditions, women's entrepreneurial activity is lower than that of men (McAdam et al., 2019: 459). Women remain underrepresented in successful entrepreneurial ecosystems (McAdam et al., 2019), and men are dominant on founding teams, in top leadership positions, and on boards of directors of all sizes of companies. However, men are especially overrepresented on those startup teams that begin as privately held companies and end up receiving external equity investment. This is important as these are the conditions that grant entrepreneurs access to the path of issuing stock on a public exchange through an initial public offering (IPO). Men are also predominant in their roles as gatekeepers who hold the power to approve or decline support for entrepreneurs. Those who hold the top administrative decision-making positions at ESOs (such as accelerators, incubators, and investment clubs) also lean heavily male. Institutional investors (including investment banks, venture capital firms, pension funds, and angel investment networks) are similarly run by a supermajority of men.

This sizable dearth of women in power is evident throughout and across entrepreneurial ecosystems. Evidence suggests that a gender system is in play, including in what are deemed to be model entrepreneurial ecosystems. Deep-set beliefs about occupational roles and gender roles in society intersect to inform beliefs about who is the best fit for running high-growth ventures. "When hegemonic gender beliefs are effectively salient in a situation, hierarchical presumptions about men's greater status and competence become salient for participants; this hierarchical dimension ... is particularly consequential for gender inequality" (Ridgeway & Correll, 2004, 517, citing Eagly, Wood, & Diekman, 2000). Specifically, men's gender is salient and signals status, competency, and best fit for leading equity-backed enterprises, and this aggravates gender gaps in entrepreneurship and in the business world.

In entrepreneurial ecosystems, these gendered hierarchies, assumptions, and biases explain large and consistent gender gaps in evaluation of performance and merit, and how this translates into inequalities in who receives support and resources and how much their ventures receive in equity funding. For example, all-male teams received 76 percent of the total invested in 2018 ($109.36 billion of the total of $130 billion).[1] In the same year, all-female founders received $10 billion less in funding than a single e-cigarette company, Juul.[2] With approximately 90 percent of all venture capital decision makers across the globe being male,[3] the system is skewed heavily toward rewarding men with financial capital and the bounty of support, and the financial, social, and political rewards that follow that investment.

In order to explain the nuanced ways in which gender is relevant to understanding entrepreneurial ecosystems, we begin with an exploration into how entrepreneurial practices are gendered such that they produce and reproduce hegemonic masculinity within and across ecosystems. Examples include prioritizing male identities, traits, and styles in investment, and technology venture incubation decisions (Balachandra et al., 2019; Brooks et al., 2014; Marlow & McAdam, 2013). This triangulation of work reveals widespread yet situated gendered practices in entrepreneurship, which raises challenges to the foundational body of entrepreneurship literature that assumes actors are economically rational and operate in a universal system

---

[1] https://fortune.com/2019/01/28/funding-female-founders-2018/ (accessed May 2, 2019).

[2] Ibid.

[3] https://news.crunchbase.com/news/inside-vc-firms-the-gender-divide/ (accessed September 9, 2020).

that is nongendered (Bruni, Gherardi, & Poggio, 2004). In order to provide a theoretical foundation for analyzing these phenomena, we first provide a literature review of multiple sociological and feminist perspectives. This theoretical grounding will help the reader better understand gender and its relevance to entrepreneurial ecosystems. Then, for deeper analysis, reflection, and understanding, we apply this body of work to a case study of gendered practices.

3.2   SEX, GENDER, AND GENDER RELATIONS

To begin with, one must differentiate among sex, gender, and gender relations to lay the foundation for a dynamic understanding of actors in entrepreneurial ecosystems. The term "sex" is best defined as the sex one is assigned at birth, or one's biological sex, with the need to acknowledge that persons born intersex may not fit into this binary categorization. Gender, on the other hand, is more recently theorized as socially constructed; that is, "as a product of socialization and experience" (Calás & Smircich, 2006: 4). The various subsets of feminist theory (e.g. liberal, socialist, radical, postmodern) focus on different salient aspects of what constitutes gender, including role socialization, cultural practices, formative development of identity and relations to others, and the processes and conditions embedded in power relations (Calás & Smircich, 2006).

According to Scott (1986), "gender is a constitutive element of social relations based on perceived differences between the sexes, and gender is a primary way of signifying relationships of power" (Scott, 1986: 1067, as cited in Acker, 1990: 145). In this respect, gender can be viewed "as both an organizing principle and an axis of power" (Calás & Smircich, 2006: 26). Scholars who focus on gender as a principle of social organization illuminate ways in which "gender is pervasive in society, operates on multiple levels, and shapes identities, perceptions, interactional practices, and the very forms of social institutions" (Sprague, 2016: viii). Gender, therefore, can be thought of as a system through which "men as a group dominate and control women as a group" (Calás & Smircich, 2006: 21). This socialist feminist perspective in particular views gender as "more than a socially constructed, binary identity"; rather, "gender is theorized dynamically in processual and material ways ... as a constitutive element of social relationships based on perceived differences between the sexes, and (as) a primary way of signifying relationships of power" (Calás & Smircich, 2006, 22 citing Scott, 1986: 1067).

The more static binary category of biological *sex* (male and female) and the more constructed, fluid, and dynamic concept of *gender* intersect in complex ways to form a powerful "organizing principle of social relations" (Ridgeway & Correll, 2004: 515). "Men" and "women," then, are conventionally used as binary categories in a heteronormative culture to refer to both sex and gender. This "sex categorization automatically activates gender stereotypes, including gender status distinctions, and primes them to affect judgments and behavior" (Ridgeway & Correll, 2004: 515, citing Blair & Banaji, 1996). These gender beliefs powerfully shape the evaluations and behaviors of individuals who are raised in the culture that perpetuates them and, importantly, in ways that are largely implicit and unconscious (Ridgeway & Correll, 2004).

According to the European Institute for Gender Equality, "gender relations" is defined as the "specific subset of social relations uniting women and men as social groups in a particular community, including how power – and access to/control over resources – is distributed between the sexes."[4] Gender relations are informed by "hegemonic cultural beliefs about gender" that impact "social relational contexts" and "maintain ... the gender system" (Ridgeway & Correll, 2004: 510). According to Witz and Savage (1991: 3), "organizational processes are central to the understanding of gender relations, and concomitantly, that organizations are gendered." In other words, gender relations are central to our understanding of organizational phenomena, human behavior in organizations, and the ways in which organizations represent situated contexts with enforcing processes

---

[4] https://eige.europa.eu/thesaurus/terms/1207 (accessed June 12, 2020).

and practices that perpetuate gender inequality in and across industries, sectors, and the greater society.

Gender or "gendering," according to the body of scholarship referenced herein, is viewed as a socially systemic "process, produced and reproduced through relations of power among differently positioned members of society, including relations emerging from historical processes, dominant discourses and institutions, and dominant epistemological conceptualizations, all of which become naturalized as 'the way it is'" (Calás & Smircich, 2006: 21). Concerned with the damaging effects of systemic inequality, activist feminists seek to change working conditions that disadvantage women. In order to better understand how gender relations disempower women, these feminists deconstruct "social, economic, cultural and knowledge relations," understanding these as "relations of power, in which gendered (and other) identities and subjectivities are formed" (Calás & Smircich, 2006: 21). Going further, feminists drawing from Critical Management Studies attempt to "denaturalize" (Grey & Willmott, 2005: 5–6) assumptions about human behavior in organizations to deconstruct existing power structures that harm women, dismantle status quos that disadvantage women, and de-essentialize persons as inherently belonging to or being identified with a particular sex or gender category.

3.3   FEMINIST PERSPECTIVES: ORGANIZATIONS

Feminist theorists have extended our understanding of organizational phenomena by analyzing the ways in which sex, gender, and gender relations explain place-based phenomenon that occurs at the level of organizations. These scholars raise concerns related to women and work in organizations, including access to resources and career tracks that stem from gender differences in evaluation, performance, pay, and promotion. Organizational practices, cultures, and norms are interrogated for how they limit women's potential as individuals as well as women's equality as a socially defined category. Sex, gender, and gender relations can influence the way one sees oneself, the way one plays out a social, personal, or professional role in society, and the way one enacts the role of entrepreneur, manager, investor, etc. (Ridgeway & Correll, 2004).

Feminist sociologist Joan Acker was among the first to raise the need for a systematic feminist theory of gender and organizations. She based this on five premises: (1) the gender segregation of work is partly created through organizational practices; (2) income and status inequality between women and men is also partly created in organizational processes; (3) organizations are an arena in which widely disseminated cultural images of gender are invented and reproduced; (4) individual gender identity aspects, particularly masculinity, are products of organizational processes and pressures; and (5) an important feminist project is to make organizations more democratic and supportive of humane goals (Acker, 1990: 140). To this end, Acker examined organizations as gendered processes in which the dominant discourse and abstract conceptualizations from the male standpoint or perspective in effect obscure processes of control in work organizations under the guise of gender-neutrality (Acker, 1990). Building on Rosabeth Moss Kanter's work on deconstructing organizations as "sex-neutral machines [whilst] masculine principles were dominating their authority structures" (Moss Kanter, 1977: 291–292 in Acker, 1990: 143), Acker illuminated gender "as a complex component of processes of control and domination" in order for us to better "understand how deeply embedded gender is in organizations" (Acker, 1990: 143). Women's experiences in male-dominated organizational contexts "tells us a great deal about how power in organizing processes perpetuates gender inequity" (Acker, 2000: 631).

This body of work reveals how organizational cultures created by dominant actors establish normative expectations for behaviors of members. Further, these studies both reveal the systemic nature of gender bias and suggest that organizations themselves are "fundamentally gendered" (Acker, 2000: 625). Widespread cultural beliefs, often referred to as stereotypes, impact "social relational contexts" (Ridgeway & Correll, 2004) that are situated in particular spaces, including inside organizations. For example, gender informs what actors at work in organizations do and do not do, say and do not say. Perceptions about and attitudes toward others are informed by the expectations that behaviors be aligned with one's sex category (West & Zimmerman, 1987). Socially constructed norms based on appropriate expressions of masculinity and femininity guide and influence "perceptual, interactional and micro-political activities" (Poggio, 2006: 226). In other words, cultural beliefs about gender constitute rules for enacting the gender system, and these social relational contexts are the arenas in which these rules are brought to bear on the behavior and evaluations of individuals (Ridgeway & Correll, 2004: 514). Given that organizations and their dominant actors both establish and reinforce these activities, normative behaviors, and social relations in a way that is gendered, organizations themselves "do gender" (Gherardi, 1994, in Poggio, 2006: 226).

In sum, feminist sociologists who study organizations and human behavior within them recognize "the centrality of gender as an organizing principle in all social systems, including work, politics, everyday interactions, families, economic development, law, education, and a host of other social domains" (Sprague, 2016: vii). These scholars illuminate how "hegemonic gender beliefs are institutionalized in the norms and structures of public settings and established private institutions" and, further, how these hegemonic beliefs are "enforced by socially advantaged actors" (Ridgeway & Correll, 2004: 517). A sociological understanding of gender offers a "gender lens" that makes "gender visible in social phenomena, asking if, how, and why social processes, standards, and opportunities differ systematically in women and men" as well as "recognizing that gender inequality is inextricably intertwined with other systems of inequality" (Sprague, 2016: viii). While our focus is on gender inequality in entrepreneurship, we recognize that other systems of inequality are at play, including class, race, ethnicity, nationality, sexual orientation, sexual identity, ability, and age, among others.

3.4 FEMINIST PERSPECTIVES: ENTREPRENEURSHIP

Entrepreneurship as a construct, practice, and economic activity is not immune to gender's pervasiveness as an organizing principle. Gender operates on multiple levels and shapes the identities, perceptions, practices, and institutions within entrepreneurial spaces. Gender gaps in entrepreneurship translate into economic, social, and political gender gaps that disadvantage women. Feminist theorists across disciplines share a concern with gender relations and social change and hold a common goal of providing "alternative ways of theorizing that may have significant social and political consequences" (Hurley, 1999: 55). Feminist perspectives on organizations reveal how actors, organizations, and institutions perpetuate gender inequality. This approach highlights how beliefs, attitudes, and perceptions translate into practices and decisions that hinder women from realizing economic gains comparable to those of men in entrepreneurial ecosystems. Fieldwork across countries, which includes narrative analysis, qualitative research, and in-depth case studies, reveals the subtle and not so subtle ways male dominance, the exclusion of women, and devaluing of the feminine play out in entrepreneurial spaces (Clark Muntean & Ozkazanc-Pan, 2016; Marlow & McAdam, 2013; see also Chapter 5). These studies also can serve to show "how the codes of a gendered identity are kept, changed and transgressed by constantly sliding between different symbolic spaces" (Bruni, Gherardi, & Poggio, 2004: 406). Recognizing that gender is a social practice and gender relations are performative, feminist theorists offer insightful perspectives for understanding these organizational phenomena in entrepreneurship. Decisions, communications, and actions may maintain, magnify, or serve to dismantle inequitable power relations within the systems in which organizations are embedded. This body of work focuses on the ways in which activities are performed in organizations to uncover the "structuring structure" (Bourdieu, 1980; cited in Poggio, 2006). These entrepreneurship scholars draw heavily on sociology, organizational theory, and feminist theory to reveal the source of gender gaps in outcomes and identify cause and effect relationships that form the foundation of inequities in the system.

According to Calás, Smircich, & Bourne (2009: 554), entrepreneurship in feminist perspectives is deconstructed and revealed not to be simply neutral economic phenomena without social and ethical considerations and consequences. To the contrary, feminist theories of entrepreneurship are "premised on the assumption that gender is fundamental in the structuring of society, with women being historically disadvantaged, and [they seek] to end this condition" (Calás, Smircich, & Bourne, 2009: 554). Liberal, psychoanalytic, and radical feminist theorists adopt a realist ontological perspective that asserts social disadvantages of women are the outcome of male-dominated structures in society, which must be dismantled to eliminate barriers to equality (Calás, Smircich, & Bourne, 2009: 554). In contrast, socialist, poststructuralist, and transnational feminist theorists focus on gender relations as a powerful cultural and material producer of social inequity (Calás, Smircich, & Bourne, 2009: 555).

Feminist theorists of entrepreneurship deconstruct the strong assumption of gender-neutrality and widespread belief that entrepreneurship is open to all equally in a free market system that assumes meritocratic systems, institutions, and practices. What is portrayed as objective, rational, and market-based logic in entrepreneurial decision-making is challenged from a feminist's perspective. Decisions including who to mentor, support, include, invite, fund, hire, promote, credit, and reward may be subject to gender bias. Yet in non-feminist theories of entrepreneurship, and commonly in practice, gender is assumed away; one's sex is considered to be irrelevant to one's potential as an entrepreneur from a gender-neutral or gender-blind perspective. These common beliefs in meritocracy and gender-neutrality further marginalize women, as they attribute lack of success relative to men to the individual, and not to gender. The subfield of "gender and entrepreneurship" or "women and entrepreneurship" is thus marginalized by the mainstream body of scholarship, which serves to further perpetrate the scientific reproduction of gender inequality (Ahl, 2004). Going further, Kiran Mirchandani raises the question of "how and why entrepreneurship came to be defined and understood vis-à-vis the behavior of only men" (1999: 224). More recently, scholars have called for integration of the subfield with so-called mainstream entrepreneurship. For example, after conducting a meta-analysis of the body of literature known as "women's entrepreneurship research," Jennings and Brush (2013) make the case that gender critically matters for entrepreneurship scholars, given that entrepreneurship itself is a gendered phenomenon that raises challenges about our assumptions and understandings of entrepreneurship more broadly.

As is argued here and will be illuminated with a case study later in this chapter, gender acts as an organizing principle in entrepreneurial ecosystems. Social relations – the interactions of humans in an ecosystem – can be gendered. In practice, the criteria used to determine who is worthy of investment at established institutions such as investment banks and venture capital firms do not appear to be solely meritocratic and gender-neutral. Despite what are assumed to be gender-blind processes, in practice we find the criteria used to determine a venture's worthiness – albeit masked by a dominant ideology of meritocracy and the assumption of economic rationality – are too often the result of unconscious bias, gendered networks, and gendered institutions. Together, these environments advantage men while disadvantaging women.

3.5 GENDER AND ENTREPRENEURIAL ECOSYSTEMS

Entrepreneurial ecosystems refer to the communities in which entrepreneurial activity takes place as well as the numerous actors and institutions that support entrepreneurs and their ventures (e.g. universities, ESOs, investors, mentors). Only recently have scholars investigated how gender as an organizing principle operates in entrepreneurial ecosystems. (For a review, see the special issue of Small Business Economics in 2019, volume 53, issue 2.) Taking an empiricist approach, in a study using GEM panel data for seventy-five countries over a fourteen-year period, Hechavarría and Ingram (2019) find that women are more prevalent in entrepreneurship when the entrepreneurial ecosystem has low barriers to entry, supportive government policy toward entrepreneurship, minimal commercial and legal infrastructure, and a normative culture that supports entrepreneurship. Other scholars have found stratifications and "disconnected social clusters" when entrepreneurial ecosystems are characterized by strong within-group network ties (i.e. bonding capital), as are found in "male-dominated strong-tie high-growth venture networks" (Neumeyer et al., 2019: 477, citing Brush & Chaganti, 1999; Edelman et al., 2010).

Patriarchal structures, free market capitalist ideology (discussed more in the next section), and gender beliefs intersect to magnify gender discrepancies in entrepreneurship. The social capital and network barriers discussed above "emerge as a by-product of skewed expectations, biases, and 'naïve theories underlying investors' conscious and subconscious search criteria" (Neumeyer et al., 2019: 478, citing Brooks et al., 2014). "As a result, women are often excluded from accessing male-dominated high-level networks in politics and industry" (Neumeyer et al., 2019: 478, citing Nikolova, 1993; Smallbone & Welter, 2001).

Seemingly objective goals of maximizing market share and financial returns in the form of revenues, profits, and returns to shareholders are broadly assumed to be the sole variables at play in decisions made in entrepreneurial ecosystems. In an ideal world, all aspiring business owners would have equal access to resources to launch, grow, and run their ventures. Yet, in practice, access to resources appears to be gendered. The gender gap in financing and other support has been recognized as producing a "missing generation" of businesses, along with the jobs, innovations, and economic value that was never created due to systemic and institutionalized bias in the system.[5] The cause and effect relationships underlying this gap warrant further investigation.

---

[5] www.kauffman.org/currents/the-value-in-knowing-what-is-missing/ (accessed June 19, 2020).

3.6   BELIEFS, ASSUMPTIONS, AND IDEOLOGIES
IN ENTREPRENEURIAL ECOSYSTEMS

Macro-level systems, beliefs, and ideologies are replicated and reinforced at the local level of entrepreneurial activity in individual ecosystems and across ecosystems under global financial capitalism. One significant factor to explore more deeply is the widespread and common belief that current practices are meritocratic and gender-neutral. This belief in meritocracy is strongest in societies where the dominant culture idealizes radical individualism, libertarianism, and free markets. Such neoliberal capitalist systems promote values and norms that strengthen a culture supportive of production, consumption, economic growth, and wealth creation by individuals. In this environment, the "ideal type" entrepreneur rises to the status of a mythological hero who brings innovation, economic growth, and inspiration in ways that are assumed to be highly beneficial for local communities as well as the economy and society at large. For example, Steve Jobs as the founder and former CEO of Apple, Inc., and Jeff Bezos as the founder and CEO of Amazon.com, Inc., are treated as the superheroes in our global capitalist system. What have become multinational corporations founded by these successful entrepreneurs are considered to be extensions of the individual owner-founders. The potentially massive amounts of wealth generated by the enterprises are treated as the rightful property of these men, earned through merit and to be shared with family/heirs, and serve to compensate those investors who bore the risk in supporting their activities and their ventures' growth. These beliefs, values, and practices ultimately result in massive wealth accumulation among these men and their families, who inherit their wealth. This result is pronounced when viewing lists of the wealthiest people in the world, who accumulated this wealth because of the rules of the game under global financial capitalism. The top ten men collectively are worth over $867 billion, nearing $1 trillion between them.

Bolstered by capitalist ideologies, global financial capitalism as an economic system perpetuates wealth, status, and power inequalities.

Despite some calling this system and the inequalities it generates and the sustainability of the model into question (Piketty, 2017, 2020), the public/voters, politicians, and policymakers generally continue to support the system, and the outcomes continue to generate further wealth inequality. Entrepreneurial ecosystems in these markets and cultures reward successful founders of firms with vast financial and social benefits. A winner-take-all economic game promotes and reinforces the rules that protect the advantageous gains accruing to the largest winners. These reward systems include equity allocation, tax policies, and a widening distribution of wealth, all perpetuating gender inequalities in entrepreneurship. The windfall of financial return on investments to shareholders – including founders and founding team members – and equity investors that remain predominantly male further magnifies gender gaps in economic, political, and social power relations. This is because vast wealth creates social status and, in countries such as the US, the ability to fund one's own or family members' and friends' political campaigns, engage in lobbying efforts, and run social media ads that influence voters. Principal owners of firms – the original founders and their family members – use the wealth generated by their firms to engage in ideological and partisan politics and to protect the interests of their firms and the owners, and they do so on a scale and magnitude much greater than hired professional managers/nonfounding CEOs (Clark Muntean, 2009).

Given that few female founders and female CEOs of firms reap these rewards and enjoy power and status under this system, male dominance is reinforced and maintained economically, politically, and socially. Yet the political Horacio Alger discourse and dominant belief that with hard work and determination, any human being can conquer all obstacles and rise to the very top of leadership mask the realities of who actually makes it to the top and why.[6] Girls and women, too, are told that anyone can rise to the top of the apex, as

---

[6] https://horatioalger.org/ (accessed June 19, 2020).

the best ideas, hardest workers, and most brilliant minds are rewarded under the myth of meritocracy. Narratives about opportunity and rewards are presented as being gender-blind and gender-neutral, despite men and male-founded and male-led firms consistently being granted the vast majority of equity investment. Given receipt of private equity finance (including angel investors, venture capital, and investment banking finance) is the exclusive gateway to going public, these structures perpetrate the glass ceiling in Fortune 500 firms, which remain consistently dominated by men, with 96 percent of CEOs being male.[7] The wealthiest CEOs are those who founded or cofounded the company (see Table 3.1). The genesis of gender gaps in corporate leadership and CEO pay, therefore, is the gender gap in equity financing and other forms of support during the founding and rapid growth phases of ventures, which occurs in gendered entrepreneurial ecosystems.

Entrepreneurial spaces, institutions, and practices are characterized by a gendered constitution that is built on hegemonic masculinity (Howson & Kerr, 2019). Women entrepreneurs face hegemonic and salient gender beliefs about their potential as entrepreneurs. In other words, women internalize gender expectations and the second-guessing of their competency and fit, which, in turn, negatively impacts their confidence while shaping their entrepreneurial behaviors and hindering their performance relative to male entrepreneurs. These gender beliefs bias the extent to which a female founder pursues equity finance, the attention she receives from mentors and investors, "her influence, the quality of her performances, the way she is evaluated, and her own and others' inferences about her abilities at the tasks that are central to the context" (Ridgeway & Correll, 2004: 519).

Male entrepreneurs, on the other hand, receive an unwarranted lift from the same gender stereotypes that hinder women. Men are more likely than women to experience overconfidence in their ideas

---

[7] https://fortune.com/2016/06/06/women-ceos-fortune-500-2016/ (accessed May 3, 2019).

Table 3.1 *World's wealthiest persons and sources of their wealth*

Billionaire-Entrepreneur	Net Worth of Individual ($ billion)	Primary Source of Wealth
1. Jeff Bezos	149.4	Amazon
2. Bill Gates	111.2	Microsoft
3. Bernard Arnault	110.6	LVMH
4. Mark Zuckerberg	85.0	Facebook
5. Warren Buffett	79.1	Berkshire Hathaway
6. Amancio Ortega	70.5	Zara
7. Larry Ellison	68.0	Software (Oracle)
8. Steven Ballmer	66.5	Microsoft
9. Larry Page	63.7	Google
10. Sergey Brin	63.1	Google

Note: Bernard Arnault (no. 3) reports his net worth as "family wealth."
Source: www.forbes.com/real-time-billionaires/#4569da6a3d78 (accessed June 2020)

and to engage in riskier behaviors. This hyper-confidence signals to investors that they have high-quality, innovative ideas and strong business models and that they would be competent managers of their enterprises. In part this is because of the images we see in the press of the ideal entrepreneur and which entrepreneurs enjoy the greatest financial success (see Table 3.1). In our media, entrepreneurship texts, case studies, and imagination, the hero on the white horse that is the ideal type entrepreneur is decidedly male and masculine in his disposition, characteristics, and dominance in entrepreneurial ecosystems (Ahl, 2004). Using media framing analysis, Wheadon and Duval-Couetil (2019) examined the content and social interactions portrayed on *Shark Tank*, a reality television show that showcases entrepreneurs pitching their business ideas to investors. They deconstructed the processes that normalize and reinforce gender stereotypes and inequalities in decision-making and who is rewarded, finding that this popular show serves to "maintain sociocultural perceptions of entrepreneurship as a gendered concept" as well showing as how media in general "plays a role in our culture in the communication, reflection, and reproduction of gender norms related to entrepreneurship" (Wheadon & Duval-Couetil, 2019: 1690).

Magnifying individual-level biased decisions stemming from gender stereotypes ubiquitous in the culture are the social dynamics of interplaying actors in entrepreneurial social contexts. Women encounter an old-boy network in the business and startup community, and these gendered networks may exclude women (Ozkazanc-Pan & Clark Muntean, 2018). Social capital and robust social networks are lauded as critical keys to entrepreneurial success among both academics and policymakers. However, according to Neumeyer et al.'s review of the literature (2019: 477), "over-reliance on social capital and strong-tie networks promotes mediocrities (Light, 2010), reduces objectivity (Locke et al., 1999), and creates barriers for historically disadvantaged groups such as novice, women, or minority entrepreneurs" (Light & Dana, 2013). When men refer, recommend, and connect men to other men, but do not do the same equally for women and/or simply have far fewer women in their social network, women do not get equivalent access to resources and opportunities in an entrepreneurial ecosystem. This results in the breakdown of the ideal of meritocracy when men's ideas and ventures percolate to the top of the lists considered "deal flow" by investors through these gendered networks, despite the idea that similar women and the ventures they form hold no less merit.

Given the discomfort people feel when being exposed to realities that suggest the current system is not actually a meritocracy, a common response is to deny that gender is at play as an organizing principle. Yet in promoting entrepreneurship and its variety of activities, resources, and support institutions as gender-blind or gender-neutral, an underlying masculine entrepreneurialism can work to diminish policies and practices for the inclusion of women in the management, promotion, and development of businesses within ecosystems (Howson & Kerr, 2019: 42).[8] These characteristics represent an important, albeit frequently ignored, variable impacting the institutionalization, growth, and development of innovation ecosystems across the globe (Howson & Kerr, 2019). Such a gender-blind perspective surrounding startups is challenged by feminist perspectives, which aim to reveal ways in which entrepreneurial activities in an ecosystem (e.g. business incubation) is a gendered process (Clark Muntean & Ozkazanc-Pan, 2016; Marlow & McAdam, 2013).

3.7   CASE STUDY: WEWORK

An example of these phenomena in entrepreneurship is evident when observing how male entrepreneurs act and how certain gendered behaviors and the perception of these behaviors are rewarded. As a case study example, Adam Neumann, cofounder and chairman of WeWork, exhibited highly masculine, charismatic, and almost prophetic behaviors while growing his enterprise with external funding from investors. Investors lauded and interpreted this highly masculinized behavior as evidence of competence, vision, intelligence, and other leadership traits requisite for disrupting markets through innovation strategies and shifting business models. The WeWork board of directors throughout 2019 was composed of seven men. Key decision makers from Silicon Valley and Wall Street (including Masayoshi Son of SoftBank Group Corp. and James Dimon of JPMorgan Chase & Co.) were also all men (Farrell & Brown, 2019). WeWork's parent company, WeCo., positioned itself as a technology startup that was going to be highly disruptive and financially successful. Despite in reality being only a "hip real-estate sublessor – not a tech company" (Farrell & Brown, 2019: B1), Neumann, his advocates and followers managed to convincingly conflate and confuse technology entrepreneurship with charismatic White male entrepreneurship. This is an example of how, in practice, the vast majority of global venture capital dollars go to

[8] Specifically, Howson and Kerr (2019) found this pattern across four business centers in Australia and four business centers in Dubai, United Arab Emirates.

enterprises founded and led by privileged White men. Further, it illuminates the social phenomena of homophily at play: privileged White men are the decision makers who dole out the investment dollars to individuals and their ventures when the individuals are very similar to them (e.g. White, male, elite economic and social status). In this respect, technology entrepreneurship may be viewed as an interchangeable term with "male entrepreneurship," yet the "male" in practice is both silenced and invisible in a system that assumes the system is a gender-blind meritocracy.

This case offers a tangible example of how entrepreneurship is dominated by Northern-Western neocapitalist ideologies supporting global financial and economic systems that reward men and prefer the masculine. In this cultural context, the undergirding belief and unquestioned assumption is that rational and sophisticated decision makers utilize financial metrics and market-based logic in choosing who to fund and support. These belief systems undergird a winner-take-all economy and zero-sum game thinking as well as a strong preference for believing in and investing in the stereotypical forceful, hyper-confident, charismatic male prototype. That this ideal type entrepreneur is solidly male (and usually a White male) is evident in lists and profiles that dominate the news (see Table 3.1). In the WeWork case, globally dominant institutional investors (e.g. Goldman Sachs and J. P. Morgan Chase & Co.) fueled irrational investment by cloaking the criteria for investment as rational given these financial institutions' status and prestige, even as the numbers, claims, business model, and actual performance defied the dollars invested (Farrell et al., 2019). This led to WeWork being compared to companies such as Salesforce, Amazon, Alibaba, Alphabet, and Facebook – all of which also have male founders and CEOs (Farrell & Brown, 2019). According to *Wall Street Journal* reporters, "founders were lionized for having giant vision, inspiration and a little bit of crazy. Mr. Neumann had all these traits, and his eccentricities only seemed to entrance investors even more" (Farrell & Brown, 2019: B6). The immature and unprofessional behaviors Mr. Neumann exhibited included spraying CEO John Zhao with a fire extinguisher, providing tequila and vodka shots to both bankers and executives, marijuana use, erratic management style, and using a company jet for his private surfing trips around the globe (Farrell & Brown, 2019). Indeed, the founder acted like a modern-day emperor who had created his own reality, using his privilege and charisma to enrich his own coffers while duping followers who might gain from his looting. While excessive ego and hubris may have ultimately led to his downfall as a respected entrepreneurial hero, he still walked away financially enriched by taking advantage of a broken system (Farrell et al., 2019).

Hans Christian Anderson's tale "The Emperor's New Clothes"[9] provides an apt metaphor for this case: Two weavers promise an emperor a new suit of clothes that they say is invisible to those who are unfit for their positions, stupid, or incompetent – while in reality, they make no clothes at all, making *everyone* believe the clothes are invisible to them. When the emperor parades before his subjects in his new "clothes," no one dares to say that they do not see any suit of clothes on him for fear that they will be seen as stupid. Finally, a child cries out, "But he isn't wearing anything at all!"

The moral of the story in this children's tale is that the arrogance and privilege of the elite brings a social expectation in the culture not to challenge the smoke and mirrors created by those in power. Only an innocent child not yet socialized to blindly support and trust the elite state the obvious truth: the emperor is pretending to have something they do not. Similarly, in entrepreneurship, much of the focus is on performativity: pitching well, exuding confidence, projecting excitement, and marketing a concept, business model, or innovation that stimulates investors to become believers and followers. That these entrepreneurs are merely men trying to gain financial wealth and fame – *not* superheroes changing the world through innovation and positive social disruption in practice – may be obvious in hindsight or to those not socialized to be blind to reality. In this sense,

[9] https://en.wikipedia.org/wiki/The_Emperor%27s_New_Clothes (accessed June 28, 2020).

gender-blind entrepreneurship can be a destructive and deceptive ideology that serves to maintain privilege for the elite and for men in particular.

Decision makers in the WeWork case were enchanted by highly masculine and charismatic performativity rather than actual merit, competence, experience, or actual financial or market performance (Farrell et al., 2019). The founder of WeWork exhibited dynamism and hyper-confidence bordering on arrogance and acted in unconventional, fraternity-style ways (Farrell & Brown, 2019). Yet this very behavior, associated with hyper-masculinity, was conflated with the ideal type entrepreneur worthy of billions of dollars of equity funding. A preference for charismatic White men, as in the WeWork example, reveals the depths to which decision makers, including investors and other resource providers, depart in practice from assumed rational, meritocratic standards and decision-making criteria. A strong and compelling performance of the hyper-masculine leadership style overshadows a grounded, rational, analytical calculus of actual market impact and sustainable financial performance metrics and/or actual value creation to multiple stakeholders. The production of gender in this case resulted in the privileging of males and exclusion of females from the board of directors and from decision-making in investment decisions in a firm valued at one time at $47 billion (Farrell et al., 2019). As a thought experiment, it is challenging to envision a woman acting with equal degrees of overconfidence, erraticism, and unprofessional behavior as Mr. Adam Neumann and receiving the same assumption of competency and billions of dollars in investment. A gender-blind or gender-neutral analysis of this example would likely miss the absence of women at the table as a contributing factor in what resulted: "a loss of $39 billion of the company's value, roughly the value of Delta Air Lines" (Farrell & Brown, 2019: B6).

Lessons learned from this case study include that investors and leaders of financial institutions are not actually using only market or financial criteria to decide who to fund and how much to invest. While behavioral economics is increasingly making us aware of how often irrationality creeps into decision-making in practice, there remains a strong assumption in entrepreneurship that professional investors – investment bankers, venture capitalists, angel investors, corporate investors – make impersonal, rational, logical decisions based on financial metrics and market potential. Yet the concept of asymmetric information (Akerlof, 1970) warns us that the use of cognitive shortcuts or heuristics is very common when one side of the table has much more information than the other in a market transaction. See also Herbert Simon (1955) and the concept of bounded rationality in decision-making.

For example, lemon laws for used car dealerships and the information service created by Carfax, Inc., were designed to address the asymmetric information and resultant unequal market power between a used car seller and a used car buyer. Similarly, potential investors listening to a pitch competition or scrolling through the pitch deck of an entrepreneur or entrepreneurial team seeking investment represent a market transaction with a highly asymmetric informational relationship. The entrepreneur knows far more about their technology, work ethic, experience, drive, knowledge, leadership potential, and dedication to the venture's success. The investor – typically having just met the entrepreneur – knows virtually nothing about these variables. In situations constituted by an asymmetric informational relationship, the investor is highly likely to rely on stereotypes, which are a common form of heuristic used when facing uncertainty and the unknown in social relations and in economic decisions. Importantly, decision makers rely, in practice, on these unconscious cognitive shortcuts, while believing they are acting impersonally, rationally, and logically. Unfortunately, investors may rely on their intuition and experience of who looks like a successful entrepreneur. Given the highly visible and dominant presence of male entrepreneurs as leaders of the companies that made it to the IPO stage or are listed on the Fortune 500 as well as our collective understanding of who the ideal type entrepreneur is and what they look like, it is clear that investors prefer stereotypical male founders.

This unconscious gender bias is magnified by popular media portrayals of entrepreneurs (Wheadon & Duval-Couetil, 2019). This strong gut feeling or instinctual preference for men and male teams short-circuits reliance on rational financial projections, actual market worthiness, or actual competence of the entrepreneur as the primary criteria determining who gets funded and who does not. When entrepreneurs seeking financing perform in highly masculinized ways, potential investors experience confirmation bias that their instinct is trustworthy in determining who to fund.

This case study provides a very recent, tangible example of how entrepreneurial ecosystems produce and reward organizational heroes that exhibit forceful and hegemonic masculinity and machismo in ways that solidify cultures which continue to exclude women (Calás & Smircich, 2006: 26, citing Benschop & Doorewaard, 1998a, b; Prokos & Padavic, 2002; Stobbe, 2005). Further, the bad behavior exhibited by the leader of WeWork was largely overlooked, accepted, and normalized by his peers. This suggests a culture comprised of a "dense cultural web of masculinities" created and reinforced through "everyday interactions, values and beliefs" surrounding entrepreneurship as a profession; such caricatures represent "powerful symbols" that reproduce a hyper-masculine culture (Calás & Smircich, 2006 citing Miller's (2004) study of women engineers in the oil industry). Further, this case study provides a tangible, albeit not uncommon, example of "the status and competence components of gender beliefs" (Ridgeway & Correll, 2004: 517) in evaluation and decision-making in entrepreneurial finance, a critical component of success in technology and high-growth entrepreneurship.

Specifically, this case illuminates the salience of gender in sophisticated institutional investors' decision-making. Adam Neumann, Founder and Chairman of WeWork, exhibited hyper-masculine behavior. Key actors in the entrepreneurial ecosystem interpreted that gendered behavior as a signal of exceptional confidence, potential, and brilliance. In expectation states theory, social relational contexts shape "self-other competence expectations," which further "affect the extent to which men and women assert themselves, whether their ideas and points of view are heard, and whether they become influential in the context" (Ridgeway & Correll, 2004: 518). Specifically, the way Neumann perceived his own competency and the ways others held high competency expectations, even in the face of an absence of experience, track record, and performance metrics to warrant such a perception, reveal how strongly evaluations of potential and performance are "shaped by gender status beliefs" (Ridgeway & Correll, 2004: 528). Widespread reliance on stereotypes in investment decisions privilege men in entrepreneurial ecosystems.

Ideology is evident in the system. The culture in which entrepreneurial ecosystems are embedded reinforces beliefs that those White men dominating the list of the world's wealthiest billionaires are there because they earned it: they had the best ideas, launched the best products, founded the best companies, and grew their businesses as the best CEOs. That they are all male is assumed to be irrelevant under an ideology that does not question their merit and is skeptical of gender as an explanatory variable. Further, this ideology does not make room for others to challenge their right to keep all of the bounty of their assumed hard work and brilliance. To do so would be to cry out that the emperor has no clothes when the system itself and those who primarily benefit perpetrate the illusion that the emperor is finely dressed in the best robes. Another lesson from this case study, also evident in the analogy of the emperor's new clothes, is that there may be social pressure not to call out smoke and mirrors type of deceptions or exaggerations. Homogenous social environments breed groupthink, conformity, and peer pressure. Such environments can lead to systemic failures in the context of entrepreneurial ecosystems, as gendered individual actions, organizational practices, and sociocultural norms are normalized while simultaneously called out as exceptions rather than rules. We beg to differ; it is the very gendered systems of entrepreneurship that allow such failures to happen in the first place, rather than the actions of lone entrepreneurs.

3.8   THEORETICALLY GUIDED FRAMEWORKS
FOR INCLUSION

In conclusion, the WeWork case study raises challenges for entrepreneurial ecosystems that are embedded in global financial capitalism and dominated by ideologies that skew decision-making about who deserves what kind of support for their entrepreneurial ventures as well as who deserves to primarily benefit from entrepreneurial activity. Without raising these challenges explicitly and enacting systemic changes, the vast gender gap in entrepreneurial funding and the consequences of that gap are not likely to narrow due to the passing of time alone. Existing approaches to narrowing the gender gap in entrepreneurship focus primarily on "fixing" the women so that they become more like their male counterparts. Too many interventions ultimately assume the gender gap is due to a talent pipeline problem. Fundamentally, these explanations for the gender gap place the impetus for change on females: girls choosing to play with dolls and makeup instead of construction toys and science kits, too few young women choosing to major in STEM fields, too few women applying for promotions or positions at technology firms, too few women leaning in and taking risks to found and lead technology ventures, women being too timid, lacking confidence, or choosing to launch businesses in feminized industries, etc.

Following these dominant explanations for the gender gap, even well-intended efforts to close the gap focus on funding Girls Who Code camps, encouraging girls to take more math and science courses, creating programming to encourage women to consider business ownership as a career path, coaching women to behave more like men when they pitch, and so forth. Fundamentally, none of these proposed explanations and solutions, and resultant interventions, challenge the system itself and the practices that continue to privilege men and the masculine in entrepreneurship. The continued expectation of and preference for a hyper-masculine style, charismatic pitches, and acceptance of marginal or unethical behavior remains present even in the rare cases in which the founder/CEO receiving venture capital money is a woman. Focusing on having individual women break through the glass ceiling on occasion under the current system may just raise more cases similar to WeWork. For example, the cautionary tale of Elizabeth Holmes, the founder and CEO of Theranos, is well documented in the 2018 book *Bad Blood: Secrets and Lies in a Silicon Valley Startup* by John Carreyrou as well as the 2019 film *The Inventor: Out for Blood in Silicon Valley*, directed by Alex Gibney. In other words, the system itself rewards and reproduces poor decisions that are gendered in ways that show preference for masculine performativity – as noted in Ms. Holmes' "acting like a man" strategy (McCarthy, 2019). In other words, documented preferences for the masculine over the feminine in high-growth/high-reward entrepreneurship not only breed problems for gender equity in the system, but also skew rationality in decision-making, threaten the sustainability of ventures themselves, and too often result in failed enterprises and loss of shareholder value.

Critical management studies and feminist theories call for more systemic change that goes beyond increasing the numbers of individual women who receive equity investment for their ventures. Inclusive entrepreneurship requires inclusive economic, political, and social systems that support a broad diversity of entrepreneurs while also being attentive to and resolving inequities in the system that privilege particular types of entrepreneurs. Instead of asking the question of how individual women might break through barriers to be the recipients of venture capital funds enjoyed by their male counterparts, this chapter interrogates the dominance of male actors in entrepreneurial ecosystems and challenges the assumption of merit as the primary determinant of who receives capital, while revealing and challenging who primarily benefits from that capital investment.

This chapter provides theoretical framing and related conceptual terms that help us make sense of what appears to be irrational (or at least not meritocratic) decision-making occurring in entrepreneurial ecosystems. Given that "extensive research has shown that exactly the same performance, idea, or product seems better to people when it comes from someone who is higher status rather than lower status in the context" (Ridgeway & Correll, 2004: 518) and that, in dominant patriarchal societies, men hold the higher status and presumption of competency and merit as entrepreneurs, efforts at inclusion must attend to deeply and widely set implicit biases embedded in the system. Interventions must include the supply side in entrepreneurial finance – that is, the investors and institutions filtering ideas, business models, and ventures and the entrepreneurs who benefit or do not benefit from gatekeepers' decision-making. The case study and supporting literature review in this chapter show the salience of gender in entrepreneurial contexts and how "gender beliefs create a double standard for judging ability, or lack thereof, from performance" (Ridgeway & Correll, 2004: 519, citing Biernat & Kobrynowicz, 1999; Correll, 2004; Foschi, 2000). Widespread implicit bias training, education about the complexity of gender stereotyping and how it affects judgment, and the imposition of transparency and accountability measures toward gender equality among investment banks, venture capital funds, angel investor groups, and the ESOs that provide them the deal flow are critical components in addressing the existing gender bias on the supply side of entrepreneurial ecosystems.

Advocates of financially sustainable entrepreneurship that is inclusive and equitable note the negative consequences of gender bias in the system. To begin to change the system, the assumption that existing criteria for investment are meritocratic and purely rational and logical must be challenged. Investors and founders require education about second-generation or implicit bias, which remains highly gendered across the world's dominant entrepreneurial ecosystems. Leaders must commit to tangible change, which includes building transparency and accountability into institutional practices. Change is not likely to happen without substantial openness to critique and commitment to, and measurement of, progress toward inclusion and equity. This all begins with the recognition that gender is a powerful, dominant, and ubiquitous organizing principle and the basis of irrational decision-making in a system that strives, but so often fails, to be fully meritocratic in practice. Further, change agents need to identify which social relational phenomena, institutionalized practices, norms, and processes create or reproduce gender inequality. Lastly, leaders can identify all of the above which furthers gender equality and other forms of social, economic, and political equality. Toward this end, scholars, policymakers, and practitioners should shift their gaze and design their interventions toward the supply side of the equation to address the structural, systemic, and institutionalized forces behind men's dominance in entrepreneurial ecosystems. To this end, we concur with the recommendations offered by Foss et al.

> If the entrepreneurial ecosystem for women is to be improved from a policy perspective, future research must move beyond consistently recommending "fixing women" through education and training. Future research needs to study both the resource providers and the connectors within the ecosystem, as well as the institutional environment embedded within it.
>
> *(2019: 410)*

3.9   CONCLUSION

Feminist theorists provide invaluable contributions "by questioning the normative expectations of a culture that associates entrepreneurship with male and masculine" (Bird & Brush, 2002; Brush, 1992, 1997; Calás, Smircich, & Bourne, 2009; Hopkins & Bilimoria, 2004). Indeed, sociology and feminism are necessary for understanding and explaining the variance between what we assume and what is true regarding who receives venture capital funds and who does not, what is invested in and what is not, and what enterprises might be more financially stable and which may not, and why. Specifically, the dominant paradigm under global capitalism assumes that economic rationality and pure meritocracy are the basis for investment decisions, including venture capital investment in technology startups. Under this ideology and belief system, gender is not an issue or relevant criteria for investment decisions or the constitution of new venture leadership. Yet as the case study of WeWork in the dominant US entrepreneurial ecosystem demonstrates, in reality, seasoned institutional investors are subject to using heuristics or cognitive shortcuts and making rash decisions based on gut feelings (Farrell & Brown, 2019: B6). Too often in this context, homophily – that is, the strong attraction to others who are similar to us – charisma, charm, attractiveness, and implicit gender bias become the basis of investment rather than compelling business models or rational analyses of financial statements and projections (Brooks et al., 2014). Charisma is a double-edged, gendered sword, as women are conditioned to be less charismatic than men across many cultures. Male founders are granted license to act theatrically and erratically – as evidenced in the case of Adam Neumann at WeWork – and are forgiven too rapidly when boyish antics or feigned innocence dismisses their culpability (Farrell et al., 2019). Too often women are called in to lead and clean up the mess and act as the adults after the crisis (e.g. in the case of Mark Zuckerberg's treatment in the media relative to Sheryl Sandberg regarding the Facebook U.S. Congressional trials).[10]

Gender stereotypes maintain a sticky gender system found in social relational contexts embedded in entrepreneurial communities. Among the myriad daily decisions made on the supply side in entrepreneurial ecosystems –whose pitch deck to review, who to mentor, who to designate a pitch competition award to, and who to invest in – there exists systematic and repeated use of gender stereotyping. Gender beliefs – and, specifically, the belief that women are less fit, competent, or innovative relative to men – bias both "men and women's behaviors and evaluations in ways that reenact and confirm beliefs about men's greater status and competence" (Ridgeway & Correll, 2004: 521). This disadvantages women as entrepreneurs and, thus, fuels gender gaps in entrepreneurial ecosystems across the

---

[10] www.theguardian.com/technology/2018/dec/22/facebook-sheryl-sandbrook-faces-axe (accessed June 19, 2020).

world. These gaps further lead to gaping gender differences in the economic rewards that accrue to founders of companies, many of whom become CEOs of multinational corporations and join the ranks of billionaires (see Table 3.1). This wealth inequality breeds power differentials and brings social and political inequality that is gendered as well.

Together, this represents institutionalization and normalization of an "essential form of gender hierarchy – that is, the cultural assumption that men have more status and authority than do women" – maintained by a gender system that sustains itself by preserving the fundamental assumption that "men are rightly more powerful" (Ridgeway & Correll, 2004: 522). These claims are evident in a culture that does not openly challenge or even find it strange that over 95 percent of all Fortune 500 CEOs are men (despite women reaching equity as professionals and as managers) and where wealth is concentrated among the founders/CEOs on the lists of the world's wealthiest multibillionaires.

Also discussed in this chapter, the gender gap in entrepreneurship is a logical outcome of an entrepreneurial ecosystem run by gatekeeping male investors who continue to fund founders who look like them and who act like the male entrepreneurs who have come before them. These entrepreneurial actors "repeatedly enact power and influence relations that predominantly favor men" (Ridgeway & Correll, 2004: 523). Male founders who promise disruption, convince investors of their brilliance and innovativeness, and demand control and rewards for their ventures are the actors who are rewarded in this environment (Farrell & Brown, 2019: B6). These practices fuel a culture in which norms, dispositions, behaviors, and conventions create a preference for the hyper-masculine founder who can act charismatically and surpass the best as a duplicate of the storied lists of the world's most lauded billionaire-entrepreneurs. As we have seen in the cases of rogue male founders and/or CEOs as well as the male investors themselves, this too often leads to organizational cultures that are fraternity-like, foster bad behavior and sexual harassment, and ultimately lead to scandals and a severe loss of shareholder value and economic waste.[11]

Institutions hold enormous power when decision makers hold the ability to include, exclude, reward, resource, develop, and integrate (or alienate) individual entrepreneurs. As argued in this chapter, "cultural beliefs about gender function as part of the rules of the game, biasing the behaviors, performances, and evaluations of otherwise similar men and women in systematic ways" (Ridgeway & Correll, 2004: 510). What happened in the entrepreneurial ecosystem with respect to WeWork reveals that hegemonic masculinity and the cultural belief that men are more competent and investment-worthy entrepreneurs perpetuate the rules of the entrepreneurial investment game that privilege men. Further, the existing gender system in and across entrepreneurial ecosystems biases behaviors toward the hypermasculine and skews evaluations of entrepreneurs and their ideas, business models, and enterprises in ways that starkly advantage men over women, masculine over feminine, in systemic and powerful ways. The collective result of this gender system is evidenced in Table 3.1, which lists the winners of the game and reveals their identities as White men who predominantly benefit from the bounty of the win in these contexts.

To conclude, feminist theorists offer gender as an explanation, given its use in practice as an organizing principle that excludes women from decision-making positions, oversight roles, and being the beneficiaries of equity investment funds for their ventures. Theories from sociology and feminism are necessary to help explain this vast gap in our belief systems and reality. ESOs and their leaders play a critical role in perpetrating or dismantling the enormous and static gender gap in entrepreneurial outcomes. Leaders and advocates of inclusion and equity would be more effective in moving the needle on the gender gap by focusing efforts to transform existing flawed

---

[11] www.bloomberg.com/news/articles/2019-03-25/after-a-sex-scandal-500-startups-and-its-former-ceo-plan-their-next-acts (accessed March 27, 2019).

paradigms and biased decision-making. By applying the theoretical insights herein to practice, there is likely to be better, more sustainable decision-making among investors and supporters of entrepreneurs, which we present as a major factor in narrowing the gender gap, using the WeWork case study.

REFERENCES

Acker, J., (1990). Hierarchies, jobs, bodies: A theory of gendered organizations. *Gender & Society*, *4*(2): 139–158.

Acker, J. (1992). Gendering organizational theory. In A. J. Mills & P. Tancred (Eds.), *Gendering organizational analysis* (pp. 248–260). Thousand Oaks, CA: Sage Publications.

Acker, J. (2000). Gendered contradictions in organizational equity projects. *Organization*, *7*(4): 625–632.

Acker, J. (2006). Inequality regimes: Gender, class, and race in organizations. *Gender & Society*, *20*(4): 441–464.

Ahl, H. (2004). *The scientific reproduction of gender inequality: A discourse analysis of research texts on women's entrepreneurship*. Malmo, Sweden: Liber.

Ahl, H., & Marlow, S. (2012). Exploring the dynamics of gender, feminism, and entrepreneurship: Advancing debate to escape a dead end? *Organization*, *19*(5): 543–562.

Akerlof, G. (1970). "The market for lemons: Quality ucertainty and the market mechanism." *The Quarterly Journal of Economics*, *84*(3): 488–500.

Balachandra, L., Briggs, T., Eddleston, K., & Brush, C. (2019). Don't pitch like a girl!: How gender stereotypes influence investor decisions. *Entrepreneurship Theory and Practice*, *43*(1): 116–137.

Benschop, Y., & Doorewaard, H. (1998a). Covered by equality: The gender subtext of organizations. *Organization Studies*, *19*(5): 787–805.

Benschop, Y., & Doorewaard, H. (1998b). Six of one and half a dozen of the other: The gender subtext of Taylorism and team-based work. *Gender, Work & Organization*, *5*(1): 5–18.

Biernat, M., & Kobrynowicz, D. (1999). A shifting standards perspective on the complexity of gender stereotypes and gender stereotyping. In W. B. Swann, Jr., J. H. Langlois, & L. A. Gilbert (Eds.), *Sexism and stereotypes in modern society: The gender science of Janet Taylor Spence* (pp. 75–106). Washington, DC: American Psychological Association. doi: https://doi.org/10.1037/10277-004

Bird, B., & Brush, C. (2002). A gendered perspective on organizational creation. *Entrepreneurship Theory and Practice, 26*(3): 41–65.

Blair, I. V., & Banaji, M. R. (1996). Automatic and controlled processes in stereotype priming. *Journal of Personality and Social Psychology, 70*(6): 1142.

Bordieu, P. (1980). L'identité et la représentation. *Actes de la recherche en sciences sociales,* 35: 63–70.

Brooks, A. W., Huang, L., Kearney, S. W., & Murray, F. E. (2014). Investors prefer entrepreneurial ventures pitched by attractive men. *Proceedings of the National Academy of Sciences, 111*(12): 4427–4431.

Bruni, A., Gherardi, S., & Poggio, B. (2004). Doing gender, doing entrepreneurship: An ethnographic account of intertwined practices. *Gender, Work & Organization, 11*(4): 406–429.

Brush, C. G. (1992). Research on women business owners: Past trends, a new perspective and future directions. *Entrepreneurship Theory and Practice, 16* (4): 5–30.

Brush, C. G. (1997). Women-owned businesses: Obstacles and opportunities. *Journal of Developmental Entrepreneurship, 2*(1): 1–24.

Brush, C. G., & Chaganti, R. (1999). Businesses without glamour? An analysis of resources on performance by size and age in small service and retail firms. *Journal of Business Venturing, 14*(3): 233–257.

Calás, M. B., & Smircich, L. (2006). *From the "Woman's point of view" ten years later: Towards a feminist organization studies* (pp. 284–346). The Sage Handbook of Organization Studies. London: SAGE.

Calás, M. B., Smircich, L., & Bourne, K. A. (2007). Knowing Lisa? Feminist analyses of gender and entrepreneurship. In D. Billamoria and S. K. Piderit (Eds.), *Handbook on women in business and management* (pp. 78–105). Northampton, MA: Edward Elgar.

Calás, M. B., Smircich, L., & Bourne, K. A. (2009). Extending the boundaries: Reframing "entrepreneurship as social change" through feminist perspectives. *Academy of Management Review, 34*(3): 552–569.

Clark Muntean, S. (2009). *A political theory of the firm: Why ownership matters.* (Doctoral dissertation in political science), defended at the University of California, San Diego.

Clark Muntean, S., & Ozkazanc-Pan, B. (2016). Feminist perspectives on social entrepreneurship: Critique and new directions. *International Journal of Gender and Entrepreneurship, 8*(3): 221–241.

Correll, S. J. (2004). Constraints into preferences: Gender, status, and emerging career aspirations. *American Sociological Review, 69*(1): 93–113.

Eagly, A. H., Wood, W., & Diekman, A. B. (2000). Social role theory of sex differences and similarities: A current appraisal. In T. Eckes & H. M. Trautner (Eds.), *The developmental social psychology of gender* (pp. 123–174). Mahwah, NJ: Erlbaum.

Edelman, L. F., Brush, C. G., Manolova, T. S., & Greene, P. G. (2010). Start-up motivations and growth intentions of minority nascent entrepreneurs. *Journal of Small Business Management*, 48(2): 174–196.

Farrell, M., & Brown, E. (2019). The money men who enabled Adam Neumann. *The Wall Street Journal*, December 14–15, 2019, B1.

Farrell, M., Hoffman, L., Brown, E., & Benoit, D. (2019). The fall of WeWork: How a startup darling came unglued. *The Wall Street Journal*, October 24, 2019. Available online at www.wsj.com/articles/the-fall-of-wework-how-a-startup-darling-came-unglued-11571946003 (accessed June 19, 2020).

Foschi, M. (2000). Double standards for competence: Theory and research. *Annual Review of Sociology*, 26(1): 21–42.

Foss, L., Henry, C., Ahl, H., & Mikalsen, G. H. (2019). Women's entrepreneurship policy research: A 30-year review of the evidence. *Small Business Economics*, 53(2): 409–429.

Gherardi, S. (1994). The gender we think, the gender we do in our everyday organizational lives. *Human Relations*, 47(6): 591–610.

Grey, C., & Willmott, H. (Eds.). (2005). *Critical management studies: A reader.* Oxford: Oxford University Press.

Hechavarría, D. M., & Ingram, A. E. (2019). Entrepreneurial ecosystem conditions and gendered national-level entrepreneurial activity: A 14-year panel study of GEM. *Small Business Economics*, 53(2): 431–458.

Howson, R., & Kerr, G. (2019). The Innovation Ecosystem: Interrogating (trans) national gender (un)sustainability in the new business centre. In J. Hearn, E. Vasquez del Aguila, & M. Hughson (Eds.), *Unsustainable Institutions of Men: Transnational Dispersed Centres, Gender, Power, Contradictions* (pp. 41–54). New York: Routledge.

Hopkins, M. M., & Bilimoria, D. (2004). Care and justice orientations in workplace ethical dilemmas of women business owners. *Group & Organization Management*, 29(4): 495–516.

Hurley, A. E. (1999). Incorporating feminist theories into sociological theories of entrepreneurship. *Women in Management Review*, 14(2): 54–62.

Jennings, J. E., & Brush, C. G. (2013). Research on women entrepreneurs: Challenges to (and from) the broader entrepreneurship literature? *The Academy of Management Annals*, 7(1): 663–715.

Light, I. (2010). The religious ethic of the Protestant ethnics. In L.-P. Dana (Ed.), *Entrepreneurship and Religion* (pp. 168–183). Northampton, MA: Edward Elgar.

Light, I., & Dana, L. P. (2013). Boundaries of social capital in entrepreneurship. *Entrepreneurship Theory and Practice, 37*(3): 603–624.

Locke, E. A., Noorderhaven, N. G., Cannon, J. P., Doney, P. M., & Mullen, M. R. (1999). Some reservations about social capital. *Academy of Management Review, 24*(1): 8–11.

Marlow, S., & McAdam, M. (2013). Incubation or Induction? Gendered identity work in the context of technology business incubation. *Entrepreneurship Theory and Practice, 39*(4): 791–816.

McAdam, M., Harrison, R. T., & Leitch, C. M. (2019). Stories from the field: women's networking as gender capital in entrepreneurial ecosystems. *Small Business Economics, 53*(2): 459–474.

McCarthy, M. May 11, 2019. Did Elizabeth Holmes delude smart men by acting like a man? *Psychology Today*. Available online at www.psychologytoday.com/us/blog/sexx-matters/201905/did-elizabeth-holmes-delude-smart-men-acting-man (accessed June 21, 2020).

Miller, G. E. (2004). Frontier masculinity in the oil industry: The experience of women engineers. *Gender, Work & Organization, 11*(1): 47–73.

Mirchandani, K. (1999). Feminist insight on gendered work: New directions in research on women and entrepreneurship. *Gender, Work & Organization, 6* (4): 224–235.

Moss Kanter, R. (1977). Women and the structure of organizations: Explorations in theory and behavior. In R. Moss Kanter & M. Millman (Eds.), *Another voice* (pp. 34–74). New York: Doubleday.

Neumeyer, X., Santos, S. C., Caetano, A., & Kalbfleisch, P. (2019). Entrepreneurship ecosystems and women entrepreneurs: A social capital and network approach. *Small Business Economics, 53*(2): 475–489.

Nikolova, M. (1993). Nyakoi demografski spekti na jenskoto predpriemachestvo (Some demographic aspects of women's entrepreneurship). *Problemi Na Truda, 9*: 46–61.

Ozkazanc-Pan, B., & Clark Muntean, S. (2018). Networking towards (in) equality: Women entrepreneurs in technology. *Gender, Work & Organization, 25*(4): 379–400.

Prokos, A., & Padavic, I. (2002). "There oughtta be a law against bitches": Masculinity lessons in police academy training. *Gender, Work & Organization, 9*(4): 439–459.

Piketty, T. (2017). *Capital in the twenty-first century*. Cambridge, MA: Belknap Press.

Piketty, T. (2020). *Capital and ideology.* Cambridge, MA: Belknap Press.

Poggio, B. (2006). Outline of a theory of gender practices. *Gender, Work & Organization, 13*(3): 225–233.

Ridgeway, C. L., & Correll, S. J. (2004). Unpacking the gender system: A Theoretical perspective on gender beliefs and social relations. *Gender & Society, 18*(4): 510–531.

Scott, J. (1986). The collectivist organization. *American Historical Review, 91*(5): 1053–1075.

Simon, H. (1955). A behavioral model of rational choice. *Quarterly Journal of Economics, 69*(1): 99–118.

Small Business Economics (2019). Special issue on women entrepreneurs in ecosystems. *Small Business Economics, 53*(2): 393–546.

Smallbone, D., & Welter, F. (2001). The distinctiveness of entrepreneurship in transition economies. *Small Business Economics, 16*(4): 249–262.

Sprague, J. (2016). *Feminist methodologies for critical researchers: Bridging differences.* Lanham, MD: Rowman & Littlefield.

Stangler, D., & Bell-Masterson, J. (2015). Measuring an entrepreneurial ecosystem. Kauffman Foundation Research Series on City, Metro, and Regional Entrepreneurship, 1–16. doi: http://dx.doi.org/10.2139/ssrn.2580336

Stobbe, L. (2005). Doing machismo: Legitimating speech acts as a selection discourse. *Gender, Work & Organization, 12*(2): 105–123.

West, C., & Zimmerman, D. H. (1987). Doing gender. *Gender & Society, 1*(2): 125–151.

Wheadon, M., & Duval-Couetil, N. (2019). The gendering of entrepreneurship on reality television. *Journal of Small Business Management, 57*(4): 1676–1697.

Witz, A., & Savage, M. (1991). The gender of organizations. *The Sociological Review, 39*(1): 3–62.

4 Individual-Level Dynamics

Beyond Motivation, Identity, and Networks

This chapter delves into the first level in our multilevel, multidimensional examination of entrepreneurial ecosystems by focusing on the individual as a means to provide insights about the intersections of gender and the lived experiences of entrepreneurs. Importantly, our use of gender here is not necessarily simply as an identity dimension of an entrepreneur or given in terms of biology. Rather, our use of gender is as a framework to understand how individual experiences take shape within gendered institutional environments and ecosystems, even if individuals self-identify as male or female (or other). That is, in contrast to conceptualizing individuals as disembodied actors with particular considerations around their economic motivations, entrepreneurial identity, and social networks as driving factors in their experiences and entrepreneurship activities, we provide an embedded gender perspective derived from feminist scholarship. In this sense, rather than being a given identity or simply a variable for comparing people, gender provides a framework for interrogating social relations and power as they are manifest in entrepreneurship and ecosystems.

Given the complexity of representing and studying such experiences, our main goal is to provide a glimpse of how entrepreneurs navigate gendered structures and social relations as they engage in economic activity in the form of entrepreneurship. Put another way, our analysis of individuals is through a gender lens that embeds them within the domain of the social and the political as gendered power relations impact the very experiences of and opportunities available to individuals. This approach is a feminist engagement with power in that it provides an important consideration of how notions of agency, choice, and action in entrepreneurship are not simply a function of entrepreneurial opportunity recognition, and behavior to take advantage of market conditions. Rather, this approach requires an analysis of how choices are structured within the context of gendered power relations and posits that traditional perspectives that do not consider the role of power fall short of the very political nature of entrepreneurship. In other words, we contend that it is only possible to understand the constraints and possibilities of entrepreneurship by recognizing the gendered institutional context of ecosystems as well as the dynamics of power and social relations. Building on these conversations, we also expand into discussion around social capital and community formation in entrepreneurial ecosystems, as these are important dimensions of individual experiences, often providing the structural mechanisms necessary for creating access and opportunities or the opposite, barriers to information and people.

To engage with these issues, we use examples from gender-focused ecosystem fieldwork in Boston, Massachusetts. The empirical data shared in this and other chapters is part of a broader effort carried out to examine ecosystems across different cities in the US including, in addition to Boston, St. Louis, Missouri, and Asheville, North Carolina (see Knowlton et al., 2015; Ozkazanc-Pan, Knowlton, & Clark Muntean, 2017). We chose these three areas as they represent the majority of research on issues such as propensity to start a business, entrepreneurial orientation, and access to knowledge and networks – the hallmark considerations of entrepreneurship research that looks at gender differences. We contend that the majority of frameworks and research on these topics provide some insights but there is much that we still do not know; this is due in part to the fact that the frameworks guiding research on gender and entrepreneurship and entrepreneurial ecosystems generally conceptualize gender as an independent variable with associated impacts on a variety of dimensions and practices. Beyond these broad areas, our research and conversations inevitably also include observations and conversations around accessing capital or pitching "the right way" to investors. Our goal is to demonstrate the limits of such frameworks, which place the onus of responsibility and change on individual actors, while offering new perspectives for rethinking gender and the complexity of social relations as they relate to economic activity within entrepreneurial ecosystems.

In this chapter, within the context of this larger research project, we focus on Boston because of the city's established history in creating and supporting startups, its prominence in receiving venture capital money, and its reputation as a progressive city in terms of politics, while at the same time recognizing the continued racial tensions and economic inequalities that are part of the city's ongoing reality. And within this context, our research explicitly examines areas of motivation, identity, and networks in terms of how they take shape for entrepreneurs and the various ways ESOs and institutional norms impact on inclusion activities.

To date, we have had opportunity to speak with eighty-two actors in the entrepreneurial ecosystem in Boston and have completed hundreds of hours of observation in coworking spaces, accelerators, incubators, and university entrepreneurship centers. Our interviewees include twenty-six individuals who represent various different roles and actors in the ecosystem, including investors, venture capitalists, lawyers, accelerator directors, and educational program directors. Also included in our research are entrepreneurs: twenty-seven women and twenty-four men, with five of those individuals (three men and two women) identifying as both entrepreneur and investor/venture capitalist. (We count the latter as two different types of actor.)

To demonstrate the ways in which gender and individual experiences intersect, we organize this chapter in the following way. First, we start with a brief overview of Boston, expanding on the resources and rich-capital context of the city. We then share vignettes representing aggregates of the experiences of entrepreneur types, as revealed during our fieldwork, to demonstrate how certain paths are followed by different entrepreneurs in ecosystems and to show how these entrepreneurs are embedded differently in social relations. We then engage in a critical analysis and reading informed by feminist frameworks to demonstrate how and why individual actions and entrepreneurial activity take shape and the complexities of inclusion in ecosystems. Presenting evidence from our interviews and observations, we show that the vignettes are representative of "typical" experiences while also recognizing they are typologies to help us categorize ecosystem experiences and, by all means, not exhaustive. This allows us to demonstrate how entrepreneurial ecosystems can be sites for the replication of existing gender and race inequalities in civil society, but with possibilities for agency and change (discussed more explicitly in our concluding chapter), a new approach to conceptualizing entrepreneurial ecosystems beyond their current standing as neutral sites for information exchange, social relations, and economic activities enabling entrepreneurship.

As a point of clarification on our methodological approach and research aims, vignettes are a well-known approach in feminist work, and they aim to highlight shared experiences of particular groups to provoke conversation and change (Blodgett et al., 2011; Calás & Smircich, 1993; McCarthy, 2017; Ozkazanc-Pan, 2020). In using this approach, our goal is to show the complexity of individual, organizational, and institutional dimensions of entrepreneurship and the embedded nature of social relations such that concentrating solely on individual-level changes (e.g. suggesting women pitch differently to investors in order to garner funding or that they expand their social networks) will not change an entrepreneurial ecosystem or its established opportunity structures. We conclude with a discussion of how feminist frameworks expand the concepts and language available to analyze individual experiences within entrepreneurial ecosystems.

4.1 OVERVIEW OF BOSTON

Boston is a well-established entrepreneurial ecosystem, often ranked as one of the top recipients of venture capital funding after Silicon Valley and New York City and one of the top cities for tech startups. Notwithstanding the gender and race inequities that permeate the tech startup scene, Boston is recognized globally as an important ecosystem for the number of startups, volume and size of deals, and availability of talent. Within this context, specialized sectors or niches include biotech, fintech, AI/machine learning, education, health services, and software. Globally, Boston is ranked in the top five ecosystems for startups, coming in fifth in 2020.[1] According to ecosystem research firm Startup Genome, Boston is generally ranked as a top ecosystem city globally based on their ranking methodology,[2] which considers ecosystem performance (40%), funding (20%), market reach (12.5%), connectedness (12.5%), talent (10%), experience (10%), and knowledge (5%). For the purposes of research, Startup Genome[3] defines an ecosystem as "a shared pool of resources, generally located within a 60-mile (100-kilometer) radius around a center point in a given region, with a few exceptions based on local reality."

According to StartHub (www.starthub.org/), an online platform dedicated to supporting entrepreneurs and startups in Boston, the number of entrepreneurship and startup-focused events that take place in Boston on a weekly basis range around 80, with many opportunities for business competitions. Based on their calculations, there are about 80 coworking spaces available, around 120 investors, and in the region of 2,700 startups in the Boston ecosystem. Similarly, Built In Boston (www.builtinboston.com/) is a central hub for all information related to startups and tech, offering information about jobs, salaries, startups, events, and news. Other platforms that offer information about jobs, startups, and networking opportunities in Boston include Startup Boston (www.startupbos.org/), Boston Startups Guide (https://bostonstartupsguide.com/), Cambridge Innovation Center (https://cic.com/), and Venture Café (https://venturecafecambridge.org).

Despite the global standing and desirability of Boston as a startup location, in many ways it is also a city that companies leave. For example, Facebook, Dropbox, Reddit, TaskRabbit, Greylock

---

[1] See https://startupgenome.com/reports/gser2020

[2] https://startupgenome.com/reports/new-science-of-ecosystem-assessment-and-methodology

[3] https://startupgenome.com/reports/gser2020 (see Key Concept on p. 36).

Ventures, LIDS, and The Timberland Company, among others, were all founded in Boston but eventually left for other cities.[4] This reputation leads to many accounts of Boston as being a city that does not have the talent, investment options, and growth opportunities to keep successful startups, a reputation that is difficult to dismantle. As many respondents remarked during our research, there is a sense that the funding gap between angel investment stage and Series A stage contributes to firm flight from Boston. Typically, angel investors invest anywhere between $5,000 and $100,000, although this figure has gone up in recent years. At the same time, Series A has ballooned to an average of $15.7 million as seed investments have grown to an average of $5.6 million.[5] This means that, on average, companies are raising substantial amounts of capital even before traditional Series A, a large change that is due in part to the inflated valuations of technology firms that have dominated the field.

In Boston, there are many different seed investors, venture capitalists, and private equity investors to provide capital for startups,[6] but similar to other ecosystems, the amount of seed capital that would traditionally come from grants, convertible notes, Series A, and other venture offerings is becoming stretched. Rather than seed investment, Series A currently looks more like the Series B of ten years ago. Thus, the amount of capital invested in firms has grown considerably as seed investments generally funded by venture capital firms, accelerators, micro venture capital firms, angel investors, and private equity firms have also grown in size. Understanding how these various ecosystem actors – ranging from individual angel investors to venture capital firms to institutional investors – evaluate firms and startup teams is a key consideration in any discussion around access and equity, but it is beyond the purview of this book.

[4] See www.americaninno.com/boston/tales-of-the-tape-companies-that-have-left-boston/

[5] https://techcrunch.com/2019/04/25/a-quick-look-at-how-fast-series-a-and-seed-rounds-have-ballooned-in-recent-years-fueled-by-top-investors/

[6] www.americaninno.com/boston/guides-boston/the-funding-index-a-roundup-of-bostons-vcs-angels-and-other-investment-firms/

Within this context, we might expect that in such a resource-rich and capital-plentiful entrepreneurial ecosystem, there would be multiple opportunities for female entrepreneurs to start, grow, and scale their ventures and that, consequently, Boston would be one of the best cities in the US and potentially in the world for women to start and grow a business. There is plenty of reason to have this expectation. For example, with government-supported initiatives, such as Women Entrepreneurs Boston,[7] nonprofit organizations such as the Center for Women & Enterprise and The Commonwealth Institute, as well as other programs that focus explicitly on women entrepreneurs and leaders, Boston offers more than most ecosystems. And while particular surveys indicate that Boston is the second-best city for women entrepreneurs,[8] other research shows that women-led startups represent only 14 percent of startups in the Boston ecosystem, the same share as in Copenhagen, Hong Kong, Johannesburg, and Moscow.[9] Our own research based on the Survey of Business Owners (2007[10] and 2012[11]), the Annual Survey of Entrepreneurs (2017),[12] and Census Data[13] indicates that Boston's women-owned businesses have hovered around a third of the city's total businesses since 2007. The percentage of female-led firms has not changed despite the resources that have become available in terms of capital, talent, and world-class educational institutions, including 35 universities and around 152,000 students who are enrolled across them.[14]

4.2   VIGNETTES

The portraits of individuals we present via vignettes are representative of typical experiences we witnessed in Boston as they related to

[7] www.boston.gov/departments/economic-development/women-entrepreneurs-boston
[8] www.fundingcircle.com/us/resources/boston-resources-for-female-entrepreneurs/
[9] https://startupgenome.com/reports/global-startup-ecosystem-report-series-2019
[10] www.census.gov/library/publications/2007/econ/2007-sbo-business-owners.html
[11] www.census.gov/library/publications/2012/econ/2012-sbo.html
[12] www.census.gov/programs-surveys/ase.html
[13] www.census.gov/quickfacts/bostoncitymassachusetts
[14] www.bostonplans.org/getattachment/1770c181-7878-47ab-892f-84baca828bf3

gender, race, and other dimensions of difference within the areas of motivation, identity, and networks. The vignettes represent aggregate experiences by entrepreneur types, and they speak to the importance of gendered and racialized social relations and their influence and impact on entrepreneurial activity. By sharing various quotes from our subjects that speak to the ways these issues are experienced, we provide rich empirical evidence for the ways in which entrepreneurial ecosystems are not necessarily sites for all aspiring entrepreneurs to access the resources and capital necessary for successful startups. Rather, they are reflective of broader society in terms of the structuring of social relations across gender and race. Beyond individual experiences, we outline the ways in which social capital is gendered and operates in entrepreneurial ecosystems, as well as the ways in which the relational, community formation aspects of ecosystems take place in a gendered fashion. In doing so, we show the ways in which social relations impact economic opportunities, but in a manner that is gendered (and racialized, as we demonstrate explicitly in Chapter 7).

Vignette 1

Mark is a single, White 32-year-old graduate of an Ivy League business school with a background in engineering and data analytics. He's been working at a consulting firm in Boston for the last year and has an idea for a fintech startup that he's been thinking about since graduate school. Through his alumni association, he's been connected to several investors and serial entrepreneurs in town to get their perspective and advice on his idea and startup plan. Over lunch and over the phone, they've all been encouraging, often putting him in touch with others they know who can provide more detailed information about the technology or providing additional connections to investors, lawyers, and talent. He's also been in conversation with his MBA school buddies, one who's got experience in investment banking and is interested in coming on board as CFO. Another would likely focus on operations and come on board as COO. Mark wants to be the idea guy and focus on strategy as CEO. It feels like the dream team.

Boston is a resource-rich town with many opportunities for startups, including educational programs; free networking events and panel discussions; office hours with lawyers, angel investors, advisors, and many others; meetups with other entrepreneurs; coworking spaces; accelerators and incubators; and university tech-transfer and entrepreneurship programs. Mark already takes advantage of a coworking space that's available for business associates at his firm and has considered applying to one of the accelerator programs in town. But he isn't sure they would help him make connections beyond those he already has; he feels that all the people worth knowing at this point are just a phone call, text, or email away. Besides, the time commitment alone would be difficult to manage given his full-time job. Mark continues working on his startup for the next year with seed funding from angel investors who were introduced to him via his alumni group. The savings he's built up from his consulting job allow him to work full time on the startup. His buddies similarly leave their positions at their respective firms, with everyone dedicating their full commitment and time to the startup. And with the seed funding, they are able to start working on the technology and business growth strategies. The following year, they have subscribers, a growing revenue stream, and new partnerships with firms who want to deploy their technology in offerings to clients. Series A is a big win at $12 million. He'll have to think about growing the organization and hiring exceptional talent – which may mean leaving Boston, an idea that he's prepared to consider, especially if it means access to additional investors like those on the West coast.

This vignette was inspired by the shared experiences of White male entrepreneurs aged between twenty-five and sixty-five, gathered during our fieldwork in Boston. While these entrepreneurs differed in terms of age and educational background, in general, they had common experiences around accessing resources, using social networks to get connected to resources and people, and the ways in which assumptions about gender played out in relation to leadership within their own organizations or their views about success in the ecosystem. Below, we share excerpts from interviews to demonstrate how these issues were expressed during our fieldwork, informing the vignette of what a traditional successful startup story looks like for White males. Specifically, these conversations focused explicitly on interrelated issues of networks and access, identity and diversity, and leadership and motivation.

In the first example, a tech founder/CEO points out the importance of access. He described his startup journey; despite not having the background traditionally considered as contributing to entrepreneurial success (he is a European immigrant who came to the US aged nine and didn't attend an Ivy League university), he has been able to gain access to valued resources, a dedicated community of support, and, equally important, access to capital. When asked about the obstacles he faced, he shared the following story.

WHITE MALE ENTREPRENEUR 20:[15] Sure. I would say one obstacle that we faced was access to certain networks within the Boston community. You know, there's two accelerators. There's MassAccelerator and TechAccelerator [pseudonyms], but outside of those two communities there's really no gateway to an authentic startup community here in Boston. I mean, there's – I had amazing professors at University B [pseudonym], I'm sure there's amazing professors everywhere else. But even Steve [pseudonym], who was an undergrad at

---

[15] We use "White male entrepreneur" to demarcate the race, gender, and actor-type within the research, the number is a coding tool to help us organize our subjects and refers to male subject number 20.

Harvard, my cofounder, he dropped out. He didn't finish. But while he was there ... while he was there, we were trying to leverage the Harvard I-Lab, but even being admitted to the program – it wasn't easy. The deadline – so there's one deadline, I think we missed it, and then you can't apply after the deadline. So it's a little – with all good reason they have their structure and they have to stick to it. But you're talking about the I-Lab. That's got to be the best kind of campus innovation program you can get in Massachusetts besides one of MIT's, but obviously we're not MIT people, so we don't have access to it. So with that said, there really was not much access to a startup community, so we had to grind our way in, I would say.

INTERVIEWER: So how did you end up getting into TechAccelerator? It's quite a feat!

WHITE MALE ENTREPRENEUR 20: Yeah, it wasn't on my radar at all. I mean, so we – at the time, the way it happened was our first money-in angel, his name is Robert Smith [pseudonym] ... yeah, he's a great guy. So he's one of our advisors; he invested in us. And as we were putting together our angel round, he was helping us assess who we wanted to partner with from an investor perspective. He was, you know, introducing me to several people from the Boston community, and then one of the people he thought of was Peter Riley [pseudonym], and he said, "He's a good guy but he's running TechAccelerator now, so maybe you could talk to him there; I think it would behoove you to at least consider the program." I had no – I mean we were working so much. We're still working like that. At that point I was working nights at a restaurant, paying my own bills, and trying to finance myself – I had no idea applications were even open. So he said, you know, "check it out". Peter said, "Hey, let's meet, fill out an application. It doesn't take long – just throw it in." And then from there I met with Peter, really liked what he stood for, learned more about the program, and thought it would really be beneficial to the company. So we decided to move forward with it.

INTERVIEWER: So once you applied, so you're part of a cohort?

WHITE MALE ENTREPRENEUR 20: We were part of a cohort of 12, yeah.

INTERVIEWER: And so once you got out of that and was part of that, where were your main sources of advice and mentoring coming from?

WHITE MALE ENTREPRENEUR 20: I would say the main sources ... so the TechAccelerator is a community itself. So Peter, who was the managing director, I spent a lot of time with him. Actually he was here this past Tuesday, so very, very close to him still. And he was probably, from TechAccelerator, the biggest source of advice. There are also two directors, who were also very involved, but Peter was probably the one I spoke with the most. Then there were, I would say, a few alumni of past TechAccelerator cohorts who would give me advice from time to time. But the majority of the other advice came from our angel investors from our angel round earlier that year. Then, during the program, we raised another round of funding, so our first institutional round, from Venture Firm A [pseudonym] and Boston Capital Firm [pseudonym], and they to date are our biggest source of advice.

Thus, while the startup journey is not an easy road, gaining access to resources, information, and the "right" person is pivotal to one's chances of becoming successful. And once successful, it is important to understand how issues of diversity are addressed, if at all. We share an example from another male entrepreneur in the healthcare space. He responded in the following way when asked about having women on the leadership team.

WHITE MALE ENTREPRENEUR 15: Not in the founding team. We have always had at least one woman involved. Either as an intern, or we had one of our ... directors of data and product ... stuff. And we hired her, god how long has it been? Well at one point, because we had to let a few people go and [we went] back to just the interns, because we were running out of funding, but yeah we've always had at least one or two women involved in the team. So the question is, what is my advice to get more women involved in entrepreneurship? That's a difficult question. I haven't thought about it much. I don't have a good answer for it. I see a lot of programs within accelerators like MassAccelerator [pseudonym; the same organization as mentioned above], you know, awards that are given specifically to women founders. I would have to look at the research to see if they're even helpful. I think that there's a lot of inspirational women that have done incredible things. I think that there are for sure plenty of barriers. I mean I feel like we have a barrier to raising funding, but I can't imagine, it's probably three times that for a woman that tries to go into a venture capitalist. And what you typically see with venture capitalists is that they're investing in people that look and sound like them, and not necessarily giving a lot of credibility to minorities and women. I think there's kind of ... if you look at both sides, right, so if you look at the women who want to be entrepreneurs, I think that there is probably societal impact that might push them in a different career direction, that if you really wanted to get them into entrepreneurship, we would have to change society. So that is difficult to ask. And then on the other side, with funding and resources, I think that there are plenty of resources that I think that anybody can take advantage of, especially if you have a good idea and you have a lot of drive. But there are other resources like funding that have significant barriers. So again, those are the two things, society and funding are the two things that I would tackle. Very easy simple solutions, right?

INTERVIEWER: Very simple. So when you're looking to grow your team, is that something you keep your eye on? The diversity – not just women – but diversity of the top management team?

WHITE MALE
ENTREPRENEUR 15:   Absolutely. Yeah, we have a very small team, so in some ways, we take what we can get if it meets a specific bar, and we determine that it's a good fit with the team. So it turns out we've gotten a lot of diversity, both ethnic diversity and gender diversity, on the team throughout the time that we've been a company. We've gotten really lucky with that, I think. And again there's studies that show that if you have a female on the board, or in a management seat in the company, then there's a net benefit to that. So we're very focused on becoming a successful company, and I think diversity is an important piece of that.

Looking at his company today, there are only five team members, all of whom are White males. Thus, while aspirationally there is commitment to being mindful of diversity and claims of how important it is, the reality is that changes and actions do not necessarily follow such discourse. In other words, the aggregate impact of the ways such beliefs and (lack of) action continue to create gendered experiences for women (and minorities) in the ecosystem is profound. And yet it is not done out of poor intent or overt sexist or racist beliefs. Rather, the rhetorical importance of diversity becomes a substitute for actual action on diversity, a practice that Ahmed (2007) coins "doing the document," where individuals or organizations end up documenting diversity issues rather than actually doing anything about them.

This is exemplified by another White male entrepreneur, thirty-two at the time of the interview, with an undergraduate, master's, and doctoral degree in biochemical engineering from Harvard. When asked "Is diversity important to you, and if so, what does that mean to you, and how would you act on that?" he responds in the following way.

WHITE MALE
ENTREPRENEUR 1:

That's a good question. It is important. It's also something that, almost getting anyone else besides yourself is as enormous a diversity of opinion. I'm trying to think. Yeah, I think it's not been the forefront of our hiring thought. I'd say the forefront has been: can we find someone who has types of skills that we're looking for (a) [because they are] a good person, (b) because most of the time everything's based off, if I'm seeking your business, I'm going to mail you some slides. And we just believe that they're true. And so, you know, having trust in a person is also important. But, too, diversity of ideas. Definitely [you] don't want – a clone of myself would not be a good thing to have. You want someone else to challenge your own ideas, [as in asking] "Why do you think this is true?" So yeah, I'd say it's important, but hasn't – we never sort of solidified it into our thinking in hiring.

The issue of connections and gaining access as well as inclusion is addressed by a White male serial founder who was sixty-two years old and the CEO of a SaaS company at the time of the interview. He stated the following when asked "In terms of connecting to others in Boston, how did you go about that?"

WHITE MALE
ENTREPRENEUR 6:

I knew them. But, if I didn't, you just do research. You look at the venture capital firms that are in your area, you will do the research to find out what stages they invest in, and then what industries and markets they invest in, then you will look at their portfolio companies to see what companies they've invested in, then you look at their partners that have invested in those companies that are similar to yours, and then you contact them. Then you go in with, you know, you just convince them to talk to you and you go in with your funding deck and pitch, and contrary to popular belief, you don't go in with a whole business plan – you go in with a slide deck.

When asked "What could be done to encourage more women and minorities in entrepreneurship?," he stated that he would encourage them to start their "careers" in entrepreneurship and said it isn't something that you just start doing, but get into it as a career.

WHITE MALE ENTREPRENEUR 6: Once you get into that ecosystem of venture capital-backed startups, all you have to be is good, right? As long as you're good, you're going to have exposure and you're going to find different opportunities and you're going to be in industries that are going. So just encouraging them to consider that a career path more than anything. I don't think that this industry, there's anything about it that would inhibit a minority or a female from getting into it, other than enough minorities or females don't choose it at the outset. And you won't see enough females and minorities as CEOs until they come in at the grassroots level and grow their careers that way.

The first vignette presented the shared views and experiences of White male entrepreneurs. Next, we present another vignette derived from the shared experiences of highly educated and accomplished White female entrepreneurs (most having gained a Ph.D.). Given Boston's success in the niche biotech industry, we focus on this category of entrepreneurs to understand their experiences. Yet we are also reminded of the fact that even in such a niche industry where women make up around 22 percent of faculty at MIT (a relatively high number for a science field), the share of companies founded by women is about half that percentage, suggesting a reverse funneling of women out of leadership and entrepreneurial roles[16] in Boston. Through our second vignette, we share the continued barriers faced by women with highly advanced degrees and business accomplishments, highlighting the seemingly ordinary ways gender norms and biases take shape in relation to entrepreneurship within ecosystems.

Vignette 2

Hard work and solving difficult problems has never been an issue for Emily. After earning a Ph.D. in biomechanical engineering and doing a postdoc at MIT, she thought about going back home to Cleveland, but got a great job offer working in a startup called BioTrue. Her work at BioTrue is quite rewarding, allowing her to bring her postdoctoral research into real-life applications. And it was only through the connections she made through her lab work that she landed the opportunity to bring her expertise to the world of startups. In reality, she did feel a sense of obligation to take up this position, given how small the community was in relation to biomedical research and startups. A startup was quite exciting, something she never thought about at all in her career plans. In many ways, Boston has been a great place to work and make new friends. And while quite often Emily works long hours, the quintessential startup experience, she wonders how things might change if she wanted to have children. Would she still be able to keep her current position as the senior science advisor overseeing many of the startups research activities? Senior leadership has said she's indispensable, but often she feels invisible in meetings and wonders whether they would replace her if they thought she

---

[16] www.washingtonpost.com/science/2020/01/29/bias-biotech-funding-has-blocked-women-led-companies/

wouldn't be as committed after becoming a mother. The work has always been intense, but that's what she's found to be most rewarding.

She wonders if it's the right time to start something up on her own. After all, she's been there almost eight years and made lots of connections. It seems inevitable that very soon she will have to choose between her career and becoming a mother; at least that's how it feels, the unrelenting realization that she is not getting younger despite knowing that she's at the top of her game in the highly specialized research field. Perhaps another startup might offer more options than this one for flexible work. Even though she hasn't even mentioned the idea of taking time off to senior leadership, Emily already knows what the response might be: we're in the middle of very important and possibly groundbreaking research and now is not the right time. But not the right time for who? And she knows that any time off would likely mean she's replaced or, worse, returns to a position that is not the one she left.

This vignette is derived from our conversations with highly educated White women entrepreneurs between the ages of thirty-five and sixty-five, who shared their stories of success but also the difficult decisions they faced in their careers because of gendered obstacles around career progression, work–life balance, and leadership opportunities. As pointed out by one of our interviewees, who has a Ph.D. in molecular biology from MIT, even if funding is not a barrier to growth, there are continued obstacles to being taken seriously as a woman founder and leader. Below, she shared her experiences within the company she founded, based on her research when outsiders were brought in by the investment team.

INTERVIEWER: So you mentioned that you found the [Boston] entrepreneurial community pretty welcoming for you. Have you had other experiences where you maybe have felt marginalized or you felt like sort of an outsider, whether it's [to do with] the broad ecosystem or just particular individuals or organizations?

WHITE FEMALE ENTREPRENEUR 20: I'd say, within my organization, I think that's what's so shocking. I think outside of my organization I'm perceived as charming and confident and competent and interesting and, you know, smart and compelling. And then within my company, I think that – I think they thought I was too young. Because I'm 35 [and] everyone else is like 20 years my senior. And so I feel like they felt like I was too young to be the face of something, because they wanted [it] to be taken seriously. They weren't concerned that sometimes their content was something that could not be taken seriously. Like that would happen and I think that they instead would shift the blame to me, like I'm the reason they weren't taken seriously, when in reality I'm like, "you're using words that show naivete, that you don't have the expertise" – you know, I was trying to give them feedback on the other thing, like the content. And so I think then I became extremely marginalized within my own company ... and I think this comes back to like what was my biggest challenge. And it was this legal knowledge.

INTERVIEWER: That's just helpful to hear, and others have said something similar, along the lines [of] they don't know how to structure the company [in a way] that would be in their best interest, and the interest of the company as well, versus benefitting a particular individual.

WHITE FEMALE ENTREPRENEUR 20: Right, and that's [what was] really interesting when I watched the concerns move away from what was good for the company to what would elevate a certain person – what would you call it, the "travelling spouse" or the "following spouse" character in my story.

INTERVIEWER: The trailing spouse. [He] wanted to come over with his best friend?

WHITE FEMALE ENTREPRENEUR 20: Right, so we had somebody, and we had his best friend, and really what I realized [was that] the mission of the company became to give that best friend a company. It wasn't to solve PTSD, anymore. And so our messaging was getting really confusing, because if the goal of your company is to give Banu [interviewer] a company, you're going to have to make a really compelling story like "I need this investment in you" versus the mission of our company – like that was always how I started any conversation: "My mission is to cure PTSD. I think I have the key."

When asked "Has the way you engage with people and organizations in Boston changed over the years? And if so, how?" she continued as follows.

WHITE FEMALE ENTREPRENEUR 20: It became very challenging. So when I was the sole founder, I could go out and say: "Hi! I'm Doctor so and so. I'm the founder of

Therapy [pseudonym], and I aim to cure PTSD by targeting the actual biology underlining [it]." But then as I became marginalized by my team, my cofounders, it became very challenging because people would have already heard about Therapy and they wouldn't have heard about me. Or the guys would introduce me as like, something else. And I was completely okay with being a junior partner, but the key word there is partner. And really I was nothing. I was just this junior person at their company. They were like, "Oh you're employee number six'" and I was like, "No, I'm employee zero." These guys would be working at – I think the CEO was about to work for some Tough Mudder thing, and the CSO, our chemist guy, was going to retire, and this other guy was moving to Singapore to like work for some random Singapore thing. And the reason we're in this room is because I had the balls to start this. And to be marginalized and feel like I couldn't talk and represent like I was part of the company, because it was causing confusion, did change how I engaged with people. But I am still a charming entrepreneur, and this scientist person. And so then I just had to go and make sure that I wasn't speaking for the company, but that I was speaking for me. Which I think was detrimental to the company. It was unfortunate that whenever I would go and engage someone, it was like: "I'm an entrepreneur. I'm working on this.

But separate from this, here are my passions." Which was wonderful, because for my long-term career, that's really, really great. I think it would have been great for Therapy had I been able to speak for them. But they were very, again, like, bullying about how to present. Because, again, they were very concerned that it would be too juvenile, or young, or junior. I have no idea. They never said it in clear terms, and it could have been female, too. I talk about this; I had three strikes against me as an entrepreneur. I do not look like what walks into any entrepreneur conference, because I'm a Ph.D. scientist. And I speak like a Ph. D. scientist, because I'm young. Like I'm younger than these people, and I think one thing that doesn't come across in your recording is I look younger. Like I'm 35, but I look – and it's great to look young, right? Except in entrepreneurship, and they want to see grey hair and lots of experience. And the third thing was being a woman. And so I'd recently realized that I was so otherly in so many ways that I don't know what ... that it is that they didn't want me representing the company. Because you look through seven pictures now on our website, you'll get an idea. Like everyone's over 50, everyone's male, and everyone's White, except for one person.

This experience was shared by another White female entrepreneur, forty-six at the time of the interview and with a degree in physical chemistry and experience as a postdoc in a laboratory at MIT, who cofounded a technology startup based on her laboratory work. While raising money was not easy, she had a very supportive male mentor. She stated the following in relation to how she came to occupy a leadership role in the startup but didn't get to make decisions.

WHITE FEMALE ENTREPRENEUR 23:   I mean our founder – there was that our founder at MIT, Professor Dan Mills [pseudonym], was a great mentor to me. And he really encouraged me to get involved in startups. He encouraged me to interact with his investors he was interacting with and brought me into very high-level discussions with our pharmaceutical sponsors and pharma companies that sponsored research. He really tried to – he was fantastic and really helped me to build my interest in entrepreneurship and business. And I didn't come in naturally with that kind of interest at all [laughs]. I was puzzled as to why I was sitting at these tables and what I was supposed to do, but he was a great person for selling big ideas and technology at a very high level.

And then at BioFirm [pseudonym] I worked very closely with our CEO ... another postdoc who had some business experience and so had wanted to take the CEO role on. And he was the CEO for several years, and then I think he ... after that, the investors brought in a more experienced life science business person and ... his role changed to – I don't know – CTO or something else.

But he was a really big mentor to me, a few
steps ahead of me, much more interested in
the business. And I was actually at BioFirm,
I was much more interested in the scientific
work and the lab development, so it was my
inclination as soon as I could to kind of leave
the business responsibilities towards him
and towards other people on our team and
focus on the lab. He was always my window
into what was going on. And so I always sort
of knew what was going on even though
I wasn't directly involved [with] the
investors anymore. And I always had this
window into it.

And so I think there is a sense that I had a
kind of back seat view of what went on at
BioFirm, and I think I learned a lot from
that. Even though I wasn't making the
decisions, I think there was an advantage for
me at least to understand what happened.
After leaving BioFirm, I became much more
interested in business, probably because
I sort of saw the mistakes that were made.
The good things – there were some very
positive things and it was successful in
many ways, but there [were] huge business
mistakes that were made. And seeing that
happen, [I'd] say, well, wait a minute.
Business people don't come in – even if they
come in with a lot of credentials and
experience, it doesn't mean that they're
necessarily – you can trust your technology
or your business to them. And I felt that I do
have my own insights and value. If I can

understand the things that they did wrong, I would have the potential to do a better job. And so I think that sort of reflected ... my role now is, oh, where I am involved in both the technology development but also the business decisions as well. And I think going forward, I see myself continuing in roles like that. I don't think I would do so well to sit back ... sort of on a purely technical level at any company anymore. So I think yes, my interactions with Dan ... [he] continues to be a friend and we get together and talk about what we're doing, and I think he's continuing to be a mentor to me.

This notion of building networks was also emphasized by another female entrepreneur who had earned a Ph.D. degree in molecular biology in 1986 and ended up coming to Boston in the mid-1990s to work at a biotech company, after having worked in a large biotech firm in the San Francisco area. She stated the following.

WHITE FEMALE ENTREPRENEUR 4: ... by working in the mainstream part of biotech longer, I created a network that I think increased my ability to be successful as a CEO at these two companies because the network existed; I didn't have to make it happen. And when you're a small company here and an entrepreneur here, your network is your infrastructure. Whether it's a human resources thing or a banking question, a finance question, a commercial question – if you can't pick up that phone and ask that question, you're dead. So people can be super innovative as young entrepreneurs and still not be hugely successful, because they don't have that network to help expedite things. And they don't have a network that basically smacks them upside the head and tells them "that's not going to work." That's very important. And so you see that all the time, these little companies especially – we're in a highly regulated industry, both from the [Food and Drug Administration] perspective and then if you're a public company, obviously by the [Securities and Exchange Commission] – if you don't have a network of advisors under those really staunch conditions of a regulatory environment, it's pretty dangerous to go forward. And just sort of hitting on the diversity issue for a moment, one of the things we've been preaching to young women in the industry for the last ten years is networking. And it can't be contrived networking. It's not just about networking to get into another company. It's about building these colleagues – your virtual colleagues. And we kind of believe – I personally believe this and I know I have a group of colleagues who agree – women network differently than men, so it's very challenging for women to break into certain networks that are primarily men. And I think that is one of our problems with female entrepreneurs, and I think you brought it up [when you asked:] "How do you find your network?"

INTERVIEWER: Can you describe that difference that you see?

WHITE FEMALE
ENTREPRENEUR 4:

So, for example, men have many sorts of informal social activities that are completely natural to them. Whether it's go out and get a beer or go play golf at these bigger conventions – you know, you go out for a drink, you go to a party, you do whatever you do. And socially, when women insert themselves into those activities, and I think it's changing now but certainly ten years ago there was sort of an awkwardness of having women just sort of jump into the network, because, you know, the way that people socialize is sort of different. So you have to kind of learn a dialogue; you have to find a common ground such that it's not this awkwardness. So I'll give you an example: when I was working at Pharmaceutical Company A [pseudonym], I was working in Switzerland a lot, and I needed to get some things done there and it was very hard on me. And I quickly found out, nobody told me this but I found out, I kept saying to people "let's get dinner." And I finally found out, they're not going to have dinner with me. They'll have lunch with me, they'll have coffee with me, but dinner is crossing the line. I was seeing my male colleagues have dinner with each other no problem. But there was something crossing the line if just a man and a woman went to get dinner together. I don't think it's as bad here [in Boston], and I don't even think it's as bad there as it was, again, ten years ago, but I think it was real. And I think that there is this social awkwardness of a woman, as she's younger, discovering it. So I think after I turned 50 it got easier. And maybe [it was] because I'd had more battle scars by then or maybe it was just because at that point in time people aren't looking at each other the same way, but it definitely changed.

INTERVIEWER: So your strategies for reaching out to your network, how has that changed over time?

WHITE FEMALE ENTREPRENEUR 4: Yeah I think that my strategies for networking when I was younger and less experienced [were] very much building mentor-type relationships and asking people for advice and asking them to advise me. And literally asking "Can we meet once a month?" or something like that. And being very subordinate, and you build that sort of apprentice relationship with people and all of a sudden the awkwardness goes away. And then they begin to really appreciate what you might be able to bring to them as well, and lo and behold they start making introductions. So now, I basically pick up the phone and say, "I need to talk to you." So ... it's a completely different thing, and it's like "I need to talk to you today."

4.3 ANALYSIS AND DISCUSSION

Here, our aim has been to demonstrate the ways in which entrepreneurship "gets done" by archetypes of entrepreneurs. In these vignettes, we showcase the experiences of male and female entrepreneurs who self-identify as White. While we recognize that there may be other experiences, our research aims to speak to those typical interactions that are experienced by White entrepreneurs in an entrepreneurial ecosystem as we saw and accounted for during field-work. In Boston, ecosystem interactions at the level of the individual are guided by the importance of social capital and networks where actors gain access to information, resources, and investors, albeit in different ways for male and female entrepreneurs (see Neergaard, Shaw, & Carter, 2005). In other words, while both male and female entrepreneurs are motivated to be successful and move forward in their startups, the trajectories of male and female entrepreneurs as well as their experiences are quite different in the sense that gendered barriers to leadership and access to information and networking emerge in the social interactions and relations that take shape between ecosystem actors.

To clarify, we saw no differences in the aspirations of male and female entrepreneurs, as both groups were equally likely to move forward in their aims to grow and scale their businesses. Where we did see differences was in the ways the motivations of women were hampered by various gendered ecosystem interactions and institutional arrangements. In addition, the motivation for expanding networks was not necessarily transactional, whereby one could engage in an exchange relationship with the aim of asking for something if needed at a later point in time; rather, expanding networks was associated with the accumulation of social capital, motivated by the benefits it brought in relation to values, trust, and community membership (see Kwon & Adler, 2014, for an overview of motivation and social capital). Even if women wanted to engage in transactional social capital accrual through, for example, social activities with professional colleagues, the ability for women to conduct business in the same way as men (e.g. over dinner) was significantly impacted by gendered norms and expectations (see Kumra & Vinnicombe, 2010, for how women have to accrue social capital in masculinized organizational cultures). Similarly, women were impeded from having leadership and decision-making roles in their own firm based on these same gendered expectations.

For men, access to information, resources, and investors was seemingly easier given the networks within which they circulated.

Their observations around the importance and relevance of diversity stayed at the level of discourse; there were no identifiable steps that were being taken by them as founders and CEOs to change the makeup of their firms or to enact change within the ecosystem through their own actions. Ultimately, suggesting women and minorities either make a career out of entrepreneurship or even expand their networks to gain access to important ecosystem actors, such as investors, does not change the existing gendered social relations that are the foundation for the ecosystem. Such gendered social relations give rise to gendered social capital, an idea we expand on next in order to explain why individual behavioral changes cannot result in systemic change in the context of ecosystems. In other words, no amount of social capital can overcome the economic inequalities arising out of gendered social structures and relations. To this end, our discussions and analyses on gender and social capital are derived from feminist economics and sociology to demonstrate the ways in which the accrual and deployment of such "capital" takes shape through gendered relations and value creation.

4.4   SOCIAL CAPITAL: A FEMINIST APPROACH

Social capital has been an important concept and unit of analysis for social scientists. This concept also has strong relevance for our understanding of entrepreneurial ecosystems, particularly in terms of how different actors may "have" different social capital and, concurrently, how trust accrued from social networks and networking may develop in different ways for different actors. Here, we provide a brief overview of the notion of social capital and relate it to entrepreneurial ecosystems, focusing explicitly on the notion of trust as the currency through which connections can yield positive outcomes. Trust comes about due to one's networks and relationships, which are formed through one's social capital in a community. Put differently, communities foster the formation of social capital, which allows particular networks and connections to take shape; and this in turn allows trust to be formed between different actors. Yet these processes and practices have gendered and racialized dimensions such that it matters in which communities one is present and accepted versus in which communities one is seen as an "outsider" or "other."

Social capital is profoundly important and relevant for expanding on gendering of entrepreneurial ecosystems, including the ways in which an individual, transactional approach to social capital versus a relational, network-based one has different consequences for our understanding of trust. Insights about social capital derived from feminist economics and sociology expand our ideas beyond our original consideration of trust to focus also on the way in which social capital is a relational formation that takes place beyond the market and the state: in the confines of the domestic sphere through the care economy. In other words, one simply doesn't carry around their social capital and cash it in as needed; rather, the formation of social capital takes place in spheres that are often thought to be beyond the purview of formal economic systems, such as entrepreneurship and ecosystems.

In the social sciences, social capital has become an important dimension and analytic focus, emanating from its use in examining how and why certain systems of government and economic development have been successful in particular states compared to others (Putnam, Leonardi, & Nanetti, 1994) and how the rise of certain social problems can be attributed to its demise (Putnam, 2000). Despite previous iterations of the concept, including that by French sociologist Pierre Bourdieu, which emphasizes conflict and power contestations (see Siisiainen, 2003 for an overview), the dominant understanding of social capital within the US has been based on the collective works of Putnam, Coleman, and Burt as the main drivers of research. Together, their ontology is based on a functionalist approach, an understanding of society through the sociology of regulation and social cohesion (Bezanson, 2006). This dominant framework has guided much of social capital research; for instance, examination of the ways in which social cohesion takes shape and impacts a variety of issues, ranging from individual experiences to organizational life to institutions (Baron, Field, & Schuller, 2000). As a refinement to social capital, scholars differentiate among bonding, bridging, and linking forms – that is, ties within social groups, ties across social groups, and ties across individuals placed in different institutionalized power positions, respectively (Urwin et al., 2008).

For Putnam (2000), social capital derives from moral obligations and norms, social values and trust, and social networks. In general, social capital has been thought of as "investment in social relations with the expectation of a return" (Lin, 1999: 30, see also Lin, 2002). Moving beyond narrow, individualistic explanations, scholars have placed the concept within social structures, disaggregating its various constitutive components to include obligations and expectations, information channels, and social norms (Coleman, 1988) to explain its emergence. In placing the individual within social contexts and structures, sociologists have expanded on the dominant understanding within the domain of economics of individuals as (only) "rational," self-interested economic actors. In providing a social explanation and context for economic activity, scholars have explained how exchange relationships contribute to social capital accrual and subsequent deployment when necessary (Granovetter, 1985).

Within the context of business scholarship, the influential paper by Adler & Kwon (2002) in the *Academy of Management Review* set the stage for relying on social capital as an important concept within the context of management, strategy, innovation, and entrepreneurship research. Adler and Kwon define social capital as "the goodwill that is engendered by the fabric of social relations and that can be mobilized to facilitate action" (2002: 17); put differently, social capital is "using the goodwill of others towards us as a resource" (2002: 18). Specifically, in the context of entrepreneurship research, scholars have considered the importance of social networks and social capital in terms of their impact on startups across nations (Estrin, Mickiewicz, & Stephan, 2013). Already, scholars have examined the ways social capital and social networks are critical to each stage of the entrepreneurial process (Amezcua et al., 2013; Hoang & Antoncic,

2003; Jack et al., 2010; Jiang et al., 2018; Slotte-Kock & Coviello, 2010). Within this context, social capital theory posits "that in addition to purely economics-driven contractual relationships, important socially driven dimensions also need to be taken into account" (Bøllingtoft & Ulhøi, 2005: 272).

Within entrepreneurial ecosystems, strategic alliances and inter-organizational networks are themselves critical forms of social capital that serve a legitimizing function, which in turn impacts venture performance (Dacin, Oliver, & Roy, 2007; Khoury, Junkunc, & Deeds, 2013; Kim & Aldrich, 2005; Koka & Prescott, 2008). Social capital, however, only supports commercial entrepreneurial activity "when supportive cultural capital is in place"; and less dominant groups may not necessarily be able to access networks of dominant groups, including across racial/ethnic divides (Light & Dana, 2013: 603). Specifically, the founder's network structure influences their founding activities, with strong ties being associated with a negative effect on founding activities and weak ties with a positive impact on founding activities (Kreiser, Patel, & Fiet, 2013). In addition to this, social competence, or the "ability of an individual to effectively utilize his or her social skills," and entrepreneurial intensity, or an "individual's commitment-related and focus-related attitudes, philosophies, and behaviors toward the establishment of a new venture," also impact on how useful social capital will be to their entrepreneurial aims (Kreiser, Patel, & Fiet, 2013: 7). Systemic gender differences in strength of ties as well as how social competence and entrepreneurial intensity are perceived, therefore, would help explain gender gaps in founding activities, including those based on lack of access to investors (see Brush et al., 2002).

To this end, Neumeyer et al. (2019) find that

> male entrepreneurs show higher comparative scores of bridging social capital in aggressive- and managed-growth venture networks, while women entrepreneurs surpass their male counterparts' bridging capital scores in lifestyle and survival venture networks.

Lastly, experienced women entrepreneurs that self-identified as white [sic] showed a higher degree of network connectivity and bridging social capital in the entrepreneurial ecosystem than less experienced non-white female entrepreneurs.

(2019: 475)

This point is also emphasized by scholars examining immigrant entrepreneurship and the ways in which network "closure" within social structures creates social capital for certain groups while leaving out entire other groups (Portes & Landolt, 1996). In other words, social capital arising from social networks and shared norms is a way to simultaneously exclude certain groups while including others. Norms, values, and attributes often thought to be shared by those in similar social structures offer a sense of community and, by extension, relationships forged on trust.

Within the context of entrepreneurial ecosystems, these observations on social capital can speak to the fundamental concern around whether or not individuals can be trusted in the various dimensions of entrepreneurship: with leading a startup, with making decisions, with investors' time and money, with leading a new technology, and so forth. The assumption is that there is an appropriate place for women within entrepreneurship activities and within ecosystems, namely within certain contexts and within certain networks, such as those of bonding ties or family/friends or potentially in those contexts in which they do well – the "lifestyle" and "survival" venture networks. Speaking about "gender differences" does not address unspoken gendered norms, especially those about trust, but aims to present the world as it is. Yet this approach cannot examine why the social world is the way it is and, in particular, the relationship between gendered social structures and their impact on entrepreneurship.

In our research, male informants were quite deliberate in using the concept of trust to speak about their concerns around leadership, technology, and business – they couldn't trust just anyone with these facets of their startups, and even if they claimed that diversity was important to them, they still had to find someone they trusted. In this sense, trust, as a dimension of social capital, is difficult to prove; put differently, it is difficult for a person to prove they are trustworthy if they are an outsider or outside of established social networks. For men, while diversity was an important consideration, it was never important enough to require action; for example, expanding one's social networks to make new connections and thereby find new people to trust. In fact, it seemed that the very notion of diversity was at odds with or challenged the implicit trust that social capital confers on people. Women, on the other hand, spoke about the consequences of lack of trust arising from lack of social capital and the impact this had on their entrepreneurial experiences, including not being able to make decisions, even when in positions of authority, or not being able to lead their own companies, even as a cofounder. Age was also a relevant factor. For example, often young White males are seen as charismatic founders and leaders despite age differences between them and those they may hire to grow their business; but for a female entrepreneur with a Ph.D., a twenty-year age gap between her and the senior leadership team was seen as a problem, and specifically as *her* problem and "overcome" by investors bringing in older males to help her out. In other words, social capital enables people to trust each other, yet gender makes a difference in the perception of whether a person has the "right" social capital, an important but overlooked dimension of social capital research which often goes unnoticed in the context of gendered entrepreneurship activities.

Feminist frameworks offer some insights. The development and deployment of social capital takes shape in the context of gendered social relations within society, and to speak only about "gender differences" within entrepreneurial ecosystems (Brush et al., 2019) falls short of understanding the complexity of gender and power relations. From a feminist analysis, structural and cultural explanations for gender inequality arise out of the unequal distribution of resources based on gender and other social dimensions, coupled with attitudes, norms, and ideologies regarding women's role in society (Norris & Inglehart, 2003). This has serious consequences for heralding entrepreneurship as a form of women's empowerment when existing economic, social, and political arrangements are not challenged or changed (see Mayoux, 2001). The development of social capital within gendered institutional contexts and arrangements is, by definition, also gendered. In effect, social capital analysis can no longer only focus on its financial or economic returns to the individual through "methodological individualism" (Van Staveren, 2002).

To this end, Franklin (2005) notes that many theories of social capital focus on networks and relationships without an explicit analysis of power *and* gender. Bruegel (2005) suggests that an alternative conceptualization of social capital would place it within the domain of public good, such that one could use social capital to enhance public good rather than use it in a narrow financialized fashion to accrue individual benefits. In her critique of existing social capital approaches which suggest that extending social networks to those outside of traditional power circles can create more opportunities for access, she argues that this simply rearranges the pieces; as she puts it, "integrationist participatory models ... only [provide] formal access to existing structures of power, rather than the resources to challenge that power" (Bruegel, 2005: 6). When the market is understood through a social lens including the ways in which social capital enables the functioning of business, it is imperative to consider how women's domestic labor and work enables the creation of such capital. As feminist economists suggest, it is necessary to include social provisioning in any analysis of the economy (Ferber & Nelson, 1993, 2003; Power, 2004). From a feminist lens, social capital is redefined from an individual-level attribute related to instrumentally increasing utility to a relational one (Van Staveren, 2002, 2010) that recognizes it as "part of a system of competing interests and values within a multidimensional space of difference, framed by large inequalities of power" (Bruegel, 2005: 14).

4.5 CONCLUSION

What we propose is that any analysis of entrepreneurial ecosystems needs to examine how power and power relations in the context of social structures and gender impact the experiences of male and female entrepreneurs. Entrepreneurial ecosystems need to be reconceptualized beyond gender-neutral assumptions and considerations of homogenous actors engaged in exchange relationships; the conceptualization should capture how the intersections of power, gender, and social capital/social structures contribute to the production, functioning, and replication of ecosystems, thereby creating opportunities for some actors and, at the same time, barriers for others. And while there is some recognition of power through the concept of linking forms of social capital, inclusion in this domain is still predicated on the assumption that certain people can hold power – this jars with the national conversation in the US right now around how to remake societal hierarchies that are racialized and gendered. Within this context, social solidarity is seen as "opening up ladders of upward mobility to individuals or small groups, rather than considering the ways diverse ideas, practices and values might be allowed to flourish" (Bruegel, 2005: 11). These considerations are often also seen within the domain of gender and entrepreneurship research where suggestions are made for women to expand their networks or to engage in training to do well in high-growth fields, or where there are calls for investors to become mentors to women and/or receive training to reduce their cultural biases against women (Guzman & Kacperczyk, 2019). Such calls are also echoed in advice to women (and men) to answer differently when they are asked questions around prevention/risk aversion versus promotion/growth during pitch contests (Kanze et al., 2018), even though scholarship denotes that feminized behaviors in assumed-masculine roles result in lower preference for both male and female entrepreneurs and their ventures (Balachandra et al., 2019). In other words, the performativity of gender, and specifically femininity, impacts how individuals are perceived in a role (i.e. that of entrepreneur) that is implicitly associated with masculinity; yet, generally, the solutions are focused on individuals rather than systems and structures. While we have spent time and space here expanding on individual experiences, we have done so by placing those individuals within gendered social structures, norms, and contexts, thereby expanding the very concepts associated with entrepreneurial ecosystems to include power relations, gendered social capital, and social structures. We have suggested that "solutions" focusing on the individual cannot address the gendered inequalities that arise from the very norms of entrepreneurial ecosystems that are predicated on social capital, trust, and communities – what we have done is demonstrate that the very foundations of ecosystems are gendered and that moving "beyond" them is not only impossible but ineffective toward gender equity. Is there a solution that could take place beyond the individual? We address this next as we focus on what inclusion efforts are taking shape through organizations, and specifically ESOs in Boston as well as in the newly emergent ecosystems of St. Louis and Asheville.

REFERENCES

Adler, P. S., & Kwon, S. W. (2002). Social capital: Prospects for a new concept. *Academy of Management Review*, 27(1): 17–40.

Ahmed, S. (2007). "You end up doing the document rather than doing the doing": Diversity, race equality and the politics of documentation. *Ethnic and Racial Studies*, 30(4): 590–609.

Amezcua, A. S., Grimes, M. G., Bradley, S. W., & Wiklund, J. (2013). Organizational sponsorship and founding environments: A contingency view on the survival of business-incubated firms, 1994–2007. *Academy of Management Journal*, 56(6): 1628–1654.

Balachandra, L., Briggs, T., Eddleston, K., & Brush, C. (2019). Don't pitch like a girl!: How gender stereotypes influence investor decisions. *Entrepreneurship Theory and Practice*, 43(1): 116–137.

Baron, S., Field, J., & Schuller, T. (Eds.). (2000). *Social capital: Critical perspectives*. Oxford: Oxford University Press.

Bezanson, K. (2006). Gender and the limits of social capital. *Canadian Review of Sociology/Revue Canadienne de Sociologie, 43*(4): 427–443.

Blodgett, A. T., Schinke, R. J., Smith, B., Peltier, D., & Pheasant, C. (2011). In indigenous words: Exploring vignettes as a narrative strategy for presenting the research voices of Aboriginal community members. *Qualitative Inquiry, 17*(6): 522–533.

Bøllingtoft, A., & Ulhøi, J. P. (2005). The networked business incubator – Leveraging entrepreneurial agency?. *Journal of Business Venturing, 20*(2): 265–290.

Bruegel, I. (2005). Social capital and feminist critique. In J. Franklin (Ed.), *Women and social capital* (pp. 4–17). London: Families & Social Capital ESRC Research Group.

Brush, C. G., Carter, N. M., Greene, P. G., Hart, M. M., & Gatewood, E. (2002). The role of social capital and gender in linking financial suppliers and entrepreneurial firms: A framework for future research. *Venture Capital: An International Journal of Entrepreneurial Finance, 4*(4): 305–323.

Brush, C., Edelman, L. F., Manolova, T., & Welter, F. (2019). A gendered look at entrepreneurship ecosystems. *Small Business Economics, 53*(2): 393–408.

Calás, M. B., & Smircich, L. (1993). Dangerous liaisons: The "feminine-in-management" meets "globalization". *Business Horizons, 36*(2): 71–81.

Coleman, J. S. (1988). Social capital in the creation of human capital. *American Journal of Sociology, 94*: S95–S120.

Dacin, M. T., Oliver, C., & Roy, J. P. (2007). The legitimacy of strategic alliances: An institutional perspective. *Strategic Management Journal, 28*(2): 169–187.

Estrin, S., Mickiewicz, T., & Stephan, U. (2013). Entrepreneurship, social capital, and institutions: Social and commercial entrepreneurship across nations. *Entrepreneurship Theory and Practice, 37*(3): 479–504.

Ferber, M. A., & Nelson, J. (Eds.) 1993. *Beyond economic man: Feminist theory and economics.* Chicago: University of Chicago Press.

Ferber, M. A., & Nelson, J. (Eds.) (2003). *Feminist economics today: Beyond economic man* (2nd ed.). Chicago: University of Chicago Press.

Franklin, J. (Ed.). (2005). *Women and social capital.* London: Families & Social Capital ESRC Research Group.

Granovetter, M. (1985). Economic action and social structure: The problem of embeddedness. *American Journal of Sociology, 91*(3): 481–510.

Guzman, J., & Kacperczyk, A. O. (2019). Gender gap in entrepreneurship. *Research Policy, 48*(7): 1666–1680.

Hoang, H., & Antoncic, B. (2003). Network-based research in entrepreneurship: A critical review. *Journal of Business Venturing, 18*(2): 165–187.

Jack, S., Moult, S., Anderson, A. R., & Dodd, S. (2010). An entrepreneurial network evolving: Patterns of change. *International Small Business Journal, 28*(4): 315–337.

Jiang, X., Liu, H., Fey, C., & Jiang, F. (2018). Entrepreneurial orientation, network resource acquisition, and firm performance: A network approach. *Journal of Business Research, 87*: 46–57.

Kanze, D., Huang, L., Conley, M. A., & Higgins, E. T. (2018). We ask men to win and women not to lose: Closing the gender gap in startup funding. *Academy of Management Journal, 61*(2): 586–614.

Khoury, T. A., Junkunc, M., & Deeds, D. L. (2013). The social construction of legitimacy through signaling social capital: Exploring the conditional value of alliances and underwriters at IPO. *Entrepreneurship Theory and Practice, 37*(3): 569–601.

Kim, P., & Aldrich, H. (2005). *Social capital and entrepreneurship*. Boston, MA: Now Publishers Inc.

Knowlton, K., Ozkazanc-Pan, B., Clark Muntean, S., & Motoyama, Y. (2015). Support organizations and remediating the gender gap in entrepreneurial ecosystems: A case study of St. Louis. SSRN. Available at http://dx.doi.org/10.2139/ssrn.2685116 (accessed May 15, 2019).

Koka, B. R., & Prescott, J. E. (2008). Designing alliance networks: The influence of network position, environmental change, and strategy on firm performance. *Strategic Management Journal, 29*(6): 639–661.

Kreiser, P. M., Patel, P. C., & Fiet, J. O. (2013). The influence of changes in social capital on firm-founding activities. *Entrepreneurship Theory and Practice, 37*(3): 539–567.

Kumra, S., & Vinnicombe, S. (2010). Impressing for success: A gendered analysis of a key social capital accumulation strategy. *Gender, Work & Organization, 17* (5): 521–546.

Kwon, S. W., & Adler, P. S. (2014). Social capital: Maturation of a field of research. *Academy of Management Review, 39*(4): 412–422.

Light, I., & Dana, L. P. (2013). Boundaries of social capital in entrepreneurship. *Entrepreneurship Theory and Practice, 37*(3): 603–624.

Lin, N. (1999). Building a network theory of social capital. *Connections, 22*(1): 28–51.

Lin, N. (2002). *Social capital: A theory of social structure and action* (Vol. 19). Cambridge: Cambridge University Press.

Mayoux, L. (2001). Jobs, gender and small enterprises: Getting the policy environment right. *ILO Working Papers* 993467093402676. Available at www.ilo.org/ public/libdoc/ilo/2001/101B09_94_engl.pdf (accessed July 20, 2019).

McCarthy, L. (2017). Empowering women through corporate social responsibility: A feminist Foucauldian critique. *Business Ethics Quarterly, 27*(4): 603–631.

Neergaard, H., Shaw, E., & Carter, S. (2005). The impact of gender, social capital and networks on business ownership: A research agenda. *International Journal of Entrepreneurial Behaviour & Research, 11*(5): 338–357.

Neumeyer, X., Santos, S. C., Caetano, A., & Kalbfleisch, P. (2019). Entrepreneurship ecosystems and women entrepreneurs: A social capital and network approach. *Small Business Economics, 53*(2): 475–489.

Norris, P., & Inglehart, R. (2003). Gendering social capital: Bowling in women's leagues. Available at www.hks.harvard.edu/fs/pnorris/Acrobat/Gendering%20Social%20Capital.pdf

Ozkazanc-Pan, B., Knowlton, K., & Clark Muntean, S. (2017). Gender inclusion activities in entrepreneurship ecosystems: The case of St. Louis, MO and Boston, MA. SSRN. Available at https://ssrn.com/abstract=2982414 (accessed May 15, 2019).

Ozkazanc-Pan, B. (2020). Feminist writing in a gendered transnational world: Women on the move?. In A. Pullen, J. Helin, & N. Harding (Eds.), *Writing differently, dialogues in critical management studies* (Vol. 4, pp. 13–24). Bingley: Emerald Publishing Limited.

Portes, A., & Landolt, P. (1996). The downside of social capital. *The American Prospect, 26*: 18–21.

Power, M. (2004). Social provisioning as a starting point for feminist economics. *Feminist Economics, 10*(3): 3–19.

Putnam, R. D. (2000). Bowling alone: America's declining social capital. In L. Crothers & C. Lockhart (Eds.), *Culture and politics.* (pp. 223–234). New York: Palgrave Macmillan.

Putnam, R. D., Leonardi, R., & Nanetti, R. Y. (1994). *Making democracy work: Civic traditions in modern Italy*. Princeton, NJ: Princeton University Press.

Siisiainen, M. (2003). Two concepts of social capital: Bourdieu vs. Putnam. *International Journal of Contemporary Sociology, 40*(2): 183–204.

Slotte-Kock, S., & Coviello, N. (2010). Entrepreneurship research on network processes: A review and ways forward. *Entrepreneurship Theory and Practice, 34*(1): 31–57.

Urwin, P., Di Pietro, G., Sturgis, P., & Jack, G. (2008). Measuring the returns to networking and the accumulation of social capital: Any evidence of bonding, bridging, or linking?. *American Journal of Economics and Sociology*, 67(5): 941–968.

Van Staveren, I. (2002). Social capital: What is in it for feminist economics?. ISS Working Paper Series/General Series, 368, pp. 1–34.

Van Staveren, I. (2010). Feminist economics: Setting out the parameters. In C. Bauhardt & G. Caglar (Eds.), *Gender and Economics* (pp. 18–48). Wiesbaden, Germany: VS Verlag für Sozialwissenschaften.

5 Organizational-Level Dynamics
Practices and Policies

5.1 INTRODUCTION

In this chapter, we begin by illuminating a variety of organization-level barriers to gender equality in entrepreneurial ecosystems. Further, we reveal how intermediary organizations serve a gatekeeping function that in practice tends to disadvantage women. To strengthen readers' understanding of these phenomena, we discuss the importance of access and how it is denied and/or granted in ways that are gendered. In order to better understand how norms, values, and practices among meso-level organizational actors impact entrepreneurs differently through their power to include or exclude, we compare and contrast the experiences of entrepreneurs and identify patterns of repeated behaviors that constitute barriers to inclusion and equity in entrepreneurship. Our three case studies are the cities of Boston, Massachusetts; St. Louis, Missouri; and Asheville, North Carolina. We offer comparisons between these cities to demonstrate how conversations and actions around diversity, equity, and inclusion take shape differently (and sometimes similarly) in different contexts. These cities have unique histories that impact contemporary experiences and actions around inclusion; at the same time, these differences allow us to recognize that there is not necessarily one path toward inclusion and that considerable and shared challenges remain. Given our extended fieldwork in Boston, we offer detailed conversations with organizational leaders in this context to support our arguments, while in St. Louis and Asheville, we provide themes and findings focusing explicitly on specific organizational practices. In Chapter 6, we speak further about the ecosystem identity of each city, locating this within a matrix of weak/strong and emergent/

established informal and formal institutional factors, building further our arguments around how and why gender inclusion is a multifaceted process and practice. Doing so allows us to locate these cities in terms of their identity and development phase and, concurrently, to speak to institutional barriers to inclusion that continue to exist despite any changes that may take shape at the level of individual actions or organizational practices. To that end, this chapter offers insights for change-makers and recommendations for how to remove organization-level barriers, while fostering intentional inclusion at ESOs – a necessary but not sufficient condition for gender-inclusive entrepreneurial ecosystems.

5.2 THE ROLE OF INTERMEDIARY ORGANIZATIONS IN ENTREPRENEURIAL ECOSYSTEMS

At the meso level, intermediary organizations can yield considerable power in determining which type of entrepreneurs is granted access, resources, and services in a particular ecosystem. More explicitly, ESOs exist to support entrepreneurs, new ventures, and entrepreneurship in general, often through an economic development strategy subsidized and promoted by politicians and other policymakers. These ESOs are often active participants in the initial and sequential stages of a new venture's creation, and they are critical providers of training, support, and mentorship. Financial service providers (such as small business lenders, banks, and equity capital investors) are critically important for a new venture's viability and growth. Professional service providers (such as law, tax, accounting, and consulting firms) are important providers of services to entrepreneurs and their ventures and, thus, also have an influential role in their success.

Entrepreneurial places contain potential resources for entrepreneurs at each stage of their enterprising endeavors, and these are delivered through these types of intermediary organizations. Access to resources is critical from the idea stage through the pre-launch and launch, and onward to the growth and development of the new venture. These resources include, but are not limited to, mentorship;

debt and equity financing; social, emotional, and psychological support; professional experts (e.g. in accounting, marketing, and global supply chain management); and high-quality business partners, advocates, and investors. Entrepreneurs primarily – and in some cases, exclusively – find out about these resources and get connected with support through their social networks. This is because many business incubators and accelerator programs, for example, do not publicly advertise their array of services. Our interviews with executive directors of these programs reveal that the dominant strategy is to limit advertising and outreach to connections inside their own social networks in order to avoid being overwhelmed with requests from candidates of unknown quality. A consistent response is that leaders of ESOs avoid communications with those they perceive to be "unqualified" or simply the wrong type of candidate, business, or industry, or candidates in what they perceive as too early idea-stage ventures (Ozkazanc-Pan & Clark Muntean, 2018).

In practice, the recipients of services access resources with ease if they are connected with the social network of insiders such as advisory board members, directors, managers, and existing tenants through their personal and professional networks. Too often a negative consequence of this approach is the exclusion of those outside of these networks from needed resources. Our research concludes that women and minority groups in particular are far less knowledgeable about existing resources in their communities, largely due to this common practice (Knowlton et al., 2015; Ozkazanc-Pan & Clark Muntean, 2018; Ozkazanc-Pan, Knowlton, & Clark Muntean, 2017). Even when made aware of resources, traditionally underserved populations more frequently experience interactions in the ecosystem differently and more problematically than members from dominant populations, such as White men from elite universities.

Organizations within entrepreneurial ecosystems may be gendered in multifaceted ways. This is evident in organizational phenomena such as the structural division of labor, the expression of symbolic images of the ideal entrepreneur, social reinforcement of gender roles, daily interactions, and cultural norms that negatively impact or effectively exclude many women (Brush et al., 2019). The absence of sufficient numbers of women at the top of organizational hierarchies and oversight boards further reduces the likelihood of decisions being made in favor of including, supporting, and promoting more women. Changing these organizational structural issues and dynamics requires commitment from the top, transparency, accountability, and continual improvement.

5.3   ECOSYSTEM MESO-LEVEL COMPARISON OF ORGANIZATIONS: BOSTON, ST. LOUIS, AND ASHEVILLE

Here we provide examples from research in ESOs with an explicit focus on gender and gender inclusion practices. The examples demonstrate a wide and varied range of ideas about the urgency of/ need for addressing gender inclusion as well as the organizational practices aimed at remediating the "gender gap." In all, the differences in organizational practices across cities, as well as within cities themselves, showcase the difficulty of having an organized and cohesive approach to gender inclusion, even if within the same city and entrepreneurial ecosystem. The quotes and observations from fieldwork shared here reflect and speak to these challenges, including some bright spots and potential ways in which change toward gender equality might be possible. In each city, we ask what ESOs are doing toward gender inclusion and equity and focus on understanding the existing actions. We start with findings from Boston, a liberal and progressive city in many ways but still lagging in gender inclusion, including in terms of a shared sense of the nature and urgency of the gender equity "problem" and the solutions offered/enacted to address it.

5.3.1   Boston

In examining the various dimensions of the entrepreneurial ecosystem in Boston, what we find is a scattered and uncoordinated set of activities undertaken by ecosystem actors over time with no clear set of gender inclusion practices, a lack of coordinated efforts, and a general lack of shared urgency about the problem (and its nature). In effect, while certain groups and individuals recognize the need for gender inclusion and are working to overcome the challenges faced by female and minority entrepreneurs in a city beleaguered by decades of racial injustice, these efforts are still quite new, emergent, and lacking in scale. This is curious in that male actors within the ecosystem recognize the relevance of diversity and, in particular, the importance of women entrepreneurs and investors as full participants. Yet the onus of responsibility still seems to fall on women to do the work of inclusion and integration. In our conversation with ESO leaders, the following themes emerged: (1) reliance on rhetoric rather than demonstrable action to remedy the situation; (2) lack of coordination and/or knowledge of gender inclusion activities across the ecosystem; and (3) lack of urgency in making gender inclusion a priority for their organization. Below, we share evidence relating to these core themes through interview quotes with ESO leadership, inclusive of both male and female directors.

INTERVIEWER:	In terms of thinking about what is being done – or what could be done – to have more women entrepreneurs in Boston, particularly in terms of scaling their businesses, what are your thoughts?
WHITE MALE ESO LEADER 22:	Well one, I think this is a much better environment for women-based startups than in the past. And I would say, starting four, five, six years ago was when there [were] a lot more support groups evolved for female founders/entrepreneurs, so there's never a better time. There's a lot more that needs to be done, so it's definitely not the ideal environment, and unfortunately it's not equal to men. But I think it's been taking big steps in that direction. There are many groups now that are

specifically formed around women founder/ entrepreneurship. There's WE BOS [Women Entrepreneurs Boston, a Boston city initiative], for example, coming up this week or next week. . . . WE BOS is a good example. But almost every organization around Boston, and there are dozens, at least the large ones have a female founder or women entrepreneur set focus at some point. Mass Innovations has a female founder focus this month. So it's a much better environment than it used to be. I think at the – what still has to be done is we need to make it equal completely. So equal to all the ideas, equal to all the resources, equal to all the funding. I think a big step would be getting more women-based venture capital representatives. So in the venture capital industry at large, women are still a much smaller percentage than men, and that's still true in Boston. Even though Boston is still expected to be much more diverse, more open, even this percentage of women-based venture capitals is much smaller. The angel community is actually pretty good. There's actually several women angel investors [who] are very active around town. Again not quite equal to men, but probably a higher percentage of women-based angel investors than there are venture capitalists.

INTERVIEWER: Any other thoughts on what can be done potentially in terms of policy, whether it's city level or somewhere else, or if you think it's something that needs to be done by the collaborative ecosystem and organizations to make these changes happen?

WHITE MALE ESO
LEADER 22:

I think the celebrating successes of women entrepreneurs a bit more so ... making sure people know about them. You know and make sure the ones who have shown great progress spend some time with the rest of the women entrepreneurs, advocating that all the startup focus organizations have some women focus on them. As well as ... not just women, but also people of color startups. You know, it's not just women, but overall diversity, and gender, and ethnic ... and I also say age.

In other words, while gender inclusion is an important element, there is resistance to focusing *just* on gender, almost as if that would be a biased response to the gender gap. This view is juxtaposed here with the perspective of another ESO leader, this time a White female. When asked the same question about what can be done to have more women entrepreneurs supported and funded in Boston, she answered as follows.

WHITE FEMALE ESO
LEADER 13:

Intentionality is key, outreach, selecting diverse groups to recruit and serve ... it's difficult being a woman and advocating for them when partners are not as passionate about that cause ... [we can get] pushback; people don't like women to be privileged in decisions. Even if they are very lacking in representation, [there is] pushback against the need to address bias against women. Women need to be explicitly extended an invitation to overcome the numbers problem and implicit bias; [we] need to be super intentional at all stages, from positively encouraging women to attend to pulling the trigger, to being invited to pitch, to found, to solicit [advice], and so forth.

She also offered some relevant statistics from her own research: among firms that got into a prestigious national accelerator (TechAcclerator) that has a location in Boston, only 5 percent had a woman of significant standing in their team; thus, 95 percent of accepted firms had male founders. She suggested that in reality the share is more than 95 percent, as, in her research, she counted women with any standing in the company as female leads, and that over time, this number has risen to 10 percent. She went on to describe the reasons for this gap, noting that women so often do not have people encouraging them to start and grow businesses, whereas men do. Her experience was that very elite women, the 1 percent, are the most demanding and get funding because of their economic privilege and access to networks.

Considering the picture for entrepreneurs from minority backgrounds, she noted that there are very few Black people in the Boston entrepreneurial ecosystem, especially in the technology sector. Her view was that the number of minority entrepreneurs, especially women of color, are not increasing. However, she suggested that they tend to lag behind White women and that there is a perception that because women are now getting funded, minorities are "next."

In thinking about how to best help female entrepreneurs generally, her observations were that women need more holistic support. She highlighted the issue of starting a family, noting that male founders with kids are not viewed as a "problem," whereas women having kids is seen as a complication. In her experience, a lot of women have a real fear of not being able to start a family if they strive to get rounds of capital. She also shared that based on her experience, women need to feel safe in order to be able to stretch and go for it, and suggested that women need to talk about things like personal goals. Her approach in this respect has been to give women permission to talk during meetings about life goals, family planning, anxieties, and fears. She noted that in her conversations with women, their fears were related to the family/private domain, such as fear of not having time with family or not being able to have a family in the future. She felt that telling women that funding is getting more competitive simply steers them away from trying. For her, the solution to gender gaps in entrepreneurship is related to governance and intentionality. She suggested that the industry needs rules to self-regulate. One policy that has been discussed is the use of quotas to bring more women onto boards, but this is not generally supported. Similarly, the idea of quotas to address funding gaps is unpopular among the investment community. She offered the idea that pension funds should dedicate a certain percentage of capital to investment in funds where a certain percentage of beneficiaries have to be women/minorities.

Simply having women in leadership positions in ESOs doesn't ensure that there will be a focused effort around gender inclusion. Another White female investor pointed out that "we/I just fund solely on merit." She went on to suggest that it is important to demonstrate "hyper-concern" with not privileging women, and reiterated several times that the funding process is based on merit. While she was open to admitting there could be implicit bias, she was quite unwilling to put systems in place to address this. When speaking about the Boston ecosystem, she had a tendency to move away from discussions of gender and speak more generally about innovation and openness of networks. In her view, gender was not viewed as a primary problem or central to the success/openness of networks in Boston.

Another White female ESO leader, working in the biotech industry, had similar views about support for women entrepreneurs and women founders. She suggested that her organization does not target women specifically; nor does it track diversity "officially."

WHITE FEMALE ESO LEADER 15: They come to us; it's self-selection. We tend to focus on individual motivation to contact us, so there is no outreach, no targeted outreach. And why do scientists come to our networking events? I don't know, but we try to work with organizations focused on diversity, like [the local university] had programming on women on corporate boards, and panel discussions; we've also worked with a marketing partner. But the problem is underdetermined. Essentially, what are we working for? Candidates on boards have to have experience at a high level, and there aren't enough women leaders. At least we attempted to start the conversation. For example, if you unpack that, it's an issue of girls in science; we partner with a high-school biotech program.

For this ESO leader, the industry is filled with male leaders and networks tend to be male. Consequently, there are not enough female leaders to take positions on panels. She noted that the lack of female representation on panels was pointed out to the ESO on Twitter, but no changes really came about. Her view was that if women just tried a little harder, they could do better, but that there was no written policy to encourage women. For her, although nonprofits tend to skew female, including her own organization, where 70–75 percent of the staff are female, most of the panels are all male. She stated that a number of women have gone through the organization's mentoring program, but when asked to describe the practices for matching mentees to mentors, she replied that this was a gender-blind and gender-neutral approach whereby they looked at quality/merit/stage of business/fit.

In all, we find that simply having women in ESO director roles does not guarantee gender-inclusive practices. Even if there is recognition of the gender gap, there is little being done in a coordinated and collaborative fashion across the Boston ecosystem. There are likely several reasons for this. First, while women occupy positions of leadership in ESOs, they may face perceived or real pressure to not appear biased toward women. In other words, women expressed hesitancy at times in supporting other women for fear of being seen to demonstrate bias, to the possible detriment of their standing or reputation in the ecosystem. (See Fisher, 2012, for an overview of how the first generation of women who were successful in *Wall Street* treated the next generation of women.)

Second, it is also possible that women in such positions simply do not "see" gender as an organizing principle and that they do not interpret their experiences from this perspective. This suggests that differences in the number of male and female founders are not assessed through a gender lens. Hence, the explanations put forward for the dearth of female founders or entrepreneurs within ESOs, and in particular in their own ESOs, were not necessarily due to gendered barriers but to pipeline issues, particularly in science. This type of explanation obscures the complexities of why women exit the field (see Clark Blickenstaff, 2005, for an overview of why this explanation persists).

Lastly, we found that in Boston, interviewees tended to expand diversity conversations beyond gender. When we brought up gender explicitly, it was frequently translated into broader concerns over diversity, including a focus on international actors, immigrants, race/ethnicity, age, and sexual orientation. And when interviewees did talk about gender, it was generally in recognition of issues associated with family and work–life balance, as these were perceived as negatively affecting women, almost exclusively.

ESOs with male leadership also spoke about gender gaps, but again put the focus (and responsibility) on "other" groups doing work within the domain of inclusion rather than ways their organizations might address it. Consequently, we found that most ESOs generally do not take responsibility for initiating action within their organizations; nor do they become involved in lobbying or pushing for policy change at the ecosystem level – for example, advocating for more public funding of efforts to support female founders and entrepreneurs. In general, when speaking with ESO leaders, we found that conversations around the "gender problem" and the proposed solutions to it were generally framed at the level of the individual.

While there were some proposed organizational solutions, such as panels focusing on female founders or conversations around lack of access to capital, the goals of such events were to empower the *individual* through information, access, and connections. They were not undertaken with recognition of the systematic nature of the gender gap in the ecosystem or with a focus on changing gendered ecosystem dynamics; rather, such actions were undertaken in a manner that preserved the status quo and existing gendered-hierarchies within the ecosystem. Ultimately, in Boston, *gender was not viewed as a major social organizing principle that impacted the entrepreneurial ecosystem; thus, there were no coordinated efforts among ecosystem actors to address gendered organizational practices that lead to gendered outcomes for entrepreneurs.*

5.3.2   St. Louis

According to the 2010 Census, St. Louis, Missouri, has a population of 319,294, and approximately half of the population (157,160) is Black or African American.[1] Racial tensions in the metropolis remain significant years after the 2014 fatal shooting of Michael Brown by a police officer in Ferguson, Missouri. In a 2013 American Express study ranking twenty-five metropolitan areas in the US according to capacity to support women-led ventures, St. Louis came in last (American Express, 2013). After conducting intensive research, including over eighty interviews with male and female entrepreneurs in St. Louis, our research found that while women express the same need for support for their enterprises as men, they are less aware of the resources available and programs offered by support organizations (Knowlton et al., 2015). Common outreach and marketing strategies, such as relying on word-of-mouth advertising, using the personal networks of insiders, and posting on social media had left many women entrepreneurs disconnected from the entrepreneurial ecosystem (Knowlton et al., 2015).

---

[1] http://censusviewer.com/city/MO/St.%20Louis (accessed August 11, 2020).

Intense discussions of the ways in which economic opportunities are stratified by race, gender, and other socio-demographic variables led to consensus that social change is required in the St. Louis region, including in entrepreneurial opportunities and outcomes (Ozkazanc-Pan, Knowlton, & Clark Muntean, 2017). These conversations led to a shared understanding and sense of urgency that leaders have translated into a variety of actions in the region. ESOs in the emergent St. Louis ecosystem have increasingly engaged in collaborative, grassroots efforts over the past several years, which has been credited with stimulating the increase in women's business ownership from 28 percent to 44 percent between 2007 and 2012 (Ozkazanc-Pan, Knowlton, & Clark Muntean, 2017). ESOs in St. Louis work in tandem with local chapters of affinity groups, such as the National Society of Black Engineers and the National Society of women MBAs, to actively recruit and support diverse entrepreneurs. Thus, these organizations act as vanguards in building an inclusive community of entrepreneurs (Knowlton et al., 2015). Their success has been attributed to a grassroots-level effort by entrepreneurs on behalf of other entrepreneurs to mitigate historical exclusion of minorities and women and to enact and implement substantive change in order to raise the stature of the city and region as an up-and-coming entrepreneurial hub (Ozkazanc-Pan, Knowlton, & Clark Muntean, 2017).

For example, in 2012, four female entrepreneurs established Women Entrepreneurs of St. Louis, which later merged with the well-established ESO Missouri Venture Forum, symbolizing the broader acceptance and support of actions toward gender inclusion (Ozkazanc-Pan, Knowlton, & Clark Muntean, 2017). In 2013, the Information Technology Entrepreneur Network launched their Inclusion Initiative with the goal of addressing the diversity gap in technology startups (Ozkazanc-Pan, Knowlton, & Clark Muntean, 2017). In 2014, a group of women founded Prosper Women Entrepreneurs with the goal of making St. Louis a wonderful and welcoming place to start and grow a business (Ozkazanc-Pan,

Knowlton, & Clark Muntean, 2017). These organizations drive diversity and inclusion efforts by finding women entrepreneurs and other leaders and asking them to engage as speakers, mentors, business plan coaches, investors, and donors in the support of up-and-coming women entrepreneurs (Knowlton et al., 2015). Along with other ESOs, several of these have partnered together and supported each other's efforts to recruit, mentor, resource, and empower diverse entrepreneurs. Organizations focused on supporting women entrepreneurs are highly integrated into the greater entrepreneurial ecosystem and are supported by ESOs not explicitly focused on gender inclusion (Ozkazanc-Pan, Knowlton, & Clark Muntean, 2017). Importantly, programming strategies mainstream diverse entrepreneurs rather than advertising them as minority speakers and presenters, presenting them, for example, as a special subset of entrepreneur (Knowlton et al., 2015). Together, several of these ESOs put on programming through Venture Café and an annual symposium aimed at building a diverse, inclusive, and dynamic entrepreneurial community while connecting diverse entrepreneurs with established organizations and the resources they offer (Ozkazanc-Pan, Knowlton, & Clark Muntean, 2017). Leading organizations in St. Louis track female participation in their membership and programming and diversify the leadership and voices internally in order to keep themselves accountable and on track for achieving inclusion metrics (Knowlton et al., 2015).

An organizational leader and model for proactive and effective inclusion by an ESO in St. Louis is BioSTL. The organization was founded in 2008 with the mission of increasing inclusion in the biosciences, a thriving sector in St. Louis. The initiation of this effort was decidedly grassroots, beginning with CEOs in the community and expanding to include over eighty-five leaders and practitioners from organizations throughout the community (BioSTL, 2020). In 2014, these efforts were formalized and expanded with a grant award from the Blackstone Foundation, which enabled them to effectively build connections for diverse individuals with the aim of finding resources, including assistance for starting new bioscience ventures

(BioSTL, 2020). Expansions in innovative programming include an STEM Entrepreneur Inclusion Initiative, Entrepreneurial Inclusion Pipeline Programming, and the St. Louis Equity in Entrepreneurship Collective, all aimed at identifying talented women and minority bioscience entrepreneurs with high potential and providing them a systematic path to the creation of high-growth businesses (BioSTL, 2020). For the past six years, this ESO has organized an annual conference that explicitly celebrates, educates, and supports emerging entrepreneurs as well as established business owners who are women, people of color, or foreign-born. Their newsletters, blogs, podcasts, panels, and programming all feature ample ambitious, talented, and successful (or on the path to becoming successful) entrepreneurs of color and female entrepreneurs. BioSTL's leadership and programming have been recognized as exemplars, including being named a "Promising Practice" by the Institute for Women's Policy Research in 2018 (BioSTL, 2020). BioSTL is highly integrated into the entrepreneurial ecosystem and a substantive collaborator in programming supported by and involving several other ESOs. Due to the efforts of this organization together with other ESOs dedicated to diversity, equity, and inclusion, St. Louis has made strides in a cohesive effort to challenge the status quo, generate a sense of urgency, and engage in grassroots efforts that are paying off for women and other historically marginalized groups in this model entrepreneurial ecosystem.

5.3.3 Asheville

Asheville in Western North Carolina (the American South) has a population of 96,000 and a relatively young entrepreneurial ecosystem that is considered by locals to be vibrant, thriving, and promising. Despite being a smaller and relatively isolated city with an economy largely dependent on tourism and without a major research university in the region, the city's centrality as a tourist destination and its high quality of life create an appeal to diverse entrepreneurs. We conducted fieldwork in Asheville during 2018–2019, interviewing leaders of ESOs as well as entrepreneurs (Carter, 2019). The focus was on how masculinity is understood in the entrepreneurial ecosystem. After transcribing and reviewing interviews, we identified several themes emerging the data, outlined below.

5.3.3.1 *Masculine Advantages and Gendered Expectations*

Both founders of firms and leaders of ESOs consistently described ideal traits of successful entrepreneurs in masculine terms, such as being aggressive, being willing to take risks, and exuding strength. Further, there was consistent acknowledgement, among both men and women interviewed, of these traits as being masculine. While exhibiting traditionally masculine traits is thought to provide a competitive advantage, at the same time, interviewees accepted that both men and women hold the capacity to exhibit both masculine and feminine traits. Thus, women expressed feeling as though they were in a double bind with respect to gender. Further, participants in the study consistently expressed gendered differences as to what level of these traits would be acceptable; and female interviewees pointed to the threat of backlash for exhibiting what might be deemed as excessive expression of masculinity. Men and women shared the view that men are perceived as worthy of support when exhibiting overconfidence and a great deal of aggressiveness, whereas women are viewed with suspicion or with prejudice for showing these traits. As a consequence, women expressed an internalized perception that they needed to take on more masculine traits, while also having reservations over being too masculine. Further, women consistently observed that male entrepreneurs are allowed to be, as one interviewee put it, "a little crazy, able to act out of the box and like renegades who don't play by the rules." Therefore, we conclude that while masculine characteristics are rewarded, men and women are not allowed to express these in the same way or to the same extent.

5.3.3.2 *Denial of Gender as Being Relevant Here*

Despite acknowledging that the expression of masculine traits provides a competitive advantage for men, while similar behaviors among women are not rewarded, participants remained consistently adamant that entrepreneurial success is not tied to the expression of gendered traits. We found that, while leaders were generally aware of the gender gap in venture finance, they consistently attributed the problem as being prevalent in other entrepreneurial ecosystems, but not present in Asheville (Carter, 2019). We interpret this finding as being due to external attribution – that is, while acknowledging gender gaps as a problem for others, it's not a problem *here* or with *us*. Leaders consistently expressed that the local entrepreneurial ecosystem and support institutions and organizations display high levels of inclusivity and equality. Despite several female entrepreneurs being aware of challenges due to their gender, leaders that are responsible for supporting entrepreneurship in this ecosystem expressed gender-blindness and a lack of awareness or acknowledgement of gender as being relevant locally. To the contrary, leaders expressed confidence that this ecosystem was a model of inclusivity and gender equality. To quote one leader:

> I have seen the bro-culture. Move fast and break things. Who cares and try to create value at all cost and a lot of that comes out of the fratty, "I'm untouchable" culture. But the values here in our area – that doesn't apply.
>
> *(Carter, 2019:15)*

5.3.3.3 *Annoyance over Pressures to Be Diverse*
While expressing confidence that they were performing very well in terms of being equally welcoming to all, leaders expressed resentment at pressures to be diverse and inclusive as well as skepticism about trying to achieve diversity for diversity's sake. Even when acknowledging a gender gap in funding elsewhere, leaders of ESOs are blind to any gender issues or gaps in Asheville, and thus are not actively seeking to close the gap locally. This is logical if they believe that gender is not an issue in the Asheville ecosystem, only elsewhere. Some leaders expressed resentment or annoyance at being asked to be "hyper-vigilant" or "overly inclusive" (Carter, 2019). Further, leaders

expressed belief that the gender of founders has nothing to do with how a firm comes to be ranked as a high-growth company. In addition, some leaders expressed distaste in discussing gender at all and a belief that everything is 50–50 between male and female founders in Asheville, though without providing evidence to support those beliefs and claims (Carter, 2019).

5.3.3.4 Updates and Conclusion: Asheville

During the time period when the qualitative research was conducted, several themes emerged. First, participants acknowledged a preference for masculine traits and behaviors, but only if presented by men. Second, while there was general awareness of gender gaps in new venture finance as well as a general culture of hyper-masculinity in entrepreneurship in general, there tended to be a lot of denial about the gender gap as being a problem or a barrier locally. ESO leaders tended to overestimate their effectiveness at being inclusive, whereas female entrepreneurs expressed various degrees of gender bias, exclusion, and frustration with the gender gap in their experiences with local ESOs and cultures. Third, there was a widespread belief in meritocracy, and in practice, ESOs assumed they are gender-neutral or gender-blind. Lastly, leaders were candid in expressing both skepticism and pushback following calls to be more diverse and inclusive.

Since the original research was carried out, there has been a positive shift toward being more openly gender inclusive as well as racially inclusive. Bottom-up pressures to attend to the concerns and experiences of women and minorities appear to have paid off, translating into more diverse representation among cohorts of entrepreneurs receiving mentoring and financing and being profiled in communications dispersed to stakeholders. The lead organization, Venture Asheville, is a high-growth entrepreneurship initiative created by partnerships of the local Economic Development Coalition for Asheville-Buncombe County and the Asheville Area Chamber of Commerce. In a recent communication, Executive Director Jeffrey Kaplan exclaimed, "Now is the time for prescient entrepreneurs to lead the way to create a truly equitable, diverse, and inclusive regional economy" (Kaplan, 2020).

5.4 DISCUSSION

Our focus in this chapter has been on the meso-level actors – those intermediary organizations that play a critical role in entrepreneurs' experiences within the ecosystem. Organizations with a mandate to support local and regional entrepreneurs, via a publicly supported, broad-based economic development strategy, hold potentially great capacity to improve the health and inclusivity of their respective entrepreneurial ecosystems. In their role as connectors, gatekeepers, and resource providers, these ESOs play a critical role in closing the gender gap in entrepreneurship.

Across three entrepreneurial ecosystems – Boston, St. Louis, and Asheville – we observe consistent patterns and themes in relation to ESOs, despite some variation among research participants and historical and cultural variation due to the histories, contexts, and geographies involved (i.e. located in the Northwest, the South, and the Midwest; cities of different sizes and with varied economies, industries, and cultures). These organizations may act as gatekeepers to important connections and resources, though as we saw in Boston, gender inclusion was not a shared concern among various different ecosystem actors, while in Asheville, change was happening rather slowly. The ways in which these organizations operate have often excluded or turned off women who would benefit from their support and resources. However, as is evident in St. Louis, it is possible for ESOs to play a leadership role in shifting the culture of the ecosystem to be more inclusive and supportive of female entrepreneurs.

In this chapter, we showcased the continued challenges and successes to motivate other positive changes among readers and leaders of organizations. In our next chapter, we focus on institutions and institutional norms that speak to the sociocultural aspects of gender norms as well as the gendered ways institutional environments impact the opportunities and choices for female founders.

REFERENCES

American Express OPEN. (2013). The state of women-owned businesses report. Available at www.womenable.,com/content/userfiles/State_of_Women-Owned_ Businesses-Report_2020.pdf (accessed July 15, 2019).

BioSTL. (2020). Homepage. Available at www.biostl.org/what-we-do/inclusion (accessed August 11, 2020).

Brush, C., Edelman, L. F., Manolova, T., & Welter, F. (2019). A gendered look at entrepreneurship ecosystems. *Small Business Economics*, *53*(2): 393–408.

Carter, C. (2019.). Working paper. Understanding the effects of masculinity on gender segregation and integration in entrepreneurial ecosystems. *UNC Asheville Undergraduate Research Journal*. Asheville: University of North Carolina.

Clark Blickenstaff, J. (2005). Women and science careers: Leaky pipeline or gender filter?. *Gender and Education*, *17*(4): 369–386.

Fisher, M. S. (2012). *Wall Street women*. Durham, NC: Duke University Press.

Kaplan, J. (2020). Announcing the 2020 Asheville Impact Micro Grant Winners. Venture Asheville. Available at http://ventureasheville.com/2020-asheville-impact-micro-grant-winners/ (accessed August 11, 2020).

Knowlton, K., Ozkazanc-Pan, B., Clark Muntean, S., & Motoyama, Y. (2015). Support organizations and remediating the gender gap in entrepreneurial ecosystems: A case study of St. Louis. Online. doi: 10.2139/ssrn.2685116.

Ozkazanc-Pan, B., & Clark Muntean, S. (2018). Networking towards (in) equality: Women entrepreneurs in technology. *Gender, Work & Organization*, *25*(4): 379–400.

Ozkazanc-Pan, B., Knowlton, K., &Clark Muntean, S. (2017). Gender inclusion activities in entrepreneurship ecosystems: The case of St. Louis, MO and Boston, MA. Online. doi: 10.2139/ssrn.2982414.

6 Gendering Institutions and Institutional Analysis

In this chapter, we underscore the role and relevance of gender and institutions in any analysis of entrepreneurial ecosystems, suggesting that it's imperative to highlight how gender impacts formal and informal institutional factors in relation to new ventures and business creation. It is important to understand how existing institutional factors that support entrepreneurship end up disproportionately favoring White males. We want to be clear that we are not necessarily stating that these institutional factors are by design or intention sexist or racist, although we still find examples of purposeful discrimination in laws across the globe that are gendered and racialized.[1] Rather, our analysis here demonstrates how institutional factors lead to gendered and racialized hierarchies within the domain of entrepreneurship that then become replicated within the relations among actors within ecosystems.

To this end, the interlocking nature of gendered institutional environments, organizational practices, and individual habits create "inequality regimes" (Acker, 2006) in entrepreneurial ecosystems. Our goal in this book is to uncover the interrelated ways individual actions, organizational practices, and institutional practices contribute to the creation and replication of such regimes. Specifically, our main argument is that the norms and organizational forms associated with institutional environments in entrepreneurial ecosystems are derived from gendered masculine values, practices, and habits. As a consequence, entrepreneurial ecosystems are conceptualized as networks of actors engaged in reciprocal exchange relationships and

---

[1] www.unwomen.org/-/media/headquarters/attachments/sections/library/publications/2019/equality-in%20law-for-women-and-girls-en.pdf?la=en&vs=5600

transactions without consideration of how gender and power relations organize and influence the shape of ecosystems by way of social relations, governance structures, and sociocultural norms.

Specifically, we demonstrate that formal aspects, such as economic and political factors, as well as informal aspects, such as social and cultural norms/values, are important elements in analyzing the organization of entrepreneurial ecosystems inclusive of actor interactions. As a caveat, while generally sociocultural influences are understood as informal factors that support and give legitimacy to particular behaviors, norms, and value systems, in some countries and contexts, norms are codified as rules and laws, at times deriving from religious tenets and/or cultural traditions steeped in history. Consequently, in certain contexts and under certain conditions, these "informal factors" may even play an outsized role in guiding actions and establishing norms, outside of formal laws, regulations and policies – for example, in countries governed by religious law (i.e. theocracies) or in those that have authoritarian rule and where personal ideologies guide official doctrines and policies. At the same time, in other countries and contexts, such as in developing nations or transition economies, formal economic and political factors may not be codified through rules and laws or not enforced due to weak governance structures and governments. In such contexts, informal factors may be more powerful than written laws in guiding behavior and sanctioning individuals and groups, and even organizations.

With these considerations, institutions and institutionalized phenomena can be both more elusive and more influential than any one organization or set of actors operating in a given entrepreneurial ecosystem. There are multiple ways in which economic, political, social, governmental, and other types of formal and informal institutions influence the routines, norms, and habits of people, so determining cause-and-effect relationships may not be possible or not make sense despite scholarship that aims to discover which sets of institutional factors support entrepreneurship activity. Within this context, gender as an analytic framework can broaden our understanding of formal and informal institutions, placing the concept as central to theorizing the formation and impact of institutions on entrepreneurship and moving it beyond its deployment simply as a categorical variable in any institutional analysis.

Specifically, a feminist analysis can uncover and address the ways societies and economies are organized through institutions, the value systems and practices that support the replication of existing societal and economic structures, and the ways in which power intersects with identities, interactions, and institutions. Guided by this framework, we deploy feminist analysis to provide insights as to how gendered institutions play a part in the organization of ecosystems as well as how they may impact the nature and strength of relationships taking place among actors within entrepreneurial ecosystems. As such, our aim in this chapter is threefold: First, we expand further on the notion of institutional environments in entrepreneurial ecosystems to highlight the ways gender impacts their constitution and replication by relying on key ideas from feminist scholars in economics and political economy; second, we focus on institutionalized sociocultural gender norms in relation to ecosystems, teasing out the ways in which they either support or prohibit particular kinds of behaviors, norms, and actions; finally, we formulate the concept of "ecosystem identity" as a typology of ecosystems derived from a gendered analysis of institutions, suggesting that certain attributes and factors contribute to ecosystems being organized in manner that can enable and support inclusion (while others are not). We start with a succinct overview of institutional approaches to entrepreneurship research.

6.1 BRIEF OVERVIEW OF INSTITUTIONAL ANALYSIS IN RELATION TO ENTREPRENEURSHIP

Broadly, institutions have been conceived as the "rules of the game" in a society that structures economic, political, and social incentives, while enforcing constraints that shape human conduct and guide social interactions (North, 1990). Within this broad concept, there are ideological, epistemological, and methodological differences in terms of the constitution of institutions, how they can/should be conceptualized, and how they can/should be studied empirically. Thus, understandings range from institutions serving a societal function in structuring the social relations between individuals to institutions as arenas of conflict and contestation over whose values/rules become dominant (see Scott, 2013, for an overview of different schools of institutionalism). There is a rich and robust history of institutional research across the social sciences including in economics, political economy, and sociology.

In relation to entrepreneurship, institutional approaches have found resonance in recent times, as a large body of research derived from economic sociology and economics has broadly influenced the trajectory of work in this area, starting with the publication of Baumol's (1968) examination of the role of entrepreneurship within economic theory. The dominant contemporary paradigm within the social sciences has been to focus on institutional economic factors examining their impact on new venture creation (Bjørnskov & Foss, 2016; Hall & Sobel, 2008), even though in previous centuries, influential scholars such as Weber, Schumpeter, and Knight set the stage for a much more complex and socially driven analysis of entrepreneurship (see Brouwer, 2002). Frameworks guided by these approaches allow for comparison of institutional factors to explain the emergence, growth, and success of ventures and entrepreneurship activity within particular nations but also to compare regions in terms of entrepreneurship rates, policies, and economic growth. This exemplifies the majority of entrepreneurship research in its focus on the role of formal institutions of the economic kind (i.e. economic policy, legal requirements to start a business, patent laws, etc.) and their impact on entrepreneurship activities across a variety of dimensions. Based on these approaches, the mechanisms through which institutional factors impact entrepreneurship can be expressed in the following manner. Governments and advocacy groups formulate and implement economic policies, thereby creating a set of institutional factors of the economic, social, and political kind. These factors, in turn, impact market conditions, among other elements of the institutional environment, which in turn influences actions that individuals can take in regards to entrepreneurship. Entrepreneurial actions then have particular entrepreneurial outcomes, such as firm creation, employment, and other economic dimensions, which are the final steps of a feedback loop that reinforces/challenges existing policies and institutional factors. While policies may change in time based on entrepreneurial outcomes (e.g. policy changes arising from difficulties associated with starting a business, obtaining a license, finding local talent, the impact of existing tax policy), in general, the mechanisms through which institutional factors impact outcomes are thought to follow this path.

Based on a systematic review of twenty years of research at the intersections of institutional factors and economic growth, Urbano, Aparicio, and Audretsch suggest that both "formal factors (e.g. procedures and costs to create a business, support mechanisms for new firm creation, etc.) and informal factors (e.g. entrepreneurial culture, attitudes towards entrepreneurship, etc.)" are relevant for understanding entrepreneurship activities (2019: 24). They suggest that while formal institutions can change in the short term, informal institutions can endure longer term, taking more time to change or be changed. Such macro-level factors can have a significant and important influence on organizations, in terms of their customs, norms, and practices, but also on the ways individuals navigate entrepreneurial ecosystems.

As such, institutions can both constrain and enable the economic and social boundaries guiding individual entrepreneurs' behavior, thus influencing entrepreneurial action, the entrepreneurial process, and new venture outcomes (Brush et al., 2019; Welter & Smallbone, 2011). Often taking the form of norms, or informal rules of the game, guiding behavior through indirect rewards and punishments (i.e. social shaming or reinforcement), institutions can frame an individual entrepreneur's sense of possibilities, venture interests, and likelihood of pursuing opportunities (Brush et al., 2019; Powell & Colyvas, 2008). Within the context of entrepreneurial ecosystems, gendered institutions and institutionalized norms can have an important impact on the institutional environment and, therefore, on the identities and social relations of entrepreneurs as well as the practices of organizations. Considerations around gender and power rising out of feminist institutionalism (Kenny, 2007) can inform debates about the gendered structuring of institutions in relation to entrepreneurial ecosystems. Feminist lenses can also elucidate how the very design of social institutions (such as norms, customs, cultural traditions, and formal and informal laws) can lead to gender inequality not necessarily due to a single policy, factor, or attribute, but through their aggregate effects (Branisa et al., 2014).

Based on these considerations, our aim here is to, first, highlight the ways institutional environments are gendered – inclusive of institutional factors, governance structures, and sociocultural norms – and, second, to coin the concept of "ecosystem identity" as a typology of ecosystems with specific considerations around institutionalized norms, structures, and pressures that lead to inclusion (or exclusion).

6.2 GENDERED INSTITUTIONAL ENVIRONMENTS AND IMPACTS ON ENTREPRENEURIAL ECOSYSTEMS

As highlighted in the previous section, an analysis derived from the intersections of economics and sociology can be helpful for identifying and examining institutional factors in relation to entrepreneurship activities. However, such an approach does not address the fundamentally gendered nature of institutions or examine the gendered assumptions guiding entrepreneurship and ecosystems research. In this section, we make the case that institutional environments are gendered, borrowing frameworks and concepts from feminist research in economics (Ferber & Nelson, [1993] 2003) and political economy (Luxton & Bezanson, 2006; Rai & Waylen, 2013), and we expand on these frameworks to demonstrate the ways in which gendered institutions give way to the gendered institutional environments for entrepreneurial ecosystems.

Broadly understood, feminist scholarship within economic and political economy calls attention to the ways in which gendered social provisioning, such as reproduction and caregiving, contributes to society and economy but is generally left out of formal economic analyses (Bakker, 2003). Such work contends that feminine values related to community, connection, and emotions are eschewed in favor of culturally masculine characteristics, such as autonomy, logic, and rational market behavior, in scholarship that examines the organization of labor, work, and the economy (Ferber & Nelson, 2003; Nelson, 1995). Strober states:

> Feminist economics is reopening questions that were seemingly answered years ago, much larger questions than those that most economists currently ask, questions about value, well-being, and power. In the process of asking these larger questions, feminist economics challenges several basic disciplinary assumptions: for example, the value of efficiency, the existence of scarcity, the omnipresence of selfishness, the independence of utility functions, and the impossibility of interpersonal utility comparisons. Indeed, feminism's basic assumption, that the oppression of women exists and ought to be eliminated is a fundamental challenge to the supposed impossibility of interpersonal utility comparisons.
>
> *(1994: 143)*

As a consequence, many of the tenets and values that guide development, economic, and trade policies are guided by masculine assumptions, assumed to be gender-neutral and universally held (see Benería, Berk, & Floro, 2015). Speaking to these points, Braunstein states:

> What is ultimately most frustrating about the neoclassical gender and growth literature is that market imperfections and the patriarchal institutions that underlie them are taken as given and

not as targets of analysis. This despite the fact that many neoclassical economists are now studying what was first termed by Anne Krueger (1974) as "rent-seeking" behavior, or efforts to claim unearned revenues ... rent-seeking can also influence the organization of nonmarket institutions, as when patriarchal property rights create male advantage in capital markets, or when norms of violence against women maintain male dominance and privileged access to resources.

(2008: 967)

Extending these concerns to the domain of entrepreneurship broadly and entrepreneurial ecosystems specifically, we demonstrate that many of the values, practices, and norms that create a particular institutional environment for "successful" entrepreneurship activities are in fact gendered (and racialized), as they are structured to create support by and for (mostly) White males.

In other words, our focus here is to expand on the ways in which formal and informal factors impact and support the creation of gendered institutional environments in entrepreneurial ecosystems. In a manner of speaking, our initial analyses in the previous two chapters "zoomed in" to understand individuals and organizations, while our analysis here "zooms out" (Nicolini, 2009) to consider institutions. In our previous two chapters, we uncovered how gendered elements took shape in relation to individual experiences, inclusive of networks, social capital, and trust dynamics, as well as how they manifest in the operating norms and practices of ESOs in different cities and contexts. Here, we add to our existing analysis to suggest that institutional factors can help create gendered institutional environments for entrepreneurship activities within ecosystems. Institutional factors that lead to gendered institutional environments are multifaceted. Our focus here is on institutional factors of the economic and social kind as they relate to entrepreneurial ecosystems. Specifically, we focus on the ways economic and social institutional factors are gendered in relation to the support and funding of new ventures and startups. We start our analysis of institutional factors with a quantitative focus and supplement this with our qualitative research as we demystify the ways in which entrepreneurial ecosystems are organized to support particular gender and race hierarchies, even if unintentionally.

A 2018 survey by the National Venture Capital Association found that 89 percent of investment partners or equivalent on venture investment teams were male and that "non-white employees comprise[d] 22 percent of the venture capital workforce, including Black employees at 3 percent and Hispanic or Latino employees at 4 percent."[2] The survey also found that "women comprise[d] 95 percent of administrative roles, 75 percent of investor relations, communications or marketing roles, yet only 15 percent of investment professional roles. Looking specifically at investment partners or equivalent on investment teams, women comprise[d] only 11 percent." Thus, the institutional environment associated with the financing of startups (particularly those requiring venture capital) is governed by decision makers who are predominantly White and male. These gender and race dynamics are also mirrored in the space of startups and established businesses within the private sector. Eventually, as successful startups grow and scale, resulting in established businesses, the gender and race dynamics do not change. Our analysis of the most recent Annual Business Survey data[3] indicates that in 2017, 70% of all employer firms were started/founded by males and, specifically, 63% of all employer firms were started/founded by White males and just 1.8% by Black males; this is compared to 26% founded by White females and 2.6% by Black females. In 2017, White people accounted for 89% of all employer firm ownership while Black people accounted for 2.5%.

[2] https://nvca.org/pressreleases/new-survey-reflects-lack-women-minorities-senior-investment-roles-venture-capital-firms/

[3] Own calculations from 2017 Annual Business Survey, https://data.census.gov/cedsci/table?tid=ABSCBO2017.AB1700CSCBO&hidePreview=true

Looking at the number of male and female executive and senior-level managers across the US private sector in 2018, the vast majority of these positions were held by White males. Our calculations indicate that White males accounted for 59% of all executive/senior-level officials, Black males and females each represented less than 2%, and Hispanic males represented just under 3% while Hispanic females represented less than 2% of these positions.[4] Conversely, women of all races/ethnicities were overrepresented in office/clerical positions and in service work compared to all males. In other words, the type of person most likely to found a business, invest in a startup, and/or be charged with growing/leading a business as an executive or senior manager is a White male. This is despite the fact that according to our calculations from 2019 population estimates, non-Hispanic White males represent 30 percent of the population in the US.[5] Thus, they are overrepresented as venture capitalists, senior executives, and founders. More importantly, these categories of actors have significant decision-making powers as they relate to which firms/teams/ideas get funded, how businesses operate/grow, and which talent to bring on board to scale. In other words, the actors within ecosystems who decide the "rules of the game" in relation to entrepreneurial behavior, community norms and values, and organizational practices tend to be White males. To understand why and how these statistics continue to be so stark despite all the ways in which various ecosystem actors (as evidenced in the previous two chapters) claim to value diversity, equity, and inclusion, it is important to focus on multiple facets that lead to the continuation of inequalities.

There are several facets related to understanding the gendered dimensions of institutional environments in ecosystems, including the gender and racial makeup of the investment community, the governance mechanisms through which networks and social capital

---

[4] Own calculations from 2018 EEOC data, www.eeoc.gov/statistics/employment/jobpatterns/eeo1/2018/national/table

[5] www.census.gov/data/tables/time-series/demo/popest/2010s-national-detail.html#par_textimage_1537638156

function as proxies for due diligence and trust, and how social norms associated with entrepreneurship take shape within entrepreneur communities. Yet in order to understand how gender- and race-based inequalities develop, it is important to deploy these analytic dimensions broadly and specifically. That is, in each city and entrepreneurial ecosystem, there can be slight variations in how governance structures are organized or how the cultural norms associated with communities of entrepreneurs develop over time. For example, political ideology (see Motoyama et al., 2017) can play an important role, as individuals decide who to rely on for gathering information and decision-making related to their businesses in certain contexts. Alternatively, grassroots efforts by entrepreneurs can play an influential and foundational role in sedimenting norms associated with behavior and information exchange; an analysis of such entrepreneur-led efforts is offered by Motoyama and Knowlton (2017) in their analysis of a startup ecosystem in St. Louis.

Further to this point, institutional factors in different cities related to affordable housing,[6] transportation, education, and workforce development/talent are thought to impact entrepreneurship activities – yet rarely are these factors considered with a gender and/or race lens to understand the disparate ways existing opportunities and resources may be accessible for individuals. In other words, feminist analysis can help uncover how gendered power relations, policies, and historic practices can lead to contemporary formations of inequalities in ecosystems. This goes beyond the dominant understanding that institutional factors are neutral and by putting the right ones in place, government officials and other policymakers can support entrepreneurship and thus economic growth. "The entrepreneur ... organizes available resources such as labor, finance, and knowledge to generate output. And here institutions determine if, how, and under what conditions entrepreneurs can get access to these inputs"

---

[6] www.uschamberfoundation.org/blog/post/path-affordable-housing-and-entrepreneurship/42397

(Bosma, Sanders, & Stam, 2018: 483). Our contention is that gender is an organizing principle of society and the economy and, hence, impacts the very ways institutions are formed, replicated, and even challenged. We question for whom are existing institutional factors "right" and who benefits from keeping them the same versus changing them?

To this end, it would be remiss of us not to mention institutional changes that are taking shape within investor communities in the US as they grapple with racial justice concerns more immediately and gender and race equity issues historically. One of the most promising changes associated with challenging existing institutions supporting entrepreneurship has been the rise of women- and minority-led funds in the venture capital space.[7] While their numbers and fund sizes are relatively small, there is a growing trend of funds that were not only started by women and minorities but also explicitly support women and minority founders,[8] including through pre-capital readiness programs[9,10] that aim to create a robust pipeline of diverse entrepreneurs ready to receive funding. This is a welcome sign in an industry where a "record-breaking year" for women-led firms in 2018 included representing 5.4 percent of all venture capital-invested firms (536 out of 9,845) and receiving 2.3 percent of all funding ($3.1 billion out of $134.7 billion).[11] At the same time, firms are also putting some effort into diversifying deal flow by setting up office hours to meet diverse entrepreneurs, expanding personal and professional networks, and working with historically Black universities, among other new trends. Just recently, ten venture capital firms have added "diversity riders" to their terms sheets, using the following language:

[7] www.sbc.senate.gov/public/_cache/files/a/b/ab045168-e00e-4d91-be68-4b6bce43ac1e/2DE1EA7748B644FDE6CA9A95C7541270.ozkazanc-pan-testimony.pdf

[8] www.reuters.com/article/us-softbank-minority/softbank-set-to-invest-in-more-than-a-dozen-u-s-minority-led-startups-idUSKBN23P3HK

[9] www.fearless.fund/getventureready   [10] https://zane.vc/pre-capital-program

[11] Own calculations from 2019 Q2 Pitchbook data, https://pitchbook.com/news/reports/2q-2019-pitchbook-nvca-venture-monitor

In order to advance diversity efforts in the venture capital industry, the Company and the lead investor, [Fund Name], will make commercial best efforts to offer and make every attempt to include as a co-investor in the financing at least one Black [or other underrepresented group including, but not limited to LatinX, women, LGBTQ+] check writer (DCWs), and to allocate a minimum of [X]% or [X] $'s of the total round for such co-investor.[12]

Concurrently, the Securities and Exchange Commission updated the definition of an "accredited investor," opening up opportunities for those to qualify to invest based on their profession and professional knowledge rather than only their wealth.[13]

While it remains to be seen whether these organizational practices can lead to substantive change in investment practices across the venture capital industry, they represent a growing shift in institutionalized norms and practices. It is possible that such practices will become codified into policies at the federal, state, and/ or local level, or through limited partners (those groups whose funds are invested by general partner firms, such as venture capitalists). Already, some limited partners are pushing for diversity on the boards of investment firms or considering diversity when choosing a general partner (investment firm) for their fund, similar to the adoption of the Rooney Rule in sports.[14] To this end, institutional change in the investment industry seems to be both gradual and contested as forces for stability and change take shape simultaneously, similar to other institutional change examples throughout history (see Mahoney & Thelen, 2010). What remains elusive but important are the ways gender impacts agency and power (Fenstermaker & West, 2002) and informal factors (Waylen, 2014) in relation to institutional change. These

---

[12] www.axios.com/venture-capital-firms-diversity-riders-cap-tables-f196b011-0559-4f00-a026-3b2618c6268c.html

[13] www.sec.gov/news/press-release/2020-191

[14] https://news.crunchbase.com/news/the-role-of-limited-partners-in-investment-inclusivity/

considerations are of particular relevance for understanding and changing gendered institutional environments that influence interactions and relational dynamics within ecosystems. To this end, our next section proposes a typology of institutional change factors as they relate to entrepreneurial ecosystems. We coin the term "ecosystem identity" to conceptualize entrepreneurial ecosystems in relation to inclusion and change, suggesting that the presence or absence of certain institutional factors can facilitate change efforts. Such an approach allows us to bridge the gap between the study of entrepreneurial ecosystems and institutional change as derived from a gender-focused perspective.

6.3   ECOSYSTEM IDENTITY: GENDER
AND INSTITUTIONAL FACTORS

Here, we explain the concept of ecosystem identity, expanding on those institutional factors, both informal and formal, that collectively contribute to the organization, functioning, and cultural dynamics of an entrepreneurial ecosystem. We suggest that even if organization- and individual-level changes in practices, habits, and even mindsets are possible, without significant changes in formal and informal institutional factors, entrepreneurial ecosystems will likely remain only partially integrated for heterogeneous actors. Change in these cases will likely be difficult and contested given different interests and power relations among actors. In this sense, ecosystem identity allows us to distinguish between different entrepreneurial ecosystems to offer insights as to how and why change, particularly toward gender equity, might be feasible or difficult in certain types of ecosystem. Thus, it is not simply a matter of having more and/or different institutional factors at play but rather, how those factors may influence the very functioning of an ecosystem. This provides a different focus from suggestions that policymakers or organizational leaders adopt one policy over another in order to "successfully" support entrepreneurship. Rather, we provide a typology of four entrepreneurial ecosystem identities (see Table 6.1) to facilitate the discussion on institutional change toward gender inclusion, focusing

Table 6.1 *Entrepreneurial ecosystem identity typology*

	Formal institutional factors: economic, political, and legal systems	
	Emergent	*Established*
Informal institutional factors: sociocultural norms and belief systems	*Strong* Communal *Weak* Nascent	Stable Bureaucratic

on a range of formal and informal institutional factors in relation to their established nature.

For informal institutional factors, we highlight the relative strength of influence associated with systems that support entrepreneurship. We denote "strong" to refer to systems of beliefs and/or sociocultural norms including shared sense of value on/about entrepreneurship among different actors, such as shared behavioral norms and mindsets that might be exemplified in group and individual actions. We denote "weak" to refer to the relative lack of informal institutional factors supporting entrepreneurship as an activity and as a social phenomenon. In such ecosystems, there is not a widely shared understanding of the value of entrepreneurship; nor are there sedimented behavioral norms and habits associated with entrepreneurial activity. In terms of formal institutional factors, we denote "emergent" to refer to newly emerging and/or partial economic, political, and legal systems to support entrepreneurship activities. Conversely, "established" refers to the existence of such systems through codified policies, rules, and regulations.

In order to understand how entrepreneurial ecosystem identities may produce change toward gender equity, it is important to understand the potential drivers of change in each type of ecosystem. Here, we want to be clear that these are "ideal types" of ecosystem identities, and most likely, in reality there are institutional factors in different ecosystems that are in the process of changing or becoming different, or simply defy neat categorization. Thus, it is likely that many cities and ecosystems do not fall neatly into any one type of identity category, reflecting the often complex social, economic, and political configurations in reality. Nonetheless, we find this typology a useful conceptual tool to organize and categorize entrepreneurial ecosystems in relation to institutional factors, both formal and informal, as a means to understand how and why drivers of change may emerge (or not).

Entrepreneurial ecosystems that are predominantly defined by weak informal institutional factors and emergent formal institutional factors are categorized as "nascent." In this type of ecosystem, there is a lack of coordinated effort in relation to entrepreneurship activities and a lack of coordinated support to engage entrepreneurs in such activities. At the same time, drivers of change can take the shape of influential ecosystem actors, including individuals acting as agents of change. In such an ecosystem, there is a real opportunity to organize the ecosystem in a manner that would support inclusion efforts, given the relative lack of established and shared belief systems about entrepreneurship. This may be the case even if sociocultural norms about women's role and ability to succeed in entrepreneurship influence how the ecosystem eventually becomes organized – in such nascent contexts, individuals may have an opportunity to become thought-leaders fostering cultural norms that are driven by the desire to be inclusive across gender, race, and other categories. Here, intentionality can be a powerful driver of influence and eventual organization of an entrepreneurial ecosystem as inclusive rather than exclusive. In other words, purposeful organization of institutions and actions, or institutionalization (Barley & Tolbert, 1997), can support the creation of entrepreneurial ecosystems that are based on principles of gender inclusion. This would require gender-aware institutionalization efforts that are embodied in the cultural norms and formal systems of the context, an ideal opportunity for building institutions that benefit rather than marginalize women, an approach to entrepreneurial ecosystem building that is based on principles of gender-mainstreaming (Moser & Moser, 2005). We would place Asheville in this quadrant.

In contrast, entrepreneurial ecosystems that have strong informal institutional factors but weak formal institutional factors can be categorized as "communal." In this type of ecosystem, there are strong and shared belief systems about the value of entrepreneurship in the context of weak or emergent formal institutions that support entrepreneurship. The value placed on entrepreneurship activities and entrepreneurship as an important phenomenon to be supported can create a sense of community or shared identity among entrepreneurs, each supporting one another through grassroots efforts, organizations, and platforms. Drivers of change in such ecosystems can come from regulatory changes or shifts that create more formalized structures to support entrepreneurship via economic growth initiatives, new political will to create the best city for startups, or legal policies aimed to ease or reduce hurdles associated with starting a new business. At the same time, in such contexts, entrenched gender norms and belief systems about women engaging in entrepreneurship may be difficult to shift without formal structures that not only support entrepreneurship but also create policies which benefit male and female entrepreneurs equally. The supportive mechanisms, such as trusted networks and social capital, which create a sense of community may also create exclusion for those who are not considered part of the community, a likely result of intentional efforts to create inclusion for particular kinds of ecosystem actors. Such entrepreneurial ecosystems can behave like traditional societies where norms and traditions rather than formal governance and institutional structures carry a strong influence in the everyday activities and lives of entrepreneurs and in the organizational practices of ESOs. Ecosystems that are organized in such a manner risk formalizing inequality through the manners and practices of actors who are not necessarily held accountable to formal institutions; in such cases, gender mainstreaming may be quite difficult without intentional recalibrating of established norms and values, and direct changes (Cavaghan, 2017) in the practices of the mostly male gatekeepers (see Connell, 2005) within ecosystems. We would place St. Louis in this quadrant.

A third type of identity is entrepreneurial ecosystems that have weak informal institutional factors but strong formal institutional factors. Such ecosystems can be categorized as "bureaucratic." In such ecosystems, there is a lack of shared understanding of the value of entrepreneurship or shared cultural norms associated with engaging in entrepreneurial activity. At the same time, these ecosystems have established formal institutions to support entrepreneurship, such as government-funded accelerators, university-based entrepreneurship education programs, or national innovation policies. Yet what such ecosystems have in terms of formal policies and structures, they lack in terms of the more informal aspects of entrepreneurial practices – the norms, shared values, and belief systems generally seen in communities of startups and entrepreneurs may not exist in such context. Drivers of change within these ecosystems can arise from influential groups interested in replicating the perceived dynamism of ecosystems in other contexts globally, bringing the "entrepreneurial spirit" to their own city through their global networks and experiences and often engaging in startups themselves to demonstrate the value of entrepreneurialism and the possibilities it can bring for economic growth. In such cases, individuals (such as serial, successful entrepreneurs) may have outsized influence in directing ecosystem activities and even in influencing policies in bureaucratic contexts. Achieving gender equity in such ecosystems can be possible if there are government or other formal institutional structures in place which play an important role in regulating (capital) markets and investment practices and/or have explicit gender-based policies to achieve equality in entrepreneurship activities, such as set-asides or dedicated capital for women-led startups. This approach would be similar to feminist approaches to restructuring economic development policies to change the very institutions creating gender inequality, as opposed to efforts to change the women at individual level (Chant & Sweetman, 2012).

Lastly, entrepreneurial ecosystems that have strong informal institutional factors and established formal institutional factors can be categorized as "stable." In such ecosystems, there can be strongly established norms, values, and sets of expected practices associated with entrepreneurship activity. In such cases, communities of entrepreneurs may have well-established habits and networks that allow them to engage in continued entrepreneurial activities while at the same time reaping the benefits of supportive and established formal institutional arrangements that support their endeavors. The existence of such institutions and systems to support entrepreneurship, such as through favorable tax policies, economic growth initiatives, and strong political will, may allow the creation and replication of an ecosystem that is generally stable. Drivers of change in such contexts may come from institutional entrepreneurship or entrepreneurs who are keen on disrupting the status quo (Levy & Scully, 2007) to restructure the institutional field, potentially in a manner that benefits them and their interests. Change toward gender equity may also come about from such institutional entrepreneurship and field-restructuring activity of the discursive and practical kind, as new norms around entrepreneurial habits, identities, and norms coupled with a push for changes in the formal institutional structures emerge as disruptions to existing fields. Formal institutional change toward gender equity would also need to include inclusive governance and decision-making structures through new political arrangements (Krook & Mackay, 2010). Importantly, such change would also need to include the domain of the informal, not simply as habits of entrepreneurs but also in terms of the household, where decisions about the division of labor (Fenstermaker, West, & Zimmerman, 2002) as well as other aspects of social capital creation impact the ability of women to engage in fully formalized entrepreneurial activities. In other words, change toward gender (and racial) equality can be most difficult to achieve in contexts that have been defined by long periods of stability, which provide little incentive or meaningful sanctions for (White) male actors to change their behaviors (see McGuire, 2002) or the institutions that support their interests. Gender inequality provides benefits of the economic, political, and legal kind for many men; entrepreneurship as a socioeconomic activity which arises out of these institutional arrangements is no different than other fields and occupations where gender equity conversations continue to take place, with decidedly small victories and a slow pace of change. We would place Boston in this quadrant.

6.4 CONCLUSION

In this chapter, we outlined the various ways the institutional structures, both informal and formal, which support entrepreneurship are in fact gendered. Our contention is that the gendering of such institutions creates opportunities that are male-centric, leading to gendered outcomes predominantly for women. The myriad informal norms and practices, such as those presented in this book, constitute largely opaque yet powerful gendered rules of the game that shape the hidden life of institutions (Chappell & Waylen, 2013), particularly in the context of entrepreneurship (see Brush et al., 2019; Marlow & Martinez Dy, 2018). At the same time, formal institutional structures of the economic, political, and legal kinds can institutionalize gender inequality, providing tacit or even explicit agreement with the tenets of inequity across different societies. In this sense, it is important to understand that gendered outcomes have racialized and other categorical and complex dimensions such that the experiences around institutionalized inequality are likely different across race, ethnicity, class, and so forth. To this end, our next chapter focuses on the ways that intersectionality as an analytic framework provides a holistic perspective on gender, race, and immigrant status in relation to entrepreneurial ecosystems as we return to our analysis of Boston through this lens. In doing so, we provide insights about the intersecting ways identities, interactions, and institutions collectively create a set of experiences, boundaries, challenges, and even opportunities in a differential manner for different individuals. Through this approach, we demonstrate that not all ecosystem actors are the same despite potentially being in the same category of entrepreneur – the complexity of such subject positions is revealed through their experiences, identities, and interactions taking shape within the context of entrepreneurship.

REFERENCES

Acker, J. (2006). Inequality regimes: Gender, class, and race in organizations. *Gender & Society, 20*(4): 441–464.

Bakker, I. (2003). Neo-liberal governance and the reprivatization of social reproduction: Social provisioning and shifting gender orders. In I. Bakker & S. Gill (Eds.), *Power, production and social reproduction* (pp. 66–82). London: Palgrave Macmillan.

Barley, S. R., & Tolbert, P. S. (1997). Institutionalization and structuration: Studying the links between action and institution. *Organization Studies, 18* (1): 93–117.

Baumol, W. J. (1968). Entrepreneurship in economic theory. *The American Economic Review, 58*(2): 64–71.

Benería, L., Berik, G., & Floro, M. (2015). *Gender, development and globalization: economics as if all people mattered.* New York: Routledge.

Bjørnskov, C., & Foss, N. J. (2016). Institutions, entrepreneurship, and economic growth: What do we know and what do we still need to know?. *Academy of Management Perspectives, 30*(3): 292–315.

Bosma, N., Sanders, M., & Stam, E. (2018). Institutions, entrepreneurship, and economic growth in Europe. *Small Business Economics, 51*(2): 483–499.

Branisa, B., Klasen, S., Ziegler, M., Drechsler, D., & Jütting, J. (2014). The institutional basis of gender inequality: The Social Institutions and Gender Index (SIGI). *Feminist Economics, 20*(2): 29–64.

Braunstein, E. (2008). The feminist political economy of the rent-seeking society: An investigation of gender inequality and economic growth. *Journal of Economic Issues, 42*(4): 959–979.

Brouwer, M. T. (2002). Weber, Schumpeter and Knight on entrepreneurship and economic development. *Journal of Evolutionary Economics, 12*(1–2): 83–105.

Brush, C., Edelman, L. F., Manolova, T., & Welter, F. (2019). A gendered look at entrepreneurship ecosystems. *Small Business Economics, 53*(2): 393–408.

Cavaghan, R. (2017). *Making gender equality happen: Knowledge, change and resistance in EU gender mainstreaming* (e-book). Taylor & Francis.

Chant, S., & Sweetman, C. (2012). Fixing women or fixing the world? "Smart economics", efficiency approaches, and gender equality in development. *Gender & Development, 20*(3): 517–529.

Chappell, L., & Waylen, G. (2013). Gender and the hidden life of institutions. *Public Administration, 91*(3): 599–615.

Connell, R. W. (2005). Change among the gatekeepers: Men, masculinities, and gender equality in the global arena. *Signs: Journal of Women in Culture and Society, 30*(3): 1801–1825.

Fenstermaker, S., & West, C. (Eds.). (2002). *Doing gender, doing difference: Inequality, power, and institutional change.* New York: Routledge.

Fenstermaker, S., West, C., & Zimmerman, D. H. (2002). Gender inequality: New conceptual terrain. In S. Fenstermaker & C. West (Eds.), *Doing gender, doing difference: Inequality, power, and institutional change* (pp. 25–39). New York: Routledge.

Ferber, M. A., & Nelson, J. A. (2003). *Feminist economics today: Beyond economic man* (2nd ed.) Chicago: University of Chicago Press.

Hall, J. C., & Sobel, R. S. (2008). Institutions, entrepreneurship, and regional differences in economic growth. *Southern Journal of Entrepreneurship, 1*(1): 69–96.

Kenny, M. (2007). Gender, institutions and power: A critical review. *Politics, 27*(2): 91–100.

Krook, M., & Mackay, F. (Eds.). (2010). *Gender, politics and institutions: Towards a feminist institutionalism.* New York: Palgrave Macmillan.

Levy, D., & Scully, M. (2007). The institutional entrepreneur as modern prince: The strategic face of power in contested fields. *Organization Studies, 28*(7): 971–991.

Luxton, M., & Bezanson, K. (Eds.). (2006). *Social reproduction: Feminist political economy challenges neo-liberalism.* Montreal, Canada: McGill-Queen's Press (MQUP).

Mahoney, J., & Thelen, K. (2010). *Explaining institutional change: Ambiguity, agency, and power.* Cambridge: Cambridge University Press.

Marlow, S., & Martinez Dy, A. (2018). Annual review article: Is it time to rethink the gender agenda in entrepreneurship research?. *International Small Business Journal, 36*(1): 3–22.

McGuire, G. M. (2002). Gender, race, and the shadow structure: A study of informal networks and inequality in a work organization. *Gender & Society, 16*(3): 303–322.

Moser, C., & Moser, A. (2005). Gender mainstreaming since Beijing: A review of success and limitations in international institutions. *Gender & Development, 13*(2): 11–22.

Motoyama, Y., Henderson, C., Gladen, P., Fetsch, E., & Davis, S. (2017). A new frontier: Entrepreneurial ecosystems in Bozeman and Missoula, Montana. Kauffman

Foundation Research Series on City, Metro, and Regional Entrepreneurship. Missoula, MT: Montana High Tech Business Alliance. Available at https://mhtbamedia.s3-us-west-2.amazonaws.com/2017/04/Entrepreneurship-Ecosystems_Montana-Report.pdf (accessed May 12, 2019).

Motoyama, Y., & Knowlton, K. (2017). Examining the connections within the startup ecosystem: A case study of St. Louis. *Entrepreneurship Research Journal*, 7(1). Online. Available at https://doi.org/10.1515/erj-2016-0011

Nelson, J. A. (1995). Feminism and economics. *Journal of Economic Perspectives*, 9(2): 131–148.

Nicolini, D. (2009). Zooming in and out: Studying practices by switching theoretical lenses and trailing connections. *Organization Studies*, 30(12): 1391–1418.

North, D. (1990). *Institutions, institutional change and economic performance*. New York: Cambridge University Press.

Powell, W. W., & Colyvas, J. A. (2008). Microfoundations of institutional theory. In R. Greenwood, C. Oliver, R. Suddaby & K. Sahlin (Eds.), *The Sage handbook of organizational institutionalism* (pp. 276–298) Thousand Oaks, CA: Sage.

Rai, S. M., & Waylen, G. (Eds.). (2013). *New frontiers in feminist political economy*. New York: Routledge.

Scott, W. R. (2013). *Institutions and organizations: Ideas, interests, and identities* (4th ed.). Thousand Oaks, CA: Sage.

Strober, M. H. (1994). Rethinking economics through a feminist lens. *The American Economic Review*, 84(2): 143–147.

Urbano, D., Aparicio, S., & Audretsch, D. (2019). Twenty-five years of research on institutions, entrepreneurship, and economic growth: What has been learned?. *Small Business Economics*, 53(1): 21–49.

Waylen, G. (2014). Informal institutions, institutional change, and gender equality. *Political Research Quarterly*, 67(1): 212–223.

Welter, F., & Smallbone, D. (2011). Institutional perspectives on entrepreneurial behavior in challenging environments. *Journal of Small Business Management*, 49(1): 107–125.

7 Intersectional Analysis

Gender, Race, and Immigrant Status in Entrepreneurial Ecosystems

In this chapter, we build on our analyses in the previous three chapters, covering individual experiences, organizational practices, and institutional norms, to speak about the ways in which intersectionality as a guiding feminist framework can shed additional light on the complexity of gender, race, and immigrant status in the context of entrepreneurial ecosystems. This is an important consideration given the watershed moment in which we currently find ourselves in early summer 2020, as centuries-old racial inequities in the US and other societies are being highlighted by the Black Lives Matter movement. While it may seem that conversations around race are now taking shape almost uniformly across different organizational spaces, particularly within the US, this change did not happen overnight, despite the seemingly rapid pace of change in opinions about racial justice.

Explicitly, the Black Lives Matter movement has become mainstreamed in such a manner that most Americans now support it,[1] an exceptional change in opinion from decades, years, and even months ago, when the movement was seen as a fringe phenomenon and its supporters spurned by most mainstream media and society. For example, Colin Kaepernick kneeling during the national anthem at football games was generally dismissed as the act of one politically radical man prior to the large-scale Black Lives Matter movement that took shape after the death of George Floyd in Minneapolis at the hands of police officers. Today, the opposite can be seen in many sporting events, which have just started back up after being shut down due to the COVID-19 pandemic (albeit with either no or reduced

---

[1] www.nytimes.com/interactive/2020/06/10/upshot/black-lives-matter-attitudes.html

audiences); in general, most of the players are kneeling, with just one or two choosing not to kneel. Beyond the arena of sports, the remarkable change in opinion has come about due to the unrelenting and largely peaceful protests for racial justice that have taken place across just about every major city in the US and continue as we write this book – there are now Black Lives Matter murals across cities, and statues associated with US confederate leaders or previous enslavers have been taken down. Universities are also attempting to dismantle centuries of colonized curriculum and ideals around progress, education, and opportunity; some of this is evidenced in the ways schools are dropping the names of former colonizers or enslavers, such as the Cass Business School in the UK which has dropped the name of Cass, a pivotal business leader in the British colonial trade.

And in an unprecedented move, several high-profile private organizations in the US, such as NASCAR, have banned the use of the Confederate flag at their events while the US Secretary of Defense has effectively banned the flag across all US military installations in a move that called for a ban on divisive symbols. Even Republicans have approved bills that remove Confederate names from US bases, planes, ships, buildings, and streets. The ban around the Confederate flag in merchandising and advertising was already in place, starting in 2015, among large private retailers including Walmart and Amazon, but in recent months, these bans have expanded beyond for-profit entities as evidence of the impact of the Black Lives Matter movement across all of society. In the months of June and July 2020, almost all major US corporations, nonprofit organizations, foundations, and other organized groups have put out media messages on issues of race, (in)equity, justice, diversity, inclusion, and so forth. These messages have also been echoed by investors, including those who have committed funds to diverse founders, such as $2.2 million by venture capital giant Andreesseen Horowitz and $100 million by SoftBank.[2]

[2] www.reuters.com/article/us-softbank-group-investments-breakingvi/breakingviews-vcs-mistake-diversity-for-a-new-asset-class-idUSKBN23J31O

By signaling the importance of this moment, such organizations have positioned themselves as progressive despite the generally stymied efforts at diversity, equity, and inclusion across most industries and organizations, most notably in the investor and entrepreneurship space. While these commitments are potentially favorable to addressing some inequities in the space of venture capital and entrepreneurship, the data suggest that currently, only 8 percent of venture capital-backed firms have female founders and only 1 percent have Black founders (while three-quarters of all founders in venture capital-backed firms are White).[3] This inequity is compounded by the fact that venture capital mega-rounds totaling more than $500 million account for around 57 percent of all capital raised (see Ozkazanc-Pan, 2019). The growing size of deals is squeezing out many firms from access to capital while, at the same time, women and minorities are being further distanced from what little capital is available to them. Consequently, understanding contemporary conversations around gender, race, and inequality requires contextualizing historically and structurally the magnitude and depth of the problems, particularly those within the space of entrepreneurship. And it seems opportune to understand how such inequities took shape and continue to take shape despite commitments (whether financial, organizational, or even rhetorical) to racial (and gender) justice.

In the US, Black communities alongside other communities of color, ethnic minorities, and immigrants have long suffered discrimination across society in terms of access and opportunity in the labor market, housing, education, and healthcare, to name a few dimensions. Within this context, understanding individual experiences requires concerted analysis of how structures, both social and economic, impact opportunities as they relate to entrepreneurship and entrepreneurial ecosystems, the main goal of this book. Thus, our focus here is to demonstrate that while we have explored the ways individual experiences, organizational practices, and institutional

---

[3] www.transparentcollective.com/who-we-are.html#/

norms create a particular set of possibilities (or not) for gender inclusion in entrepreneurial ecosystems, they also need to be reconsidered through intersectionality. In other words, to truly understand the heterogeneity of actors in entrepreneurial ecosystems including entrepreneurs, it is vital to see the ways in which gender, race, and immigrant status intersect as categories of power relations, impacting social capital and community formation aspects of entrepreneurship.

Through our analysis, we want to point out that entrepreneurial ecosystems are not gender- or race-neutral sites for entrepreneurial activity, but rather communities that engage in economic activity in the same unequal historic and structural context as society broadly – ecosystems are in some ways, a reflection of society, complete with racialized opportunity structures, gendered norms and values, and institutionalized inclusion policies and practices across different organizations. Thus, while ecosystems may be replete with resources, as is the case in Boston, this is not a guarantee that opportunities will be available to all entrepreneurs and other actors. And ensuring equal access to resources, either by way of ESOs or individual investors, is not a case of individuals having to behave differently, but rather a structural consideration around how the very functioning of an ecosystem requires particular forms of social capital and entrepreneurial community. That is, despite the fact that highly popularized renditions of entrepreneurial communities are shaping the social imaginary of entrepreneurs and entrepreneur-hopefuls, the gendered and racialized complexity of such ecosystems is rendered invisible despite acknowledgement of their interactive and dynamic nature.

This is probably best evidenced in the highly popular work of Brad Feld, Techstars cofounder and venture capitalist at the Foundry Group in Boulder, Colorado. In his influential 2012 book *Startup Communities*, he introduces the Boulder thesis: entrepreneurs are the leaders of startup communities, leaders must have a long-term commitment, startup community must be inclusive of anyone who wants to join, and these communities must have continual activities that engage the entire entrepreneurial slack (Feld, 2012). In his new book, which is co-authored, *The Startup Community Way*, Feld and Hathaway (2020) rework the Boulder thesis to argue that ecosystems must be understood through complexity theory, what they call complex adaptive systems, whereby ecosystems are conceptualized as highly complex interactions of various actors that cannot be controlled or fully understood and must be understood holistically. This approach results in expansion of the Boulder thesis to include several other factors: openness, support, and collaboration as critical behaviors in an ecosystem; the primary purpose of a startup community is to help entrepreneurs; startup communities can be guided and influenced but not controlled; and each startup community is unique and cannot be replicated. Most profoundly, they introduce the following new premise: "Startup communities are organized through networks of trust, not hierarchies" (Feld & Hathaway, 2020: 18). This acknowledgement and recognition is important, but yet again, while structural reasons are tangentially acknowledged as contributing to a lack of participation or access (and even trust), what is missing in this premise is an understanding of interactions between heterogeneous actors working within gendered norms and racialized leadership opportunities and power relations. Without such considerations, the idea of "networks of trust" does not address the ways in which trust happens (such as through social capital) and what it looks like in the ecosystem, something we've focused explicitly on in terms of the ways gender impacts the very notion of trust. Here we extend our observation and critique around gender to include race and immigrant status, two additional dimensions that are intertwined with how individuals experience and participate in ecosystems.

As such, in the midst of gender- and race-based stereotypes, suggesting to entrepreneurs, particularly women and minorities, that they need to "pitch" correctly (Brooks et al., 2014) will not change structural barriers that leave them outside of startup communities and entrepreneurial ecosystems. In fact, it seems antithetical to suggest that women entrepreneurs figure out how to correctly speak back to investors who are essentially asking them "not to lose" pitches (Kanze et al., 2018) rather than suggesting that male investors listen differently or ask questions in a manner that does not make assumptions based on the gender (or gender performance) of the entrepreneur. These concerns are rarely raised in the highly popularized versions of entrepreneurial ecosystems analyses, such as in Feld's books, or even in academic scholarship. For example, research suggests that success in pitching is a nuanced combination of passion and preparation and not related to gender even though the study uses a sample of 126 Executive MBA and MBA students that is 70 percent male to make this argument (see Chen, Yao, & Kotha, 2009). To move beyond such "findings," even if they acknowledge the complexity of interactions among ecosystem actors, requires a framework that focuses not just on individual actions, mindsets, and decision-making, no matter their aggregate outcomes – a hallmark assumption of methodological individualism – but also on social relations and structures. What is necessary is a careful analysis of historic context, interactions, and structural considerations as a way to understand how certain people and groups are unable to benefit from startup communities and entrepreneur ecosystems, how they are unable to become part of networks of trust even if they are located in the same place and geography as other entrepreneurs. To this end, intersectionality offers a feminist framework informed by Black feminist perspectives and critical race theory and simultaneously takes into account multiple dimensions or levels of analyses as they relate to experiences, opportunities, and structures: identities, interactions, and institutions to be explicit.

As a framework, intersectionality speaks to the ways in which intersecting dimensions of gender and race are needed to understand the differential experiences of women of color – that is, beyond a new identity category, intersectionality addresses structural, political, and cultural elements that lead to particular experiences of marginalization as well as empowerment for women of color (Crenshaw, 1989, 1990). Collins and Bilge (2020) build on this notion to suggest that while a plethora of definitions and concepts have been examined under the broad umbrella of intersectionality, as an analytic framework it offers a distinct observation of power relations across social categories such as gender, race, ethnicity, etc. and the ways in which these categories are formed in relation to each other across people. Nash suggests that while intersectionality has successfully exposed the problematic liberal ideology of wanting society to see "beyond differences," it also grapples with four fundamental issues: "the lack of a clearly defined intersectional methodology, the use of black women as prototypical intersectional subjects, the ambiguity inherent to the definition of intersectionality, and the coherence between intersectionality and lived experiences of multiple identities" (2008: 4).

Guided by these concerns and aims, the chapter delves into how intersectional differences (McCall, 2005; Sayce & Acker, 2012) between women entrepreneurs result in additional biasing forces for women of color and/or immigrant women entrepreneurs, which reflect potentially different experiences than White women engaging in entrepreneurship. To make this argument, we rely explicitly on intersectionality as a framework to examine the ways in which identities, interactions, and institutions impact opportunities for entrepreneurship – and the ways in which historic context and power relations impact the structuring of social relations. Here, our understanding is that even if economic opportunities take shape within embedded social structures, the embedding develops differently across different ecosystem actors, even if they are of the same kind, such as entrepreneurs.

To this end, we focus not only on the experiences of Black women entrepreneurs but also include those of Latinx and an Asian immigrant women to provide distinct insights into the ways entrepreneurial ecosystems foster a community for some entrepreneurs but not necessarily for others and the ways ESOs grapple with diversity and inclusion across gender and race. As a note, we rely predominantly on excerpts from our interviews to showcase the points around intersectionality and to demonstrate the value of such a framework for expanding the language and concepts we have available to study entrepreneurial ecosystems. Thus, while not all Black female entrepreneurs (or others) may have had the same experience as the entrepreneurs we spoke to during fieldwork, our research aims to highlight the complexity of ecosystems in order to move the scholarly field forward and to provide policy recommendations. It is not the aim of this book to speak for and about all types of entrepreneur, but it is the aim, in line with feminist politics and research, to bring visibility to those elements of entrepreneurial ecosystems that may end up replicating inequalities that take shape across gender and race. By focusing on gender, race, and immigrant status, we expose the complexities of entrepreneurial ecosystems in terms of their differential and dynamic structuring.

Moreover, we demonstrate how ESOs can contribute to structural inequalities through their practices and policies, that paradoxically, in their aim to get the "best entrepreneurs and companies," end up replicating existing gender- and race-based inequalities. We show how this may be possible by focusing on the recruitment and evaluation practices at a tech accelerator. At the same time, we also highlight the struggles faced by an accelerator that intentionally supports minority entrepreneurs despite a sea of seemingly available resources and investors in Boston. In doing so, we highlight the importance of understanding the intersections of gender, race, and other relations of difference or intersectionality in any entrepreneurial ecosystem analysis.

As a point of clarification, while there is research that attends to gender (Ahl & Nelson, 2010; Elam, 2014; Fischer, Reuber, & Dyke, 1993; Marlow & McAdam, 2013) or race (Fairlie & Robb, 2010; Gold, 2016; Light & Rosenstein, 1995; Walker, 2009) or immigrant status (Bhachu, 2017; Fairlie & Lofstrom, 2015; Portes, 1995; Portes, Haller, & Guarnizo, 2002) in relation to entrepreneurship activities, very few scholars attend in a manner that is intersectional, though there are notable exceptions (see Abbas et al., 2019; Knight, 2016; Romero & Valdez, 2016; Wang, 2019). We expand on intersectionality not only as an identity dimension but as a set of conversations on identity, inter-actions, and institutions such that we consider the intersecting ways relations and structures impact opportunities for individuals and groups within the context of entrepreneurship. For entrepreneurial ecosystems research, we expand on our earlier analyses to consider how gender, race, and immigrant status impact the ways in which power, social capital, and social structures influence individual experiences and organizational actions within the historic context of institutionalized norms. This means we return to our previous discussion on Boston but with an intersectional lens such that our examination and discussion now locates contemporary individual experiences and organizational practices within a racialized, institu-tional context that unfolded historically across several domains, such as housing, education, and leadership opportunities.

7.1   ANOTHER BOSTON

In contemporary Boston, it is not difficult to see signs of prosperity in and around the city, such as around MIT, Harvard Square, and the newly developed Fort Point areas. But one can travel not too far outside the center of the city and its affluent sections and see race-based inequalities in the neighborhoods of Roxbury, Mattapan, and Fairmont, to name a few. A report examining income inequality at the city and metropolitan levels by the Brookings Institute (Berube, 2018) finds Boston ranks seven in the top ten cities for income inequality while coming in at tenth place for metropolitan-level inequality. In terms of wealth, a 2015 joint study by Duke University, the New School, and the Federal Reserve Bank of Boston (see Munoz et al., 2015) found that in Boston, White households have a median wealth of $247,500 while the median wealth of Dominican and Black families is about $8 (eight dollars). The study also found that

> close to half of Puerto Ricans and a quarter of U.S. Blacks don't have either a savings or checking account, compared to only 7% of whites. Whites and nonwhites also exhibit important differences in

assets that are associated with homeownership, basic transportation, and retirement. Close to 80% of Whites own a home, whereas only one-third of U.S. Blacks, less than one-fifth of Dominicans and Puerto Ricans, and only half of Caribbean blacks are homeowners. And while most white households (56 percent) own retirement accounts, only one-fifth of U.S and Caribbean blacks, and 8 percent of Dominicans have them. Although members of communities of color are less likely to own homes, among homeowners they are more likely to have mortgage debt. Nonwhite households are more likely than whites to have student loans and medical debt.

Munoz et al. (2015: 1)

This comes as no surprise given that, historically, Boston has been segregated both in terms of education and housing (see Kantrowitz, 1979) and is infamous for efforts from the mid-1970s through 1988 to desegregate schools by busing Black students into predominantly White schools. These efforts resulted in inflamed racial tensions, as Whites harassed and assaulted Black children on buses by throwing rocks and hurling racial slurs and other epithets at them. While there was some initial success, a 2018 *Boston Globe* analysis found that 60 percent of Boston City schools meet the definition of segregation (Vaznis, 2018). Currently, Boston is a minority-majority city, where White people represent 44.5 percent of the population but around 63 percent of business ownership. Minority business ownership hovers around 30 percent[4] (see U.S. Census, 2019 Boston Quick Facts).

A 2017 *Boston Globe* research series highlighting race and racism in Boston found that Black people represent less than 1 percent of partners at Boston-based law firms – only eight Black partners among the thousand-plus partners overall. The report also found that in Boston, fewer than one in fifty senior managers are Black while

---

[4] www.census.gov/quickfacts/bostoncitymassachusetts

only about 1 percent of board members at publicly traded companies are Black (Boston Globe, 2017). At the time of the report, there were only two Black executives in the 200 publicly traded companies in Boston. Similarly, a 2017 report by the Boston Foundation found that 85 percent of foundation and nonprofit leaders in the Greater Boston area are White (The Boston Foundation, 2017). Given these institutionalized norms in government and the for-profit and nonprofit sectors, access to economic opportunity and leadership remains racialized in Boston given the historic ways the city has and continues to be structured in terms of politics, policies, and practices. To understand how this landscape of gendered and racialized institutional norms impact entrepreneurial ecosystems, we tease apart the ways in which gender, race, and immigrant status intersect to create different experiences around entrepreneurship. Specifically, we focus on the experiences of self-identified Latina, Black, and Chinese immigrant female entrepreneurs and the perspectives and practices of ESO directors with respect to diversity and inclusion. We then highlight a new kind of ESO that provides a very different experience and set of opportunities for women of color by explicitly addressing the structural inequalities of the city: an entrepreneurship program that provides young women of color with coding, life, and leadership skills in a dorm-style housing and coworking environment located within a predominantly minority neighborhood.

7.1.1   Gender, Race, Immigrant Status, and Entrepreneurship

We share quotes from research to suggest how the city can be a lonely place as individuals strive to find a sense of belonging in different communities, including in startup communities. To this end, a self-identified Latina woman entrepreneur stated the following when asked, "Is Boston a welcoming city for minorities and women?"

LATINA FEMALE
ENTREPRENEUR 2:

[Laughs.] Well, Boston is traditionally known as this very insular place, you know, unfriendly, cliquey. And when I first came

here in 1994, you know, it's been a long time
and there certainly are visible changes.
When I first came here, I hated it here ...
Boston was a shock because it wasn't
diverse. It was segregated, literally
segregated. And I came here and it took me a
long time – law school was my sole network.
It's super challenging to develop that
network of people that make you feel like
you belong, you feel they are your support
system and resources.

To address this lack of connection, she got involved with a
Latino professional association after law school, which helped her
get to know the Boston community better.

LATINA FEMALE
ENTREPRENEUR 2:

And you know, there are places you can go,
there are certainly innovation centers,
there's district hall, there's accelerators, etc.,
but I'm in the South End and we don't have
anything in the South End. So, I knew about
District Hall, and so that's how I knew to
sign up for those emails [information about
startup relevant events], but you have to
have someone that either tells you about it
or you're hearing about it maybe from the
City. And I mean it's funny because I never
went to the SBA, people mention SCORE,
they mention SBA, but I didn't leverage
those, only because I felt that those were at
the extreme opposite ends. For some reason
I view those as, if you want to start a hair
salon or, I don't know, something much
more on the ground, very grassroots, that's

more the resource you would look at. But not really for this fitness idea [her startup was focused on fitness], I didn't think that would be helpful.

The idea of connecting with different people and networks was also mentioned by an immigrant Asian female founder who was twenty-eight at the time of the interview. In her words:

ASIAN FEMALE ENTREPRENEUR 9: And the one thing nobody talks about in the entrepreneur world is how psychologically difficult the process is. It's not about the glamour or the things that people see. A lot of entrepreneurs are depressed. A lot of them. I was depressed for a long time because I almost went out of business. You need an emotional support network for that, and I think that's really missing in the female entrepreneurship circle. . . . Maybe the need is even greater for guys. Because I don't often hear guys say, "this is difficult for me." It's more like, "we've done great things and our company is growing like crazy and we're great!"

It's almost a shameful thing to reach out [in the] minority [community for] help, in a sense. I don't see a lot of people, myself included, purposefully seeking out Asian entrepreneurship help. I think we're all just trying to do whatever gives us an advantage in surviving, and if being Asian is part of that, that's fine, but that's not something I personally promote a lot.

If I get rewarded with an award, for example, I want to be awarded because I'm awesome.

I don't want to be awarded because they need a female minority to fill in the gap. But it does happen.

The ways in which gender and race intersect in relation to economic opportunity were explicitly addressed by a Black female entrepreneur with a tech startup, who was raised in Boston and twenty-seven at the time of the interview. She states the following when asked about changes in the Boston entrepreneurial ecosystem as it relates to women and minority entrepreneurs and their businesses.

BLACK FEMALE ENTREPRENEUR 17: We are an afterthought. All of the entrepreneurs were Caucasian men, as they were getting started, and they still take on problems that they understand. It's a very bro culture, like, "Hey, man, happy to help you. This is exactly what I want." And believe it or not, all White male founders that I have ever been associated with are pretty much like ... very focused on their business and they just want to talk about how to get things done and make things happen. I believe that their businesses will be successful. It's a very different approach. Most men are unfamiliar with it, don't know how to handle it, don't know if they want to support it, but don't want to put money in it, so they say things like, "Oh, yeah, I love your business, but I can't give you any money because I don't understand your problems."

INTERVIEWER: Can you tell me more about that? Because that's to me sort of the core of this issue of being in a liberal, progressive city that abstractly says, "Diversity is interesting and I value it," but practically –

BLACK FEMALE ENTREPRENEUR 17:
Yeah, we don't do anything about it at all . . . I went to a meeting with investors that are like, "Yes, we are committed to helping diversity, entrepreneurs, things like that." . . . I had . . . a conversation and went and met with them, heard their whole story about how they want to help and commit. And I was like, "Yeah, we're looking to raise money." And she's like, "Yeah, cool. I'll introduce you to other Black entrepreneurs or other Black angel investors that can help you."

INTERVIEWER:
. . . this person was White?

BLACK FEMALE ENTREPRENEUR 17:
Yes.

INTERVIEWER:
Right.

BLACK FEMALE ENTREPRENEUR 17:
Like, "Wait, what? Why am I talking to you just to get more introductions to other people? Is it that you don't believe in my business? Is it that you don't think this is being helpful? Or do you not really resonate with this problem? I thought you just told me you were about diversity." Like I think that even as a business owner, my business challenge is that I am constantly talking about diversity, a lot of it for many companies is just conversation. They're not committed to actually making change and coming up with tangible steps in order to get us to the next place. And so I think that's a challenge that's here, having people of

diverse backgrounds who want to be a part of the tech ecosystem. They are looking to connect [to] resources, they are looking to engage with people that have the power and the wealth, but for some reason, there is a disconnect, which means when people hear "diversity," they aren't ready to sign a check. It's two different things.

Deploying an intersectionality approach, the highlighted interactions speak to the ways in which networks of trust are simply not taking shape for these female entrepreneurs, who self-identify as Latina, Asian immigrant, or Black. In other words, while White female entrepreneurs also express similar interactions related to being outside of trusted networks and needing introductions, they were able to find male allies who supported them and investors who funded their ideas and companies. The ways in which identities and interactions intersect for women of color are quite different: the intersections of their gender, race, and/or immigrant identities create different considerations around finding community, getting support, and/or creating a sense of legitimacy around their business. These hurdles are neither explicit nor necessarily intentional on the part of other ecosystem actors and startup community participants, but it is this lack of awareness about intentions versus outcomes that results in the replication of inequalities. The implicit ways in which entrepreneurial ecosystems have norms and expectations about interactions – such as being transactional in connecting with others or having conversation over dinner if you're both male, or thinking that connecting women of color to other women and/or people of color is a kind, helpful, and nice thing to do in a liberal city – are based on fundamental ideas people have about others.

These highlighted interactions and resultant experiences speak to the myriad ways in which race, gender, and immigrant status "get done" in the context of entrepreneurship: ecosystem behavioral norms are implicitly gendered and racialized and only surface during explicit interactions across social categories. This is an important consideration for entrepreneurial ecosystems analysis. It is not enough to recognize that complex interactions among actors give rise to startup communities and entrepreneurial ecosystems. Rather, it is imperative to understand and analyze how these interactions are not neutral across gender, race, or immigrant status and how actors are not homogeneous even if they are of the same type, like entrepreneur. The complexity arising from the multiple, simultaneous, and ongoing social interactions among and between ecosystem actors is based on gendered and racialized assumptions (including those around trust) about other people within the startup community and within society. These assumptions have significant consequences for being recognized as part of *the* startup community (rather than *a* startup community), having access to important people, resources, and opportunities within the community, growing one's business, accessing capital, receiving support and advice, and other dimensions that contribute to successful entrepreneurial ventures.

Our analysis shows that there are subsets of communities within an entrepreneurial ecosystem with distinct and diverse experiences such that existing conversations around complexity or examining only gender, race, or immigrant status can miss their intersections. It is not the aim of this book to suggest that such subsets are positive or natural, but rather to demonstrate that entrepreneurial ecosystems are complex not because they are made up of disembodied actors engaged in relational exchanges but because they are made up of heterogeneous actors whose identities and interactions within the context of institutionalized norms reflect alternative paths and (im)possibilities that cannot be highlighted with existing ecosystem scholarship. Yet beyond individual interactions, organizations are also an important dimension related to how ecosystem actors engage in exchanges. These actors can serve as gatekeepers to resources, people, and information while, at the same, playing a significant and positive role in mitigating inequalities.

7.1.2 Gender, Race, and Organizations

Given our explicit focus on gender, race, and immigrant status, we highlight conversations with two different ESOs: TechAccelerator (mentioned in Chapters 4 and 5), an accelerator that focuses on high-growth tech startups across the US and which also has international connections/locations; and Inclusion Labs [pseudonym], an accelerator with an explicit focus on minority entrepreneurs, located in a minority neighborhood within Boston city limits. We start by highlighting the recruitment and assessment efforts at TechAccelerator. As discussed in Chapter 5, the accelerator has diversity aspirations that are based on goals and programs put together by individual directors rather than a general, firm-level policy on the issue. We then share a conversation with Inclusion Labs around the challenges of growing minority entrepreneurship within the city. Following this, we highlight an example of a new ESO model that has emerged in Boston, G|Code (actual name as the information we use is based on publicly available data), that tackles the challenge of inclusion within tech and entrepreneurship by addressing its structural determinants: housing, education, and networks. We begin with a portion of our interview with TechAccelerator.

INTERVIEWER:	So, can you tell me a little bit more about how you go through the initial process of filtering, so that you do have these smaller focus cohorts? You know, what is that application process like, and that filtering like [at TechAccelerator]?
WHITE FEMALE ESO DIRECTOR 3:	So, we actually receive direct applications. Like I can tell you in the last cohort, we had about 500 applicants that wanted Boston, specifically, as their first city, and another 500 that wanted Boston as a second city. Meaning, for example, they wanted the New York program, but the second option would

be Boston. So *we look at those ... about 1,000 applications, potentially. But out of those 1,000 applications, we only take maybe two or three. The rest comes from referrals. Real cold calls, the number of companies that we take from that pool is very small. The bulk comes from referrals* [authors' emphasis]. We do have a strong network in Boston, but globally as well. So, for example, we were just discussing Harvard, you know, we need to go to Harvard, and we have to talk to this company, that company, because we get referrals from other companies at Harvard, people that work at the incubator at Harvard, and professors, and whatnot. The same kind of relationship we have at MIT, Babson, Olin, all the schools in Boston. And globally, through other accelerators. Because the accelerators that exist, for example, in Chile, Brazil, France, etc., a lot of times they are actually launching pads to an accelerator like TechAccelerator so these companies can enter the US market. So, they start locally in their original companies, but then they come to TechAccelerator so they can become global companies and enter the US market. So, we also tap those, and through, you know, venture capitalists, angel investors, mentors, we connect with all those stakeholders, and we ask for referrals, and that's how we source the bulk of the successful applicants. And the process is simple. We review each and every application.

INTERVIEWER: Every single one?!

WHITE FEMALE ESO
DIRECTOR 3:   Yes. We read from top to bottom, we watch their videos – each application has two videos – and we, you know, if it's looking decent, we call for an interview. We just finished one today, and we interview the company for about an hour, and that's enough to say, "Do we want to interview again? Do we want to give them some homework? Do we want to have other questions answered by the next meeting? Or do we just want to make an offer?" So, sometimes a one-hour meeting is enough to make an offer; sometimes it requires multiple meetings. But it's not a long process, because it's a pre-seed fund, an accelerator, so you can't really be dwelling on the decision for months, and, you know, it's not the model. So, we make quick decisions.

INTERVIEWER: You mentioned you sort of read through everything, what is it that you're looking for that differentiates people that are ready to be in TechAccelerator versus those that are not?

WHITE FEMALE ESO
DIRECTOR 3:   We look at their execution track record. Have they accomplished anything in life, at all? So, you know, if they already had a failed startup, that's a sign that they got to some point. Ok, it failed, but they actually tried. Or, with the startup that they're applying for, do they have a working product, have they gotten any traction, have they signed people up, you know, have they built a good team? Because sometimes it's just a one-person team, and that's not the best sign. It just shows that that

person wasn't even capable of attracting, you know, engaging other people to be as excited as he or she is about the company. So, building the team, that's one sign of being able to actually execute, and sell it to you. Traction is another sign, and previous execution, track record, be it through a startup, success or failed, or through some kind of project – some sign that the person can get, you know, get things done. *And also, to be brutally honest, we do look at some credentials, as well. It's at a lower priority, but, for example, we enjoy quite a bit of success working with, you know, MIT and Harvard, so we know that, typically, entrepreneurs coming from those schools are worth at least an interview. So, we do look at some of these credentials, but it is at a lower priority than the execution track record itself* [authors' emphasis].

There are several points we want to address based on this example. The first is that despite having multiple and different directors of various TechAccelerators focused on diversity programs at their specific locations, there is no cohesive policy or requirement at the level of senior organizational leadership at TechAccelerator. This means that while these various programs run, essentially idiosyncratically and at the will of the director, there is no oversight or accountability, no reporting of metrics or any established goals or targets in terms of cohort diversity efforts. And this leads to our proposition that while there may be individual efforts by directors at their program/location, the fact is that existing recruitment and assessment practices can undermine any diversity and inclusion effort. As the director of TechAccelerator in Boston indicated, in about 1,000 applications, only 2 or 3 make it into the cohort (which is generally up to 10 teams) based on their track record rather than referrals and connections to elite local universities. Since our interview with this director in 2017, there has been a change in the TechAccelerator leadership in Boston; the current leadership seems more committed to diversity and inclusion, as evidenced by some of the new cohort teams. Yet if we examine the website for the main TechAccelerator, the tab around diversity and inclusion points us to various blogs on the topic and highlights particular founders rather than sharing data or numbers associated with efforts on this issue. In all, we see that while diversity and inclusion efforts have become mainstreamed in entrepreneurial ecosystems, there is little being done to hold ESOs accountable for their organizational practices and their role as gatekeepers in ecosystems – a role that acknowledges their position and power rather than simply as connectors within ecosystems. And more importantly, gatekeeping requires a conversation on power relations. Simply having a few more diverse founders does not change the structural inequities that benefit TechAccelerator and other high-growth accelerators who have the luxury of choosing from among thousands of applicants but still rely largely on referrals from their trusted networks as the primary way to assess the team and their potential success with the program.

Yet what about those ESOs who are much more explicit about their role within the entrepreneurial ecosystem with respect to minority entrepreneurs? Here, we highlight our conversation with a Boston-based accelerator focused explicitly on founders of color.

INTERVIEWER:	In terms of connecting, once they're leaving the accelerator, connecting them to potential funders, what has that experience been like?
BLACK MALE ESO DIRECTOR 8:	Well, it's been very difficult because – well, actually, it's not connections – connecting them to funders has not been difficult. It's are they investable or are they investment ready is

the bigger question, because you can actually put as many entrepreneurs in front of a funder as you want, but that doesn't mean they're ready to actually receive money. The real battle is getting them ready to receive funding. But as far as just getting them a front seat or an interview, or a face-to-face meeting with funders, that has not been a problem at all. That happens all the time.

INTERVIEWER: So can you sort of maybe explain a little more for me about what is the challenge with being investable? What is that barrier around being investable?

BLACK MALE ESO DIRECTOR 8:   Well, usually being investable requires that you have your balance sheet in order. The financial health of your company should meet a certain criteria. Your balance sheet, your [profit and loss statement], your income statement, your cash flow statement – you want to make sure you have all of those things in order. Not only that, but you want to make sure that you have some kind of collateral, because when you are receiving funding, you have to – in essence, you have to be willing to give something away. It could be a small piece of your business, it could be a piece of your house. But you have to make sure that you have enough collateral. And three, you've got to make sure that you understand what it takes to actually run an enterprise and not just a small business or a hustle that brings you like money on an annual or a monthly income. You really have to start looking at your business as an actual enterprise. So as soon as you get the operational management skills required, you have the collateral and equity that you're willing to give away on the business, then you can actually sit down at a table and begin to discuss, "Hey, this is how much I would like for the business" or, "This is how much equity I would like to give away in the business."

INTERVIEWER: Got it. In terms of Boston, do you find that the venture capitalists in Boston are amenable to investing in minority entrepreneurs?

BLACK MALE ESO DIRECTOR 8: Well, not really, because they have a hard time understanding the minority market and so therefore they don't see the value of what's being presented to them. So it does require a lot of education, a lot of homework, and a lot of due diligence. And that usually comes by way of the actual entrepreneur educating these venture capitalists, because again, this sector, this market, this industry, they don't have that much familiarity with.

INTERVIEWER: Right, right. And so when [you say] "industry," you mean sort of the creative arts?

BLACK MALE ESO DIRECTOR 8: Right, not just the creative sector, but I would say just minority businesses as a whole. They really don't understand the value that they bring to the table and so, therefore, like they don't really get the funding they need.

INTERVIEWER: Yeah. So can you tell me more about that? I find that really interesting. What is it that is different about the minority businesses that you think the venture capitalists aren't getting?

BLACK MALE ESO DIRECTOR 8: Well, some of the projects or some of the undertakings tend to be a little bit more culturally based. By which I mean if you take for example like Black haircare, which is a multibillion dollar industry in America. A lot of venture capitalists don't understand the kind of money that is spent on Black haircare per annum to make a sound decision and say, "Oh, you know what? I'm definitely going to get my return on this venture." It requires a lot of due diligence on their part. Usually they don't have that knowledge like at hand for them to say, "I should be able to make a sound decision moving forward." So it does require a little bit of homework.

We present the above portions of our interview to demonstrate that while access to investors may not be such a hurdle for minority entrepreneurs, at least in the view of the ESO director, there still exists the challenge that the majority of White venture capitalists and investors (in Boston and likely elsewhere) do not have the background, relationships, or understanding of Black/minority businesses to be able to assess them. Without this knowledge of minority markets and without a trusted network that is diverse, there seem to be very few individuals that investors can rely on to help them with due diligence in relation to minority businesses, and consequently most White venture capitalists/investors opt to not invest. Further exacerbating this situation is the fact that many Black/minority people in Boston do not have the requisite capital or collateral that would be necessary to start a business, get a bank or other type of loan, or dedicate their efforts to full-time entrepreneurship without paid employment. This is a structural problem that is manifest in the individual experiences and interactions of minority entrepreneurs – and without addressing the root cause of the problems through institutional change that includes intentional organizational practices and inclusive economic development policies, entrepreneurship cannot become a sustainable or meaningful path to social and economic mobility by communities that have been historically marginalized from wealth-creation, even though individuals may see some positive returns on their ventures. Intersectionality allows us to "see" the complexity of these issues by placing social identities and social interactions within the context of a racialized institutional environment that values trusted networks to make investment decisions (i.e. the gendered and racialized structure of the venture capital industry). And these dimensions take shape within the context of a city that has a history of racial tensions despite being considered a liberal and progressive city. In terms of entrepreneurial ecosystems, several themes emerge from our observations, including identifying how various structures, interactions, and practices intersect to create barriers or, at times, new economic opportunities for entrepreneurs, something we discuss explicitly in the next section when we focus on G| Code, a new kind of entrepreneurship support organization.

Intersectionality as a theoretical framework also allows us to consider how power is a relevant part of any entrepreneurial ecosystem analysis, as such an analysis requires an acknowledgement of institutional arrangements and an environment that favors and rewards, even if unintentionally, certain genders, races, or immigrant backgrounds over others, thereby exacerbating existing inequalities across social categories. Often, power is a missing dimension from entrepreneurial ecosystem analysis even if the role and importance of networks and embeddedness are acknowledged within institutional environments. By using trusted networks and social relations as proxies to reduce transaction costs (i.e. due diligence), White venture capitalists/investors are acting rationally, by any neoclassical economics argument. Yet this approach assumes that reducing transactions costs is the only measure of economic success under conditions of uncertainty and bounded rationality – it misses the point that such "rational" behavior and decision-making creates gendered and racialized economic inequality. If ecosystem players are assumed to be disembodied rational economic actors embedded in social relations that are thought to generate trust and reduce malfeasance, then these assumptions undermine the complexity of entrepreneurial ecosystems in terms of how they replicate the very gendered and racialized institutional environments (as discussed in Chapters 2 and 6) that allow certain people and groups to succeed. In other words, the existing institutional environment and network relations among actors within an entrepreneurial ecosystem can end up marginalizing certain entrepreneurs by inadvertently sanctioning them in the pursuit of opportunities.

In effect, entrepreneurial ecosystems exist neither as hierarchies nor as organizations, but behave more like networks based on trust, as described by Adler (2001). Ecosystems can be seen as resulting from the information and trust requirements of the knowledge economy taking shape under late capitalism. In such instances, it seems likely that the plethora of resources available within an ecosystem would allow for knowledge-based trust, networks, and exchange relationships to flourish, but as we have demonstrated, this is not true for *all* actors within the category of entrepreneur. Ecosystems are assumed to have a self-modulating quality, whereby those who "break" or "violate" norms would be sanctioned, but in reality, such sanctioning doesn't formally happen unless it involves litigation, and even then, systemic changes can be difficult. Consider the high-profile cases where venture capitalists have been accused of sexual harassment, such as the very public case of Ellen Pao vs. Kleiner Perkins, or where a tech startup founder created a toxic work environment for female employees, such as the company culture Travis Kalanick created at Uber (Williams, 2017). In these and similar cases, there was little change in the structure of the venture capital industry or in the very standing of a startup within an entrepreneurial ecosystem, even if some individuals were potentially sanctioned. Ironically, or perhaps not because of irony but gendered norms and sexism, Pao's gender discrimination case was dismissed by a jury that seemed to be confused about the facts as she was repeatedly painted as "resentful" and "combative" by attorneys for Kleiner Perkins in court,[5] replaying gendered stereotypes about women in powerful positions. In contrast, Uber's Kalanick, while forced to leave the firms' board of directors, still managed to sell stock worth around $2.5 billion and profit off the situation before moving on.[6] He's currently investing in a new hotel startup that uses 3-D technology, his reputation seemingly intact and his ability to invest, unfettered.[7] In regards to the claims of a toxic work culture, Uber paid around $4.4 million to settle sexual harassment claims.

In all, as these examples demonstrate, bad and illegal behavior can result in fines and sanctions against a firm or an individual, but not in a manner that would change the institutionalized practices of the venture capital industry or startups, or change the behavior of individuals and their ability to continue circulating in entrepreneurial ecosystems, albeit in a different city, as ecosystem actors. In other words, problems of equity and inclusion are blamed on organizational culture or particular individuals rather than being the result of a systemic problem: deeply rooted and normalized practices and assumptions which are presumed to lead to successful entrepreneurial ecosystems through the interactions of entrepreneurs, venture capitalists, ESOs, and others actually create inequalities across social categories. Social relations guided by trust give rise to new investment opportunities within entrepreneurial ecosystems and seemingly start a virtuous cycle of entrepreneurs giving back time, resources, and advice to other entrepreneurs. This is the shadow side of entrepreneurial ecosystems. White male actors are able to engage in behavior, intentional or not, that is detrimental to other actors, such

---

[5] www.nytimes.com/2015/03/28/technology/ellen-pao-kleiner-perkins-case-decision.html

[6] www.marketwatch.com/story/ubers-travis-kalanick-is-leaving-the-board-and-thats-a-good-thing-analyst-says-2019-12-24

[7] https://skift.com/2020/02/10/uber-co-founder-travis-kalanick-backs-hotel-company-using-3d-printing-tech/

as women and minorities, with few significant consequences in the pursuit of entrepreneurial success and investment deals.

This is surprising given that scholarship attending to the violation of norms and opportunism assumes that

> market mechanisms can be designed that would allow joint profit optimization for any transaction. It is only in the case of opportunistic behavior (given a set of other conditions) that hierarchical control mechanisms such as fiat, monitoring, and incentives represent the only reliable safeguards for effective exchange.
>
> *Ghoshal and Moran (1996: 18)*

In other words, behavior only becomes sanctioned when it inhibits profit maximization for firms and violates the norms of trust as they relate to economic exchange – not when such behavior limits opportunities for women and minorities. Highly masculinized, aggressive, and risk-taking behavior is normalized as part of the institutionalized practices of the venture capital industry and depends on trusted networks to continue replicating. In other words, trusted networks, the very foundation of "successful" startup communities and entrepreneurial ecosystems are also the very foundation of inequalities and injustices across gender, race, and immigrant status in certain circumstances. Without acknowledging how such networks within gendered institutional environments can contribute to the creation of inequities as they relate to identities, interactions, and institutions, no single change in behavior or organizational practice – such as suggesting women find male allies or pitch differently or that ESOs have more representation of female entrepreneurs on panels – can change entrepreneurial ecosystems toward becoming more inclusive. In our final chapter, we expand on why inclusion matters particularly in relation to entrepreneurship and economic development and suggest policies to that end while recognizing that some might see policies as a kind of sanction on the "free market." Specifically, changing institutional environments at the nation state, regional/state, organizational, and individual levels through policies can be a holistic solution that can address the widespread ways in which gendered outcomes in entrepreneurship and gendered opportunities in entrepreneurial ecosystems continue to be the norm. But meanwhile, such change can be local and needs to start with a fundamental understanding of the structural and institutionalized drivers of inequality in entrepreneurial ecosystems: education, housing, and leadership opportunities. We highlight the work being done by G|Code, a successful entrepreneurship program led by a self-identified Black woman in Boston, to demonstrate that intersectional (and multilayered and multileveled) problems need intersectional solutions. We do not anonymize this organization, as our research comes from publicly available online sources. The program can be a good case study for other researchers interested in studying inclusion efforts in entrepreneurial ecosystems.

7.1.3 G|Code: Rethinking Entrepreneurial Ecosystems from the Ground Up

G|Code is the brainchild of Bridgette Wallace, a self-identified Black woman who served as the Program Manager for Boston's Public Health Commission and the Department of Public Health. Bridgette earned her Master's in Urban Planning with a concentration in Economic Development from Tufts University.[8] She serves on the Roxbury Neighborhood Council, and her "goal [is] to create and support additional pipelines that enhance Boston's innovation mix by focusing on women, housing, technology, and entrepreneurship" (thegcodehouse.com). G|Code offers young women of color between the ages of eighteen and twenty-five an opportunity to engage in the entrepreneurial ecosystem through an intersectional solution. Their mission statement is as follows: "G|Code offers young women of color a safe co-living, working, and learning community where they will learn cutting-edge technology skills, gain employment experience and

---

[8] www.thegcodehouse.com/whoweare

connect with our world renown network of mentors, advisors and enterprise partners." There is no fee associated with the offered programs, which include a twenty-four-month residential program and a ten-month nonresidential one, although cohort members still have access to the G|Code house and space. The programs are supported by partners, funders, and volunteers and an operational team to ensure sustainability. The G|Code house is located in Roxbury, a predominantly Black neighborhood in Boston, and was redeveloped with support from Sasaki, an architectural design firm in town. The goal in locating the property within Roxbury was to address concerns around gentrification and create opportunities for young women in their own neighborhoods so that they would not feel displaced.

We highlight this program for several reasons. First, the leadership at G|Code understands that solving the inequities in entrepreneurship, particularly in the tech startup space, cannot be solved simply by teaching young women to code. That is an individual solution to a structural problem with many facets. The solution requires a holistic approach: offering residential and coworking space that is safe for women of color within their neighborhoods, offering educational courses on tech and leadership to change mindsets and behaviors, and offering a network of mentors and advisors during and beyond the program. Second, G|Code is designed and located intentionally in a predominantly minority/Black neighborhood such that issues of access, belonging to a community, and trust become established without requiring additional work on the part of the young women. The location alongside the connections to a network of mentors allows for the building of social capital in a manner that is not transactional or exploitative. In other words, young women learn coding skills and become highly employable, not as tokens in an organization that aims to be attuned to gender equity and racial justice, but as competitive individuals within the talent landscape of Boston with a strong network of mentors and advisors who can support them. Finally, G|Code aims to dispel the notion that no innovation or opportunity exists in minority communities – a strong stereotype that often plays out in media outlets when mostly crimes or other negative daily ongoings in such neighborhoods are highlighted rather than positive community developments, such as new businesses that start up in such areas. This stereotype propels individuals to believe such areas are not safe and that the only possibilities for entrepreneurship and innovation in the Boston area take place in Kendall Square, Harvard, and MIT (among other gentrified areas).

In all, G|Code paves the way for our next chapter as we discuss holistic frameworks for creating inclusive economic opportunities and entrepreneurship opportunities. The intersectional challenges highlighted in this chapter speak to the ways in which the multiple dimensions of identities, interactions, and institutions intersect to create unique challenges that are experienced by women (and men) differently in terms of race and immigrant status. Yet shared within their experiences is the broader context of entrepreneurial ecosystems, not only as trusted networks but also as contested communities (Ozkazanc-Pan, forthcoming): an institutional environment that is structured to benefit mostly White males through intentional and unintentional practices, expectations of reciprocity, and implicit assumptions about behaviors and trust. The complexity of these issues allows us to rethink entrepreneurial ecosystems in terms of the varied and heterogeneous nature of actors within the same category of entrepreneurs and their diverse experiences within the same ecosystem and city – in the case of our research, Boston. Our findings have some significant implications for how we conceptualize and study entrepreneurial ecosystems, a point we address explicitly in our final chapter, as well as the ways in which scholarship attending to ecosystems is fraught with assumptions about the very actors being studied. Our goal has been to demonstrate that differences matter, and by providing a framework derived from feminist insights and intersectionality, we have expanded conversations on how entrepreneurial ecosystems operate inclusive of the ways in which inequalities may take shape for some actors but not necessarily for others. Finally, we hope that by focusing on the structural, we have highlighted how inequities take shape but also how they can be solved, as the example of G|Code demonstrates. Next, we discuss our contributions to entrepreneurial ecosystem research and offer insights about policies that can lead to inclusion in entrepreneurship and economic development for women (and others).

REFERENCES

Abbas, A., Byrne, J., Galloway, L., & Jackman, L. (2019). Gender, intersecting identities, and entrepreneurship research: An introduction to a special section on intersectionality. *International Journal of Entrepreneurial Behavior & Research*, 25(8): 1703–1705.

Adler, P. S. (2001). Market, hierarchy, and trust: The knowledge economy and the future of capitalism. *Organization Science, 12*(2): 215–234.

Ahl, H., & Nelson, T. (2010). Moving forward: Institutional perspectives on gender and entrepreneurship. *International Journal of Gender and Entrepreneurship, 2* (1): 5–9.

Berube, A. (2018). City and metropolitan level income inequality data reveals ups and downs through 2016. Brookings Institute, Washington, DC. Available at www.brookings.edu/research/city-and-metropolitan-income-inequality-data-reveal-ups-and-downs-through-2016/ (accessed July 15, 2019).

Bhachu, P. (Ed.). (2017). *Immigration and entrepreneurship: Culture, capital, and ethnic networks*. New York: Routledge.

The Boston Foundation. (2017). Opportunity in change: Preparing Boston for leader transitions and new models of nonprofit leadership. Available at www.tbf.org/-/media/tbforg/files/reports/nonprofit-leadership-final.pdf?la=en (accessed July 15, 2020).

The Boston Globe. (2017). For blacks in Boston, a power outage, December 2017. Part of series on Boston, Racism, Image, Reality. Available at https://apps.bostonglobe.com/spotlight/boston-racismimage-reality/series/power/ (accessed July 15, 2020).

Brooks, A. W., Huang, L., Kearney, S. W., & Murray, F. E. (2014). Investors prefer entrepreneurial ventures pitched by attractive men. *Proceedings of the National Academy of Sciences, 111*(12): 4427–4431.

Chen, X. P., Yao, X., & Kotha, S. (2009). Entrepreneur passion and preparedness in business plan presentations: A persuasion analysis of venture capitalists' funding decisions. *Academy of Management Journal*, 52(1): 199–214.

Collins, P. H., & Bilge, S. (2020). *Intersectionality*. Cambridge: John Wiley & Sons.

Crenshaw, K. (1989). *Demarginalizing the intersection of race and sex: A black feminist critique of antidiscrimination doctrine, feminist theory, and antiracist politics.* Chicago: University of Chicago Legal Forum.

Crenshaw, K. (1990). Mapping the margins: Intersectionality, identity politics, and violence against women of color. *Stanford Law Review, 43*: 1241–1299.

Elam, A. B. (2014). *Gender and entrepreneurship.* Northampton, MA: Edward Elgar Publishing.

Fairlie, R. W., & Lofstrom, M. (2015). Immigration and entrepreneurship. In B. Chiswick & P. Miller (Eds.), *Handbook of the economics of international migration* (Vol. 1, pp. 877–911). New York: North-Holland.

Fairlie, R. W., & Robb, A. M. (2010). *Race and entrepreneurial success: Black-, Asian-, and White-owned businesses in the United States.* Cambridge, MA: MIT Press.

Feld, B. (2012). *Startup communities: Building an entrepreneurial ecosystem in your City.* Hoboken, NJ: Wiley.

Feld, B., & Hathaway, I. (2020). *The startup community way: Evolving an entrepreneurial ecosystem.* Hoboken, NJ: Wiley.

Fischer, E. M., Reuber, A. R., & Dyke, L. S. (1993). A theoretical overview and extension of research on sex, gender, and entrepreneurship. *Journal of Business Venturing, 8*(2): 151–168.

Ghoshal, S., & Moran, P. (1996). Bad for practice: A critique of the transaction cost theory. *Academy of Management Review, 21*(1): 13–47.

Gold, S. J. (2016). A critical race theory approach to black American entrepreneurship. *Ethnic and Racial Studies, 39*(9): 1697–1718.

Kantrowitz, N. (1979). Racial and ethnic residential segregation in Boston 1830-1970. *The Annals of the American Academy of Political and Social Science, 441*(1): 41–54.

Kanze, D., Huang, L., Conley, M. A., & Higgins, E. T. (2018). We ask men to win and women not to lose: Closing the gender gap in startup funding. *Academy of Management Journal, 61*(2): 586–614.

Knight, M. (2016). Race-ing, classing and gendering racialized women's participation in entrepreneurship. *Gender, Work & Organization, 23*(3): 310–327.

Light, I. H., & Rosenstein, C. N. (1995). *Race, ethnicity, and entrepreneurship in urban America.* New York: Aldine de Gruyter.

Marlow, S., & McAdam, M. (2013). Gender and entrepreneurship. *International Journal of Entrepreneurial Behavior & Research, 19*(1): 114–124.

McCall, L. (2005). The complexity of intersectionality. *Signs: Journal of Women in Culture and Society, 30*(3): 1771–1800.

Munoz, A. P., Kim, M., Chang, M., Jackson, R. O., Hamilton, D., & Darity Jr., W. A. (2015). *The color of wealth in Boston.* Federal Reserve Bank of Boston. Available at www.bostonfed.org/publications/one-time-pubs/color-of-wealth.aspx (accessed July 20, 2019).

Nash, J. C. (2008). Re-thinking intersectionality. *Feminist Review, 89*(1): 1–15.

Ozkazanc-Pan, B. (2019). Statement of record, U.S. Senate Committee on Small Business and Entrepreneurship Reauthorization of SBA's Small Business Investment Company Program. Available at www.sbc.senate.gov/public/_cache/files/a/b/ab045168-e00e-4d91-be68-4b6bce43ac1e/2DE1EA7748B644FDE6CA9A95C7541270.ozkazanc-pan-testimony.pdf (accessed December 21, 2019).

Ozkazanc-Pan, B. (Forthcoming). Rethinking social capital: Entrepreneurial ecosystems as contested communities. *Research in the Sociology of Organizations.*

Portes, A. (Ed.). (1995). *The economic sociology of immigration: Essays on networks, ethnicity, and entrepreneurship.* New York: Russell Sage Foundation.

Portes, A., Haller, W. J., & Guarnizo, L. E. (2002). Transnational entrepreneurs: An alternative form of immigrant economic adaptation. *American Sociological Review, 67*(2): 278–298.

Romero, M., & Valdez, Z. (2016). Introduction to the special issue: Intersectionality and entrepreneurship. *Ethnic and Racial Studies, 39*(9): 1553–1565.

Sayce, S., & Acker, J. (2012). Gendered organizations and intersectionality: Problems and possibilities. *Equality, Diversity and Inclusion: An International Journal, 31* (3): 214–224.

Vaznis, J. (2018). Boston's schools are becoming resegregated. *The Boston Globe,* August 4, 2018. Available at www.bostonglobe.com/metro/2018/08/04/boston-schools-are-becoming-resegregated/brwPhLuupRzkOtSa9Gi6nL/story.html (accessed July 20, 2019).

Walker, J. E. (2009). *The history of black business in America: Capitalism, race, entrepreneurship* (Vol. 1). Chapel Hills: University of North Carolina Press Books.

Wang, Q. (2019). Gender, race/ethnicity, and entrepreneurship: Women entrepreneurs in a US south city. *International Journal of Entrepreneurial Behavior & Research, 25*(8): 1766–1785.

Williams, J. (2017). Why sexual harassment is more of a problem in venture capital. *Harvard Business Review.* Available at https://hbr.org/2017/07/why-sexual-harassment-is-more-of-a-problem-in-venture-capital (accessed May 15, 2019).

8 Holistic Solutions for Inclusive Economic Development through Entrepreneurship

This chapter examines individual, organizational, and societal approaches to addressing gender inequality in the context of entrepreneurship, businesses, support organizations, and economic development strategies. Beginning with an evaluation of the types of arguments made for gender equality in the workplace, this chapter provides an overview of existing rationales and interventions to address gender inequity from a critical perspective. This holistic framework for building inclusive entrepreneurial ecosystems incorporates strategies and tactics of organizational actors, policymakers, change agents, and activists across micro, meso, and macro levels. Recommendations and resources for implementing change provided in this chapter will be useful for leaders, activists, practitioners, and other change-makers.

8.1 ARGUMENTS FOR GENDER EQUITY

Institutional pressures for gender equality in the workplace fall into two categories. The "business case" line of reasoning for having women represented in decision-making roles, including on top management teams and boards of directors, focuses on organization-level benefits. Improving gender equality promises to increase revenues through multiple mechanisms. The presence of women in leadership roles in business firms improves decision-making, generates new revenue from innovation, and enhances organizational performance (Lorenzo et al., 2018). Strong representation of women appeals to female stakeholders, such as actual or potential investors, customers, clients, and employees. Demographic diversity leads to less group-think, more intersectional thinking, and higher levels of innovation as the sources of ideas and challenges expand (Ribberstrom, 2013).

The combination of increased market share (increase in sales revenues) and decreased costs raises profits for businesses and, thus, promises higher share prices for publicly traded firms. Given this line of reasoning focuses predominantly on the benefits to businesses and their bottom lines (profit margins), these arguments are purely instrumental and strategic. While individual women might benefit from improved gender relations, equity in pay, promotions, appointments, evaluations, and a more inclusive culture, such business case arguments do not ultimately focus on direct benefits to individual women or to women as a group or category. The ultimate beneficiaries are the owners of the firm (stockholders in a publicly traded corporation), who benefit the most from any increase in profits that comes with effective gender inclusion efforts. If improving inclusion and equity raises more costs than benefits to shareholders, managers will not pursue these actions, as this would be a violation of the legal fiduciary duty to shareholders. Normative arguments based on social justice rationales or ethical principles such as justice, fairness, human flourishing, or reducing harms are notably absent.

The exclusion and underrepresentation of women is costly to organizations, and this can negatively impact the bottom line, or profit margins, of businesses. Female executives are perceived to be less costly than male executives given the evidence that women command lower pay packages and are less likely to negotiate or to win negotiations for pay raises and other forms of compensation. Problematically for gender equality in pay, organizations typically save money by hiring women, and decision makers understand these savings in their hiring logic, particularly with regard to top-level positions. Other costs of too few women include the negative consequences of tokenism. The visible absence of sufficient numbers of women at the top of organizational hierarchies has led to the common practice of putting an individual woman or person of color in a leadership position to deflect criticism based on lack of diversity. Putting a token woman or person of color in a visible position of representation in organizations (such as on panels, management teams, and boards of directors) is a limited strategy that may backfire. Organizations that have women represented in higher ranks but in a much smaller proportion relative to men are more likely to experience higher rates of sexual harassment and associated consequences, including negative reputational effects, lawsuits, high staff turnover, absenteeism, alienation, disengagement, and a hostile or toxic work environment, particularly for women from marginalized groups. Ellen Pao's gender discrimination lawsuit against the lauded venture capital firm Kleiner Perkins Caufield & Byers is a widely known example of this phenomenon. According to her own account, Pao experienced forms of sexual harassment, including a hostile work environment, discrimination, and exclusion as a token female (Pao, 2017). The lawsuits and negative public relations that ensue in these cases are costly to organizations' bottom lines and reputations.

Very different arguments for gender equity involve the welfare of individual women and the collective equity of women as a marginalized group. Social justice arguments attend to intrinsic values, normative claims, and ethical and moral dimensions of gender equity in organizational and societal life. Claims that promoting and appointing women on their merits and paying them equal to men because it is "the right thing to do" have a foundation squarely in ethical and moral principles: fairness, justice, benevolence, equity of treatment based on desert, attention to human flourishing, holistic well-being of individuals, reduction of harms, etc. These types of arguments and principles are missing from business case arguments for gender diversity, and so decision makers do not focus on these in boardrooms, shareholder meetings, or strategy sessions. Further, well-argued ethical and moral rationales for gender equality in the workplace and at the apex of business organizations and financial institutions are rare in the popular media and in coverage by the business press.

8.2 INDIVIDUAL STRATEGIES: LEAN IN AND ITS LIMITS

Despite three waves of feminism and widespread women's movements and social media campaigns, women remain underrepresented in critical decision-making roles across the globe. In the US in particular, individual-level approaches to addressing the gender gap in pay, promotions, and appointments dominate discussions, while systemic and institutional solutions are less common. Further, women as a group are expected to solve their own "gender issues" rather than assigning any responsibility to men who hold the power to affect change in the organizations they lead. An example of the onus being placed squarely on individual women is the popularity of the Lean In movement. Sheryl Sandberg, the COO of Facebook, popularized this term in a 2010 TED talk and in her book *Lean In: Women, Work and the Will to Lead* (Sandberg, 2013). The book became a national bestseller and led to the creation of Lean In Circles and a movement of individual women collaborating with others toward improving their own prospects in the workplace. While noting the organizational, institutional, and societal context in which individual women attempt to climb the corporate ladder, her primary argument is that individual women hold themselves back from success and thus need to solve their own deficiencies relative to men who hold power. She advises individual women to take more risks, make their own seat at the table, speak up, self-advocate, lean forward, and eschew worrying about pleasing people or being liked. While sales of the book and the establishment of Lean In Circles and social media promotions suggest the book and the movement has been a success, Sandberg received substantial public and scholarly criticism.

Critics decry the hyper-individualistic solutions, which focus primarily on highly educated, largely White, economically and socially privileged women and give insufficient attention to the structural, institutional, and systemic barriers that women face as a marginalized group and the ways in which these barriers are intersectional. In addition, Facebook and other Silicon Valley technology firms are notably poor models of gender equality and inclusion, particularly at the top rungs of these firms. Further, recent scholarship suggests that women are punished for carrying through with advice to forego being liked and to boldly assert themselves given entrenched double binds. Specifically, women who exhibit what is perceived to be too much ambition or masculine traits such as being vocal and assertive are not liked and are penalized (Exley, Niederle, & Vesterlund, 2016). Focusing on individual women developing self-confidence, self-advocacy, and taking a seat at the table avoids direct challenges to systemic male privilege. Thus, focusing solely on individual women or women in groups as the solution has the effect of retaining the systemic, institutionalized privileges men hold with the status quo. The existing power structure deflects accountability for instituting necessary changes. Men continue to hold super-majorities in offices, with decision-making power across all sectors of the economy, including media, finance, technology, and other critical social and political institutions (Catalyst, 2021). Token successful women, like Sandberg, may yield unique situational power, but insufficient numbers of women at the apex suggest a severe lack of institutionalized efforts toward gender equality and access to power for sufficient numbers of women and especially for women with diverse sociocultural and socioeconomic backgrounds.

Given that entrepreneurial activities take place in patriarchal cultures, this "patriarchal nature of the entrepreneurship domain" raises challenges for women, including the perceived need to engage in identity work, to resolve tensions that arise, and to fit in as women with culturally ascribed femininity in a highly masculinized field (McAdam, Harrison, & Leitch, 2019: 466). Women have expressed a perceived need to imitate the practices of men to increase their credibility (McAdam, Harrison, & Leitch, 2019), and yet acting more like a man through Lean In-type strategies (e.g. pitching or speaking more like a man, exhibiting overconfidence) can backfire and make one less likeable or lead to feelings of not being authentic to one's self. In sum, individual-level solutions are overrated and largely ineffective, as they fail to address the myriad institutional, structural, and systemic barriers that explain men's advantage and privilege relative to women in entrepreneurship.

8.3 ORGANIZATION-LEVEL EFFORTS TOWARD GENDER INCLUSION

Broad societal shifts in gender, race, and class dynamics over the past few decades place heightened managerial demands on organizations competing globally for talent and market opportunities (Clark Muntean, Ozkazanc-Pan, & Still, 2013). Labor markets consist of more women than ever before in the workforce, a rise in dual-income households, and increasing numbers of women out-earning their male partners (Rouse, 2010). Addressing and taking advantage of these labor force changes is integral to strategic management, particularly as firms continue to grow their operations locally, nationally, and globally. In effect, labor force trends necessitate change in how businesses formulate their strategies and conduct their day-to-day operations to attract and retain talented employees, comply with legal requirements, and signal a commitment to achieving greater equality and inclusiveness. Within this context, human resources as a business function take on the strategic role of finding and maintaining talented employee and managerial pools under the rubric of diversity management, including specific practices and programs focused on attracting and retaining female employees with managerial and executive potential.

As record numbers of women enter the workforce and begin to break glass ceilings, the assumption is that there will be better diversity overall and that this will bring in a wider scope of opinions and ideas that will, ultimately, improve organizational performance (Jayne & Dipboye, 2004). This constitutes the business case argument for gender equity. Companies may strategically adopt inclusive hiring and retention practices to improve decision-making within the firm, better serve a diverse customer base, and signal an inclusive image to its stakeholders. In addition, external institutional pressure and recommendations from women's groups and corporate governance advocates have pushed organizations to follow more inclusive hiring, retention, and promotion strategies with respect to women.

Thus, not surprisingly, findings suggest that organizational responsibility for diversity (rather than a pure focus on diversity training or aims to end social isolation) yields the most positive return on increasing managerial diversity (Kalev, Dobbin, & Kelly, 2006).

Brush et al. (2019) identify three common areas in which organizations themselves may be gendered within entrepreneurial ecosystems: (a) in the construction of divisions such as division of labor, work roles, and opportunities; (b) in the construction of symbols and images (including language, ideology, and cultural artifacts) that serve to reinforce gender divisions and in relation to how these are represented in the media, including who is visible and showcased as the ideal entrepreneur; and (c) in the gendered social structures and everyday social interactions within and across organizations. Together, the production and reproduction of gender norms, gendered practices, and gendered structures serve to disadvantage women, relative to men, as entrepreneurs seeking to launch and grow their businesses.

Even the lauded Silicon Valley technology firms receive negative report cards on social media and in the press, and they continue to be pressured to be more attentive to issues surrounding gender diversity and inequality. Hostile work environments, toxic masculinity and misogyny in organizational culture, and sexual harassment result in women's exodus from technology companies and their avoidance of pursuing leadership roles in technology ventures or career tracks in STEM fields.[1] Entrepreneurial firms and ESOs play important roles in initiating broader efforts at gender inclusion through addressing these problems that continue to plague women's experiences. Founding teams and startup companies can improve their performance in this regard by establishing clear commitments to diversity and inclusion from the top management team and advisory board or board of directors. Expressing a desire to be inclusive is a necessary but insufficient condition for improvement. Leaders need to have a tangible strategy

---

[1] www.newyorker.com/magazine/2017/11/20/the-tech-industrys-gender-discrimination-problem (accessed June 23, 2020).

and action plan with clear metrics and accountability for following through. Transparency and measurement provide the opportunity for stakeholders to keep leaders accountable for their commitments to diversity and inclusion, as opposed to simply expressing that they care about it. These metrics must measure the impact of the organizational culture on women's experiences of inclusion or exclusion. One simple-to-adopt practice is conducting exit interviews with women to document and make transparent their reasons for leaving.

Organization leaders and other decision makers might address gender inequality by making organization-level changes. In theory, a manager can seek organization-level change through the adoption of practices, programs, and policies and/or procedures that address gender inequality and promote inclusion. In practice, popular approaches such as adopting women's leadership development and mentoring programs, adopting zero tolerance sexual harassment policies, and making regular public proclamations that the organization and its leadership value women have been largely insufficient in ameliorating systemic gender inequity, particularly at the top ranks of organizational life. Gender equality has been notably absent across the professions. Male-dominance remains pronounced across lucrative sectors and industries, including in high-tech and venture-backed entrepreneurial enterprises and investment firms as well as in C-Suites and boards of multinational corporations, on Wall Street, and in Silicon Valley.

Gender gaps are evident at every stage of the life cycle of a woman's (potential) career at an organization. Leaders of organizations can make intentional interventions at each stage of the leaky pipeline across a woman's career, whether in a nonprofit ESO, a startup business, or an established entrepreneurial firm. The first aspect that may require change is in the wording of job descriptions; for example, avoiding use of superlatives or gendered terms such as "aggressive," "hustler," and "hacker," while expressing commitment to being inclusive in hiring.[2]

---

[2] See www.glassdoor.com/employers/blog/10-ways-remove-gender-bias-job-listings/

In addition, human resource departments and recruiters should avoid placing job descriptions in venues that may be exclusive and conducting outreach through social networks that are homogenous and male dominated. Next, hiring decisions should attempt to be gender-blind through anonymous application processes. If this is not possible during job interviews, interviewers should be gender aware (Clark Muntean & Ozkazanc-Pan, 2015). Starting compensation packages should not have gender disparities. Search committees and hiring professionals should have implicit association bias training and be held accountable for their performance with respect to gender-inclusive outreach and hiring decisions. For many more ideas on how to close the gender gap in hiring, see Model View Culture.[3]

Gender gaps are also a problem in talent development, which includes training but also mentoring and appointments to challenging projects and assignments. Gender gaps may also be apparent in appointments to lucrative committees, clients, and boards. Women should not be relegated to less prestigious and more time-consuming service roles and tasks while men are appointed the most lucrative committee assignments, clients, projects, and board positions. In a similar vein, evidence suggests that men may be resourced more generously than women in the workplace. In a Catalyst study of 1,600 business school graduates, researchers found that on average men's projects had double the budget and three times the staffing of women's projects (Silva, Carter, & Beninger, 2012). These gaps can play out in the entrepreneurial world – for example, if females have access to fewer investment dollars or lack access to appointments to boards of directors, executive positions, and decision-making roles.

Well-documented gender gaps in performance evaluations disproportionately negatively impact women's careers compared to men's careers, resulting in slowed and side-tracked careers and lower compensation of women relative to men (Lyness & Heilman, 2006). Finally, gender gaps in promotions include the different speed or rate

---

[3] https://modelviewculture.com/pieces/25-tips-for-diverse-hiring

at which women and men climb the corporate ladder, gendered roles and inequality in responsibility, and unequal access to prestige positions and titles. Further, compensation gaps over a lifetime result in a gender gap in wealth; this negatively impacts the pool of women-controlled equity funds, which are more likely to invest in female-founded firms and startups with a female CEO. For more ideas on how ESOs, including venture capitalists, can close the gender gap and be more inclusive, see Project Include (http://projectinclude.org/recommendations/).

8.4   SOCIETAL-LEVEL EFFORTS: GENDER-INCLUSIVE ECONOMIC DEVELOPMENT POLICY

8.4.1   *Interventions in Workplace Gender Equality: Exemplars and Lessons Learned*

Recognition of the importance of women's actual and potential contributions to economic growth through business ownership is on the rise. On a global scale, social, political, and economic equality for women is a primary economic development tool. Given that women comprise just over half of the world's population and yet remain systemically underrepresented in the most well-compensated sectors, industries, and careers, gender equality in the workplace promises to offer considerable economic gains to countries able to achieve it. In the US, formal governmental policies explicitly focused on establishing and enforcing gender equality in the private sector are rare and have stagnated over the past decades. Social movements and special interest groups have largely replaced more formalized interventions by legislators, the executive branch, or the courts. For example, the 2020 Women on Boards (www.2020wob.com) campaign strives to exert public pressure on businesses to appoint more women on corporate boards of directors. Women 2.0 (www.women2.com) is a for-profit media and technology company that seeks gender parity in the US entrepreneurial ecosystem and beyond through activism, social media campaigns, educational campaigns, consulting, and partnerships. The #MeToo movement's success has resulted in corporate law firms on *Wall Street* adopting the so-called Weinstein clause as part of the due diligence process for merger and acquisitions (Jaeger, 2018).

In the developing world, economic development efforts focus on establishing basic human rights for women, including the legal capacity to own property, open banking accounts, and have access to small business loans. The focus is particularly on impoverished women with lack of access to education and, thus, not in skilled careers. In this respect, microenterprise is offered as an alternative to job training, the provision of education, or the provision of government subsidies such as a universal basic income. Microlending operations and institutions have been criticized for practices that are exploitative and/or bring unintended negative consequences for the very women who they are trying to serve (Clark Muntean & Ozkazanc-Pan, 2016).

In the developed world, country-level interventions to address gender equality are highly varied. Given the lack of urgency exhibited by industry to adopt effective gender inclusion strategies, interest groups have emerged that demand public policy interventions from federal and state governments. As Esping-Andersen (2009) argues, given the institutional biases against women in the labor force and the internalization of costs to employers who take on the responsibility to fix them, public policy is necessary to ensure equity. In classically liberal, democratic regimes with neoliberal, free market economic systems, the slow track to gender equality in the workplace has led to growing dissatisfaction and a concomitant call for government intervention into corporate decision-making with respect to appointment of directors to corporate boards (Dahlerup & Freidenvall, 2005). To address these demands, many countries across the globe have adopted corporate quotas, including nine that have adopted comprehensive hard quotas for private sector and state-owned companies, seven who have adopted limited hard quotas for state-owned companies only, and seven that have adopted soft quotas for private sector and stated-owned companies (Piscopo & Clark Muntean, 2018).

In the wealthiest countries in the world, gender equality is still a problem. Despite some viewing the US as an exemplar in high-growth entrepreneurship and technology innovation, there remain persistent gender gaps in entrepreneurial outcomes. One underlying variable may be the lack of institutionalized, country-level interventions to address gender equality, such as legislated gender quotas for legislative bodies and corporate boards of directors. An exception is recently passed Senate Bill 826, which required publicly traded companies headquartered in the state to have at least one woman on their board of directors by year end 2019, with a requirement to have larger ratios met by 2021 (Piscopo, 2018). As an anomaly, the US ranks at the bottom of comparable countries in terms of its lack of provision of a universal legal right to early childhood education or any form of universal paid parental leave (Livingston, 2016; Whitehurst, 2017). Yet even in European countries with more progressive and aggressive policy interventions, including family-friendly provisions and labor market laws covering gender equity, motherhood penalties stemming from the inherent bias in the system continue to limit women's progress in the workforce (Iverson & Rosenbluth, 2010). In both the US and Canada, "women-owned enterprises are less likely to benefit from government-funded small business and innovation support services compared to male-owned enterprises" (Orser Elliott, & Cukler, 2019, 6; citing Amezcua & McKelvie, 2011; Brookfield, 2017).

8.4.2 Interventions into Gender Equality in Entrepreneurship

Across the globe, politicians and their agents have developed policies, programming, and initiatives to promote entrepreneurial activity as an economic development strategy (Auerswald, 2015; Isenberg, 2014). At the local as well as the regional and federal levels, governments and governmental agencies have invested considerable effort in developing the local conditions, programming, and supportive policies to encourage entrepreneurship, innovation, and dynamic economies (Brush et al., 2019; Isenberg, 2010; Stam & Spigel, 2016). Institutional, sociocultural, and economic variables heavily impact the strength and quality of entrepreneurial ecosystems (Brown & Mason, 2017), gender as a root cause is often omitted (Brush et al., 2019). Scholars find "persistent gender bias" in economic development policy and the ways in which policymakers talk about entrepreneurship that "perpetuates hetero-normative assumptions that women are failed or reluctant subjects" (Harrison, & Leitch, 2019: 460; also Ahl & Marlow, 2012; Ahl & Nelson, 2015; Ely & Meyerson, 2000; McAdam, 2013). Given that "regulatory institutions can have a hidden gender dimension which reduces the feasibility and desirability of entrepreneurship for women" (Brush et al., 2019: 397), impactful interventions would unhide the gender-related causes behind what are framed as women's individual choices.

In the developing world, many economic development strategies focus on empowering impoverished women through promoting microenterprise and microlending. This predominant economic development strategy receives broad support from world economic, health, and development organizations and the policymakers and funders that support them. Yet limiting the conceptualization of women to need-driven subsistence "entrepreneurs" has the unfortunate consequence of aggravating the dichotomization of women and men into separate entrepreneurial domains, with men continuing to dominate the high-growth, opportunity-based world. The types of women-led businesses this conceptualization is thought to be best suited to are subsistence-related, craft-based, micro, small and marginal businesses, largely in feminized industries such as caregiving and retail (Clark Muntean & Ozkazanc-Pan, 2015). The metacommunication in our narratives about gender and entrepreneurial fit and in the actual programming and policies across the globe is that women require empowerment, saving, and fixing, while men deserve attention for their innovative and high-growth potential and are a better fit for technology entrepreneurship given their dominance in the STEM fields. Further, men dominate in their role as financiers who do the empowering through their microlending programs as well as their role in funding high-growth ventures.

Cautionary tales abound surrounding well-intentioned policy interventions aimed at encouraging women's entrepreneurship. The root cause of unintended consequences in these cases ultimately lies in the ways in which entrepreneurs are "portrayed as disembodied, sex-less and gender-less" in the heteronormative and gender-blind approaches to the development of entrepreneurial ecosystems (McAdam, Harrison, & Leitch, 2019: 470). For example, women-only networks are an established policy intervention across multiple jurisdictions (McAdam, Harrison, & Leitch, 2019; see also EU, 2015; OECD, 2004). The intentional top-down creation of formal women-only networks, combined with teaching women that they have to learn and play by the dominant rules of the game, has been shown to have the effect of generating gender capital that leads to gender inequality: women-only entrepreneurial networks create the situation in which women are "unable to access sufficient economic, social, cultural and symbolic capital, restricting their ability to establish credibility as field players" (McAdam, Harrison, & Leitch, 2019: 470). The result is further isolation, ghettoization, and underrepresentation in the entrepreneurial ecosystem (McAdam, Harrison, & Leitch, 2019). Thus, policy initiatives that are gender-blind, on the one hand, or gender-attentive but misguided, on the other hand, are largely ineffective and serve to reinforce and reproduce masculinity that advantages male entrepreneurs.

Recent gender and entrepreneurship scholarship argues that women as a category do not need to be "fixed" and that women are not in deficit with respect to their capacities as entrepreneurs relative to men (Ahl, 2004). To the contrary, many scholars have argued that systemic, institutional, and cultural phenomena are squarely at the root of the gender inequality that we observe in entrepreneurial ecosystems. Summing up these findings, Brush et al. conclude:

Research has indicated quite a few regulatory, normative, and cultural-cognitive institutions with a potential gender impact. These include the constitution providing for gender equality in society; labor market rules giving equal access to employment positions; family and tax policies, such as specific tax regulations and the overall infrastructure for childcare; and property rights that may allow or prevent female ownership of land; together with the predominant gender ideology and gender stereotypes in a particular society.

(2019: 398)

Policy recommendations in the women's entrepreneurship literature continue to focus on developing programming, such as mentorship programs, training programs, and advising for individual women as a subcategory, which in itself assumes that women are at a deficit relative to their comparable male counterparts, while ignoring structural, systemic, institutionalized, and cultural barriers to women's equality. As Foss et al. note, "noticeably absent (are) suggestions for *actually changing policy*, such as new legislation, gender quotas, new government purchasing rules, or changes to the welfare systems – suggestions that might add value to the entrepreneurial ecosystem" (2019: 421). These deficits in attending to gender are magnified post-COVID-19, when policymakers' interventions across countries to attend to the economic impact of stay-at-home orders have consistently been blind to, discriminative of, or hostile toward women-owned businesses (DIRI, 2020). Leading scholars of women's entrepreneurship emphasize the need for gender-aware policy formulation and government responses to the crisis that include attention to societal attitudes, structural barriers that more negatively impact female founders and self-employed women, and the increased vulnerability of the most physically embodied work, such as caregiving, retail, and personal services, where women are overrepresented relative to men (DIRI, 2020). Scholars also stress that government policy must conduct gender-based analysis, make significant investments, and provide clear supports to female entrepreneurs in order to prevent the widening of the gender gap in entrepreneurship given the gendered precariousness of their enterprising.[4]

In sum, the capacities and ambitions of women as successful entrepreneurs, managers, and leaders in lucrative industries, including technology entrepreneurship, banking and finance, and advanced manufacturing, are not fundamentally dissimilar from those of men who currently occupy the C-suites and boards and who benefit from their dominance in leadership and decision-making roles. Instead, the culprits are damaging stereotypes and harmful perceptions of powerful women and women leaders, as well as structural, cultural, and institutional barriers to their equality. This recent line of argument suggests that the responsibility for the full inclusion of women at the apex of social, economic, and political power requires reassignment away from individual women or women as a disadvantaged interest group/minority category. What is required is a concomitant assignment of responsibility to the men – individually and collectively – who benefit from retention of their privilege through enforcement of the status quo, thereby excluding women's rise and full equality at the table. Furthermore, the field needs to shift to comprehensive, ambitious, and targeted recommendations for policymakers going forward. For example, Rosa and Dawson (2006: 363, cited in Foss et al., 2019: 421) note that there is no existing policy on, nor has there been any effort to draw attention to policymakers about, the anomaly of how gender impacts the process of academic spin-offs and commercialization within universities. In a similar vein, Gupta, Goktan, and Gunay (2014) note the need for "public policy aimed at eliminating gender stereotypes in the popular press and mass media to level the playing field," while Jayawarna, Rouse, and Macpherson (2014) refer to how class intersects with gender and "recommend governments to provide child care in order to make it possible for the less privileged to engage in entrepreneurship" (Foss et al., 2019: 421).

---

[4] Women's Enterprise Policy Group, 2020 (see DIRI 6.24.2020 slides).

8.5   BRINGING IT ALL TOGETHER: BUILDING INCLUSIVE ENTREPRENEURIAL ECOSYSTEMS

An example of how to reframe the research questions and problems, and how the focal point of the research itself is gendered in a way that continues to systemically disadvantage women, lies in how we problematize the gender gap in equity funding. The problem: Brush (2014) found that of all US venture capital-funded businesses (2011–2013) only 15 percent had a single woman on the executive team, while only 3 percent had a woman as CEO (Brush et al., 2019). Brush et al. (2019: 394) cite statistics indicating that "of 43,008 global technology companies with founders achieving initial funding between 2009 and 2017, about 16 percent had one female founder" (it is assumed that the rest had zero female founders, and not multiple female founders). The vast majority of approaches that identify the root of these problems and the research questions formulated focus on disparities or deficits in women as individuals. Existing theories and research questions focus on how women lack important types of capital or resources, how they lack the same skill sets, dispositions, risk profiles, and intentions as men. Further, these explanations focus on women's choices of industry, business model, funding source, and growth objectives, as if these were cleanly endogenous and natural – that is, emanating intrinsically or fundamentally from the woman herself. Such approaches too often tend to essentialize and naturalize women as being lesser than or lacking as potentially high-growth, high-performance entrepreneurs. In other words, how we "scientifically" study women entrepreneurs and the societal discourse surrounding how we talk about women in relation to entrepreneurship reproduces their inequality (Ahl, 2004). Reframing the problem looks like this: reformulating the research question to ask: Why do venture capitalists fail to invest in worthy women-led ventures? (Brush et al., 2019). Theories that explain these supply side issues would focus on the implicit biases, faulty decision-making, and gendered treatment of women at each stage of the entrepreneurial process, by (mostly) men.

Solutions emanating from these findings might look like: sophisticated implicit gender bias training for decision makers, including investors and heads of ESOs, and designing transparency, accountability, and performance metrics for resolving these biases and producing gender equity in outcomes.

Activists, organizations, and their leaders hold the potential to work together to foster environments and cultures that are welcoming to female entrepreneurs. ESOs in particular play a critical role in shaping the culture and experiences of entrepreneurs in the ecosystem. Given their mission to connect entrepreneurs with important resources, including access to networks, mentors, professional services, human capital, and financing to launch and grow their enterprises, ESOs may act as connectors, advocates, and incubators that equalize the playing field or, alternatively, as gatekeepers and enforcers of the status quo, which privileges men as entrepreneurs. For example, in high-growth and technology-focused business incubators and accelerator programs and spaces, "stereotypical gendered expectations surrounding high technology venturing reproduces masculine norms for entrepreneurial behavior" (Brush et al., 2019 citing Marlow & McAdam, 2012; see also Ozkazanc-Pan & Clark Muntean, 2018). Leaders in these organizations that support entrepreneurs should, then, be held to account for their expectations, norms, and cultures that skew outcomes to disadvantage women relative to men. Leaders and activists together need to attend as well to the "policy dimension of entrepreneurial ecosystems (which) continues to be underplayed," including specified targets, functions within government, and legislative intervention that is "immediately actionable" (Foss et al., 2019: 422).

Closing the well-documented gender gap in equity finance will require multiple interventions at all levels and across all domains in the pipeline. Women-backed investment funds and other funds are starting to focus investments into women-founded companies and startup teams with female CEOs and gender-balanced boards (Hoey, 2018). The gender composition of prominent private equity firms, venture capital firms, and angel investor networks will need to substantively change in order for systemic change to occur. Further, men in power on existing male-dominant boards and making the decisions who to fund and who not to will need to be transformed in terms of their awareness of gender issues, their commitment to eliminating the gender gap, and their willingness to be transparent and held accountable for real change.

For all ESOs, a recommended first step is to assess current and past performance through gathering data and mapping the networks in the entrepreneurial ecosystem. This involves investigating the gender balance in coworking spaces, incubators, accelerator programs, and events, such as hackathons, pitch parties, and startup weekends. Further, the leadership offices, management teams, boards of directors, and advisory boards should be assessed for their own performance on gender inclusion. If these spaces are dominated by men, then the likelihood of ESOs exceling at serving women will be greatly reduced due to homophily and gendered network effects. Thus, resolving the gender gaps in entrepreneurship requires strategic formulations and changes to entrepreneurial ecosystems that clearly include metrics and accountability measures, in which "targeted outcomes and responsibilities are clearly defined and monitored" (Foss et al., 2019: 422).

Additionally, ESOs need to identify the change-makers, resisters, partners, and advocates. Crucial decision makers, investors, influencers, and gatekeepers represent nodes in a network and thus are central to affecting change. While the gender of these individuals is important to note, their acknowledgment of the challenge women face in entrepreneurship relative to men and their willingness to act at their own ESOs and in the community are paramount. This requires having conversations with leaders about their diversity and inclusion goals and experiences, and assessing their attitudes, assumptions, and intentions. It should not be assumed that all women are gender aware or that simply the presence of a gender-identified woman will itself automatically lead to better performance with respect to gender inclusion. Women as well as men may need to be educated about the ways in which entrepreneurship as practiced and supported may be gendered in such a way that disadvantages women. In addition, enlightened men and male allies play a critical role in their capacity to amplify inclusion efforts and to move the community toward closing the gender gap (Ozkazanc-Pan, Knowlton, & Clark Muntean, 2017).

Furthermore, leaders should set SMART (specific, measurable, achievable, realistic, and time bound) goals and be held accountable for their progress on meeting these targets (Doran, 1981). Depending on the mission and role of the particular ESO, metrics might include dollars invested, entrepreneurs mentored, program participants, event attendees, loan recipients – all disaggregated by gender. Gender-aware practices include being mindful of who is being portrayed as an entrepreneur, investor, mentor, and leader. Websites, promotional materials, flyers, and social media should be checked to ensure women are in equivalent proportion to men. Mentors, advisors, panelists, and presenters should also be intentionally balanced in their composition.

Given policy is a context-specific force embedded in a nation's or region's institutional frameworks, legal and regulatory interventions are critical tools for influencing entrepreneurial behavior at the macro level (Foss et al., 2019; Welter, 2011). Recent work shifts the gaze from fixing the individual women entrepreneurs to addressing systemic, structural, and cultural bias and barriers in the entire entrepreneurial ecosystem and the culture in which it is embedded. The ecosystem concept enables scholars, policymakers, and practitioners to recognize the interdependence among actors, ventures, and organizations and design policy interventions to address inequities from a more accurate, nuanced, and complex perspective (Foss et al., 2019). This body of work identifies the ways in which women are disadvantaged in many aspects of the entrepreneurial process, including at the individual, organizational, and institutional levels (Brush et al., 2019).

There is a stark disconnect between feminist theorizing that seeks "to explain how societal and structural conditions affect women in the labor market and in organizations" and the existing sole focus on "individual level remedies" along with the absence of policy recommendations that would address structural-level problems (Acker, 2008; Ahl & Nelson, 2015; Foss et al., 2019: 423; Kvidal & Ljunggren, 2014). This is perhaps even more surprising given the field's acknowledgement that "policy is the most powerful and hence, the most important ecosystem component" (Mazzarol, 2014; Stam, 2015) "because its inherent sub-policies and scope of influence overlap with other ecosystem components" (Foss et al., 2019: 423). The design and introduction of initiatives to close the gender gap in entrepreneurship, therefore, must shift dramatically in order to effectively address the major culprits behind the sticky gender gap: that is, the systemic, cultural, and structural issues embedded in the entrepreneurial ecosystem that privilege men and disadvantage women.

Policymakers must begin by debunking the myth of meritocracy and rejecting the common assumption that there exists a level playing field and that all types of capital are equally accessible to all without sex or gender being an issue. Failure to take these initial steps and to deeply examine "both the process and content of policy interventions" can serve to perpetuate men's structural advantages while reproducing "the idea that women are a problem to be fixed" (Feng, 2015; McAdam, Harrison, & Leitch, 2019: 471). In scholarship, public policy, and program design across entrepreneurial ecosystems, there is consistent and an exclusive focus on women, the female gender, and the feminine as being the problem. For instance, "the emphasis on training women serves to reproduce the second-ordering of women that characterizes so much of the gender research in entrepreneurship" (Ahl, 2006; Foss et al., 2019: 423). Overall, the focus on "fixing the women" serves to silence and make invisible the dominance, privilege, and assumed norm of the male entrepreneur and the preference for the masculine style (e.g. in pitching). A revolutionary approach would flip this on its head and interrogate the assumed superiority of the masculine. For example, scholars would research the negative impacts of hyper-confidence among male entrepreneurs, deficits in mostly male networks, and negative outcomes that arise by mostly men receiving venture capital and heading the unicorns that receive this oversized investment, rather than researching the negative impacts of relatively lower confidence or risk tolerance among women, assuming women-only networks are the best strategy for addressing the gender gap, and celebrating the very small percentages of women that succeed in the male-dominated domain.

Furthermore, it is important for change-makers to realize that "women" are not a homogenous group. One-size-fits-all approaches and policies that are offered in isolation have been found to be ineffective (Foss et al., 2019; Mason & Brown, 2014). Women come from a variety of experiences and contexts, and they differ in their needs at the micro, meso, and macro levels. The cultural component in entrepreneurial ecosystems is both highly influential and resistant to rapid change. Despite challenges involved in changing long-held beliefs, attitudes, norms, and customs in a society, a holistic approach would tackle cultural elements that disadvantage women and negatively impact their entrepreneurial outcomes. Two categories of intervention offer promise: legal/regulatory solutions and shifting cultural conventions through grassroots movements and community leader contracting. Cultural practices harmful to females such as foot binding and female genital mutilation have been successfully mitigated through both types of intervention.

In sum, leaders can instigate positive changes in awareness, attitudes, and practices both inside and outside of their respective organizations. This begins with publicly expressing commitment to these changes and then executing a clear strategy and action plan. Within the organization, this can include implicit bias assessment and training, educational programming on best practices, and circulation of research findings, case studies, and exemplar models of inclusive organizations and communities. Much work is also needed to shift the culture and remove systemic barriers at the macro level. Activist approaches such as campaigns to hold the media responsible for who is portrayed as a successful entrepreneur and holding organizers to account for including women as keynotes and panelists are also effective grassroots interventions.

8.6 NEW DIRECTIONS FOR THEORIZING ENTREPRENEURIAL ECOSYSTEMS

Based on our fieldwork and analysis, we suggest several new directions for scholarship attending to entrepreneurial ecosystems, and most notably we suggest that the siloed approach of looking at gender only in respect to women or creating parallel research streams that do not change or challenge existing gendered norms and assumptions in the entrepreneurship field are quite problematic. We start with considerations around the study of the "gender gap" in entrepreneurship to suggest that the very conceptualization of it has to change. For instance, effective policy focused on women's entrepreneurship is a critical component of thriving entrepreneurial ecosystems, enhancing economic development through the resources they provide female entrepreneurs (i.e. mentors, financing, business development training) as well as providing women access to networks and markets (Foss et al., 2019; Kantis & Federico, 2012). Yet in a systematic literature review, Foss et al. (2019) found that the body of research on women's entrepreneurship over the past thirty years offers only vague and conservative policy implications. Even when analyzing feminist theoretical perspectives applied to study the gender gap in entrepreneurship – namely those of feminist empiricism, feminist standpoint theory, and post-structural feminism – Foss et al. (2019) found that irrespective of the theoretical stance, the policy analysis and recommendations still remained sparce and limited. What has been consistently recommended in the field of women's entrepreneurship, even in scholarship with a critical stance, is developing the skills of individual women through education and training programs (Foss et al., 2019). As the authors note, this constitutes a universal and dominant recommendation that implies women need to be "fixed," rather than recommending that the systemic, structural, and cultural gender biases that constitute barriers to women's equality of entrepreneurial outcomes relative to men need to be fixed. Other research suggests women can experience a multitude of explicit and implicit ways in which their competence is questioned or they are assumed to be ignorant during entrepreneurial training programs (Knowlton et al., 2015). In all, individualizing inequality in the domain of entrepreneurship does not yield institutional or organizational change that can impact the opportunity structures of economic development. Rather, scholarship must attend to the simultaneous and concurrent ways in which gender gaps take shape, with impacts that are felt globally and across economies.

That is, given gender gaps are endemic to entrepreneurial ecosystems across the globe, new directions for research should focus on how to remove structural barriers, shift cultural norms, address implicit gender bias, and develop skills and capacities of decision makers who act as gatekeepers to women rising to the top. In other words, removing gendered barriers to entrepreneurship should be an important scholarly ambition across the domain of entrepreneurship scholars, rather than assumed to be the sole responsibility of those focusing on gender. As an example of a public policy that addresses structural barriers to women's equality in entrepreneurship, programs and subsidies that support childcare encourage and facilitate women's participation in entrepreneurship and in the broader economy (Brush & Greene, 2015; Elam & Terjesen, 2010). And this kind of consideration should be included in discussions around what makes an entrepreneurial ecosystem successful in terms of formal institutional factors that support entrepreneurship; currently, such conversations only take shape in relation to women and entrepreneurship, not in the context of broader discussions around entrepreneurship as a highly socialized economic activity. (See Chapter 6 for discussion on different types of ecosystems and mechanisms for change.) For example, in a multi-country comparative analysis of the institutional and cultural factors that lead to more opportunity-based entrepreneurial activity among women, Clark Muntean (2013) found the greater the women's legal and social status, institutional presence, and economic empowerment, the greater the support for women to exploit market opportunities and effectively translate their ideas, creativity, and skills into high-potential, high-growth ventures. Specific recommendations resulting from this study include improving access to collateral and, ultimately, business loans by strengthening the property rights of women, increasing women's representation at the top in all levels of society (including banking, government, academia, and business firms), and developing policies and programming that intentionally empower women and drive their economic equality with men (Clark Muntean, 2013). Countries that are effective in these institutional measures are more likely to yield positive results for all in the form of greater job creation, prosperity, and greater equality for girls and women.

Beyond the ways that ESOs can engage in practices toward gender equality in the context of entrepreneurship, this text also offers insights for how actors in entrepreneurial ecosystems are theorized and studied and how policies for inclusive economic development can be realized if gender is understood as an organizing principle of society and, hence, of ecosystems. For policymakers, creating and supporting policies that can support economic development in an inclusive fashion has recently meant the emergence of business-friendly policies (i.e. ease of starting a business, regulations, availability of real estate, tax incentives, etc.) that generally deploy public funds to spur entrepreneurship activities. Such efforts were most readily visible in the competitive ways in which cities tried to lure the second HQ for Amazon in the hopes that it would create jobs and have positive spillover effects. These approaches are based on the assumptions that the benefits of economic development policies by way of entrepreneurship will benefit *all* entrepreneurs. In turn, the creation of new ventures will create new jobs and economic opportunities in the city, as businesses in retail, service, and food, among other sectors, will emerge to support the core firms. This assumes that all actors in ecosystems are homogenous and act in ways that are similar. There is little consideration of the ways in which ecosystem actors, such as entrepreneurs, differ on various dimensions across identity, experience, practices, and networks.

Moreover, there is little examination of whether and how supporting particular kinds of startups and ventures, such as those in the high-tech sector, really provides benefits for other sectors and types of workers. Feminist research on political economy sheds light on these issues by highlighting the "who, what and how in the relationship between social, political and economic structures of power, resources and access to them" (Isakovic, 2018: 2). In the context of entrepreneurship and entrepreneurial ecosystems, gender, power relations, and social structures are critical considerations when it comes to how and why certain groups continue to be marginalized in resource-rich contexts. For example, given that the high-tech sector is predominantly White and male, supporting the growth of this kind of business may not necessarily spur inclusive economic growth, as is evidenced in various innovation districts in the US (i.e. Kendall Square in Cambridge). These kinds of efforts generally yield a growth in income inequality, as wealth becomes concentrated in particular sectors and locations in the city while housing and transportation costs in the "tech boom" area skyrocket. By adopting a feminist and critical approach, our contributions are to highlight how existing scholarship in the domain of entrepreneurial ecosystems not only misses these complexities but also does not consider them as being within their domain. We cannot disagree more, as the very funding of particular kinds of ventures over others is itself already worth examining in terms of whose interests are being served by the funding and scaling of such firms, as are the kinds of ideas, ventures, and solutions to ongoing social, economic, and political problems that remain invisible, underfunded, or ignored in the existing economic system that predominantly seeks and supports high-tech, high-growth ventures.

Building on this point, for policymakers and ESOs who want to provide resources and mentorship to entrepreneurs, understanding how differences create opportunities for some entrepreneurs while they also work to distance others from the resourcing organizations of the ecosystem is vital. As our work shows (Ozkazanc-Pan Knowlton, & Clark Muntean, 2017), gender is a differentiator for how entrepreneurs organize and access resources, how they connect with and become engaged with ESOs, and how they network in the context of sociocultural gender norms. The simultaneous interplay and relational dynamics of individual, organizational, and societal factors create entrepreneurial ecosystems that are not necessarily neutral in terms of how they are organized, replicated, and resourced. Gender becomes an organizing principle in regard to how resources are distributed, how information is exchanged, and how networks are both established and accessed in entrepreneurial ecosystems. Stemming from this gendered organization of entrepreneurial ecosystem, women's experiences can be negatively and dramatically different than men's, despite existing in the same ecosystem. Thus, it is vital to differentiate ecosystem actors in the ways they are gendered, embodied, and relational. We have aimed to demonstrate how and why these differences take shape and their consequences with respect to experiences and access throughout the book.

Similar to other scholars' recommendations, future research should focus on the intersection of the entrepreneurial process and cultural and institutional contexts, and how these shape the outcomes of entrepreneurial efforts in ways that systematically disadvantage women relative to men (Aldrich & Martinez, 2007; Foss et al., 2019). Yet our contribution to such research endeavors is to create awareness around the ways gendered social relations and structures impact identities, interactions, and institutions, particularly in the context of entrepreneurial ecosystems. Such a holistic approach to strategically developing an ecosystem acknowledges interdependencies among actors and contextualizes local culture and systemic conditions (Foss et al., 2019). To this end, researchers should progress toward suggested policy solutions that attend to the "regulatory and contextual policy components" of entrepreneurial ecosystems and which directly involve "legislation, market regulation, taxation, [and] welfare provision," which scholars have tended to avoid in the past (Foss et al., 2019: 422). Policy changes should therefore be specific, targeted, and designed with attentiveness to the interconnecting and interacting components in the local/regional ecosystem (Foss et al., 2019; Isenberg, 2010) such that a supportive environment for women is created that puts their chances of entrepreneurial success on par with men. This is not only a good policy for gender equality but it is a good policy for inclusive economic development. Globally, "gender inequality in earnings could lead to losses in wealth of $23,620 per person" and "human capital wealth could increase by 21.7 percent globally, and total wealth by 14.0 percent with gender equality in earnings" (Wodon & de la Brière, 2018). Given the finding that entrepreneurial ecosystems are gendered (Small Business Economics, 2019: special issue; Gicheva & Link, 2015), politicians, policymakers, and other leaders need to design formal public policies that effectively address and resolve existing rules of behavior, processes, mechanisms, and contexts that continue to exclude and disadvantage women relative to men (Foss et al., 2019). Such an approach can create inclusive economic development and contribute significantly to the well-being of the economy and society.

In all, how entrepreneurial ecosystems are theorized requires paying attention to the way actors are conceptualized. From our perspective, actors are gendered, embodied, and relational individuals who derive strategies, experiences, and practices based on their identity and networks in the context of overarching societal gender norms. Such norms are predicated on ideas of who can be what kind of entrepreneur. In the world of entrepreneurship, gender norms and gendered practices marginalize women from information, access, and networks that are valuable resources to their ventures. For scholars, understanding how the very dynamics and relational aspects of entrepreneurial ecosystems are already gendered and embodied can provide new insights for research, as they recognize that actors are not homogeneous. Guided by gender as a framework for re-theorizing entrepreneurial ecosystems, the field of entrepreneurship can begin to provide clear and relevant policy solutions toward ending gendered economic inequality in cities and regions across the world.

REFERENCES

Acker, J. (2008). Feminist theory's unfinished business: Comment on Andersen. *Gender & Society, 22*(1): 104–108.

Ahl, H. (2004). *The scientific reproduction of gender inequality: A discourse analysis of research texts on women's entrepreneurship.* Copenhagen: Copenhagen Business School Press.

Ahl, H. (2006). Why research on women entrepreneurs needs new directions. *Entrepreneurship Theory and Practice, 30*(5): 595–621.

Ahl, H., & Marlow, S. (2012). Exploring the dynamics of gender, feminism and entrepreneurship: advancing debate to escape a dead end?. *Organization, 19*(5): 543–562.

Ahl, H., & Nelson, T. (2015). How policy positions women entrepreneurs: A comparative analysis of state discourse in Sweden and the United States. *Journal of Business Venturing, 30*(2): 273–291.

Aldrich, H. E., & Martinez, M. A. (2007). Many are called, but few are chosen: An evolutionary perspective for the study of entrepreneurship. In Á. Cuervo, D. Ribeiro, & S. Roig (Eds.), *Entrepreneurship* (pp. 293–311). Berlin, Heidelberg: Springer.

Amezcua, A. S., & McKelvie, A. (2011). Incubation for all? Business incubation and gender differences in new firm performance (summary). *Frontiers of Entrepreneurship Research, 31*(8): 3.

Auerswald, P. E. (2015). Enabling entrepreneurial ecosystems: Insights from ecology to inform effective entrepreneurship policy. *Kauffman Foundation Research Series on city, metro, and regional entrepreneurship.* Available at: www.kauffman.org/wp-content/uploads/2019/12/enabling_entrepreneurial_ecosystems.pdf (accessed July 15, 2019).

Brookfield Institute of Innovation + Entrepreneurship (2017). Empowering women in entrepreneurship and social capital enterprise design workshop. Available at http://brookfieldinstitute.ca/?s=women4 (accessed June 20, 2020)

Brown, R., & Mason, C. (2017). Looking inside the spiky bits: A critical review and conceptualization of entrepreneurial ecosystems. *Small Business Economics, 49*(1): 11–30.

Brush, C. G. (2014). Exploring the concept of an entrepreneurship education ecosystem. In *Innovative pathways for university entrepreneurship in the 21st century* (Advances in the Study of Entrepreneurship, Innovation and Economic Growth, Vol. 24, pp. 25–39). Bingley: Emerald Group Publishing Limited.

Brush, C. G., Edelman, L. F., Manolova, T., & Welter, F. (2019). A gendered look at entrepreneurship ecosystems. *Small Business Economics, 53*(2): 393–408.

Brush, C. G., & Greene, P. G. (2015). Women's entrepreneurship. *Wiley Encyclopedia of Management*, 1–5. Available at https://doi.org/10.1002/9781118785317.weom030101 (accessed July 15, 2019).

Catalyst (2021). Women in the workforce: Global – A quick take. Available at www.catalyst.org/research/women-in-the-workforce-global/ (accessed April 17, 2021).

Clark Muntean, S. (2013). Wind beneath my wings: Policies promoting high-growth oriented women entrepreneurs. *International Journal of Gender and Entrepreneurship*, 5(1): 36.

Clark Muntean, S., & Ozkazanc-Pan, B. (2015). A gender integrative conceptualization of entrepreneurship. *New England Journal of Entrepreneurship*, 18(1): 27–40.

Clark Muntean, S., & Ozkazanc-Pan, B. (2016). Feminist perspectives on social entrepreneurship: Critique and new directions. *International Journal of Gender and Entrepreneurship*, 8(3): 221–241.

Clark Muntean, S. Ozkazanc-Pan, B., & Still, M. (2018). Work-life balance programs as a case of institutionalized and socially entrenched gender inequality. *Inequality, Institutions and Organizations Conference*, Vancouver, BC, June 6–8, 2013.

Dahlerup, D. & Freidenvall, L. (2005). Quotas as a 'fast track' to equal representation for women. *International Feminist Journal of Politics*, 7(1): 26–48.

DIRI – Diana International Research Institute Roundtable (2020). COVID-19 impact on women's entrepreneurship research: New questions, approaches, and methods. Webinar attended by Clark Muntean, S., June 24, 2020.

Doran, G. T. (1981). There's a S.M.A.R.T. way to write management's goals and objectives. *Management Review*, 70(11): 35–36.

Elam, A., & Terjesen, S. (2010). Gendered institutions and cross-national patterns of business creation for men and women. *The European Journal of Development Research*, 22(3): 331–348.

Ely, R. J., & Meyerson, D. E. (2000). Theories of gender in organizations: A new approach to organizational analysis and change. *Research in Organizational Behavior*, 22: 103–151.

Epsing-Andersen, G. (2009). *Incomplete revolution: Adapting welfare states to women's new roles*. Cambridge: Polity Press.

EU (2015). Promoting entrepreneurship: Support networks for women. Available at http://ec.europa.eu/growth/smes/promoting-entrepreneurship/we-work-for/women/support-networks/index_en.htm (accessed June 20, 2020).

Exley, C. L., Niederle, M., & Vesterlund, L. (2016). Knowing when to ask: The cost of leaning in. NBER Working Paper No. 22961, pp. 1–53.

Feng, L. (2015). Your rolodex matters, but by how much depends on your gender. Available at http://knowledge.insead.edu/career/your-rolodex-matters-but-by-how-much-depends-on-your-gender-3862#dhrXj1CeKITM4qq5.99 (accessed April 11, 2017).

Foss, L., Henry, C., Ahl, H., & Mikalsen, G. H. (2019). Women's entrepreneurship policy research: A 30-year review of the evidence. *Small Business Economics*, *53*(2): 409–429.

Gicheva, D., & Link, A. N. (2015). The gender gap in federal and private support for entrepreneurship. *Small Business Economics, 45*(4): 729–733.

Gupta, V. K., Goktan, A. B., & Gunay, G. (2014). Gender differences in evaluation of new business opportunity: A stereotype threat perspective. *Journal of Business Venturing, 29*(2): 273–288.

Hoey, K. (2018). 10 Female founded venture capital funds you should have in your network. *Forbes.* July 12, 2018. Available at www.forbes.com/sites/kellyhoey/2018/07/12/ten-female-founded-venture-capital-funds-you-should-have-in-your-network/#4220eef97565 (accessed November 11, 2018).

Isakovic, N. P. (2018). A WILPF guide to feminist political economy. *Women's International League for Peace & Freedom.* Available at www.wilpf.org/wp-content/uploads/2019/07/WILPF_Feminist-Political-Economy-Guide.pdf (accessed March 14, 2020).

Isenberg, D. J. (2010). How to start an entrepreneurial revolution. *Harvard Business Review, 88*(6): 40–50.

Isenberg, D. J. (2014). What an entrepreneurship ecosystem actually is. *Harvard Business Review, 5*: 1–7.

Iverson, T., & Rosenbluth, F. (2010). *Women, work, and politics: The political economy of gender inequality.* New Haven, CT: Yale University Press.

Jayne, M. E. A., & Dipboye, J. (2004). Leveraging diversity to improve business performance: Research findings and recommendations for organizations. *Human Resource Management, 43*(4): 409–424.

Jaeger, J. (2018). The "Weinstein Clause": M&A deals in the #MeToo era. October 12, 2018, *Compliance Week*, published by Wilmington plc. Available at www.complianceweek.com/news/news-article/the-weinstein-clause-ma-deals-in-the-metoo-era#.W-h-RpNKiUk (accessed November 11, 2018).

Jayawarna, D., Rouse, J., & Macpherson, A. (2014). Life course pathways to business start-up. *Entrepreneurship & Regional Development, 26*(3–4): 282–312.

Kalev, A., Dobbin, F., & Kelly, E. (2006). Best practices or best guesses: Assessing the efficacy of corporate affirmative action and diversity policies. *American Sociological Review, 71*: 589–617.

Kantis, H. D., & Federico, J. S. (2012). Entrepreneurial ecosystems in Latin America: The role of policies. *Liverpool: International Research and Policy Roundtable.* Published by the Ewing Marion Kauffman Foundation.

Knowlton, K., Ozkazanc-Pan, B., Clark Muntean, S., & Motoyama, Y. (2015). Support organizations and remediating the gender gap in entrepreneurial eco-systems: A case study of St. Louis. SSRN. Available at https://ssrn.com/abstract=2685116 (accessed May 27, 2018).

Kvidal, T., & Ljunggren, E. (2014). Introducing gender in a policy programme: A multilevel analysis of an innovation policy programme. *Environment and Planning C: Government and Policy, 32*(1): 39–53.

Livingston, G. (2016). Among 41 nations, U.S. is the outlier when it comes to paid parental leave. Pew Research Center. September 26, 2016. Available at www.pewresearch.org/fact-tank/2016/09/26/u-s-lacks-mandated-paid-parental-leave/ (accessed November 11, 2018).

Lorenzo, R. Voigt, N., Tsusaka, M., Krentz, M., & Abouzahr, K. (2018). How diverse leadership teams boost innovation. *Boston Consulting Group.* January 23, 2018. Available at www.bcg.com/en-us/publications/2018/how-diverse-leadership-teams-boost-innovation.aspx (accessed November 13, 2018).

Lyness, K., & Heilman, M. (2006). When fit is fundamental: Performance evalu-ations and promotions of upper-level female and male managers. *Journal of Applied Psychology, 91*(4): 777.

Marlow, S., & McAdam, M. (2012). Analyzing the influence of gender upon high–technology venturing within the context of business incubation. *Entrepreneurship Theory and Practice, 36*(4): 655–676.

Mason, C., & Brown, R. (2014). Entrepreneurial ecosystems and growth oriented entrepreneurship. *Final Report to OECD, Paris, 30*(1): 77–102.

Mazzarol, T. (2014). Growing and sustaining entrepreneurial ecosystems: What they are and the role of government policy. *Small Enterprise Association of Australia and New Zealand ("SEAANZ") White Paper.*

McAdam, M. (2013). *Female entrepreneurship.* New York: Routledge.

McAdam, M., Harrison, R. T., & Leitch, C. M. (2019). Stories from the field: Women's networking as gender capital in entrepreneurial ecosystems. *Small Business Economics, 53*(2): 459–474.

OECD (2004) Women's entrepreneurship: Issues and policies. Background Report for 2nd OECD Conference of Ministers Responsible for Small and Medium-sized Enterprises (SMEs): Promoting Entrepreneurship and Innovative SMEs in a Global Economy: Towards a More Responsible and Inclusive Globalisation, Istanbul, Turkey, June 3–5, 2004. Available at: www.oecd.org/cfe/smes/31919215.pdf (accessed November 3, 2019).

Orser, B., Elliott, C., & Cukler, W. (2019). Strengthening ecosystem supports for women entrepreneurs. Telfer School of Management, University of Ottawa. Retrieved from Telfer, Ottawa. ca/i2-report at https://telfer.uottawa.ca/assets/

documents/2019/5515_TELFER-Orser-Inclusive-Innovation-report_0419_final-aoda.pdf (accessed June 23, 2020).

Ozkazanc-Pan, B., & Clark Muntean, S. (2018). Networking towards (in) equality: Women entrepreneurs in technology. *Gender, Work & Organization, 25*(4): 379–400.

Ozkazanc-Pan, B., Knowlton, K., & Clark Muntean, S. (2017). Gender inclusion activities in entrepreneurship ecosystems: The case of St. Louis, MO and Boston, MA. SSRN. Available at https://ssrn.com/abstract=2982414 or http://dx.doi.org/10.2139/ssrn.2982414 (accessed July 7, 2019).

Pao, E. (2017). This is how sexism works in Silicon Valley. My lawsuit failed. Others won't. *New York Magazine*, August 21, 2017. Available at www.thecut.com/2017/08/ellen-pao-silicon-valley-sexism-reset-excerpt.html (accessed July 8, 2020)

Piscopo, J. M. (2018). Bringing women to the table in California's corporations. *The Gender Policy Report* published by the University of Minnesota. http://genderpolicyreport.umn.edu/bringing-women-to-the-table-in-californias-corporations/ (accessed August 21, 2018).

Piscopo, J. M., & Clark Muntean, S. (2018). Corporate quotas and symbolic politics in advanced democracies. *Journal of Women, Politics & Policy, 39*(3): 285–309.

Ribberstrom, K. (2013). Using diversity to drive innovation. TEDxSpringfield. December 2, 2013. www.youtube.com/watch?v=7mhKfyRtFB0 (accessed September 23, 2017).

Rosa, P., & Dawson, A. (2006). Gender and the commercialization of university science: Academic founders of spinout companies. *Entrepreneurship and Regional Development, 18*(4): 341–366.

Rouse, Cecilia. (March 31, 2010). "The Economics of Workplace Flexibility". The White House. Blog post. Available at https://obamawhitehouse.archives.gov/blog/2010/03/31/economics-workplace-flexibility (accessed April 17, 2021).

Sandberg, S. (2013). *Lean in: Women, work, and the will to lead.* New York: Random House.

Silva, C., Carter, N., & Beninger, A. (2013). Good intentions, imperfect execution? Women get fewer of the "hot jobs" need to advance. Catalyst, 2012, in *Harvard Business Review* September 2013, p. 87.

SBE (*Small Business Economics*) (2019). Special issue: Women entrepreneurs in ecosystems. *Small Business Economics, 53*(2): 393–546.

Stam, E. (2015). Entrepreneurial ecosystems and regional policy: A sympathetic critique. *European Planning Studies, 23*(9): 1759–1769.

Stam, E., & Spigel, B. (2016). Entrepreneurial ecosystems and regional policy. In *Sage handbook for entrepreneurship and small business* (p. 407, Chapter 21). London: SAGE. doi: 10.4135/9781473984080.n21.

Welter, F. (2011). Contextualizing entrepreneurship – Conceptual challenges and ways forward. *Entrepreneurship Theory and Practice*, 35(1): 165–184.

Whitehurst, G. (2017). Why the federal government should subsidize childcare and how to pay for it. The Brookings Press. March 9, 2017. Available at www .brookings.edu/research/why-the-federal-government-should-subsidize-childcare-and-how-to-pay-for-it/ (accessed November 11, 2018).

Wodon, Q. T., & de la Brière, B. (2018). *Unrealized potential: The high cost of gender inequality in earnings. The cost of gender inequality.* Washington, DC: World Bank. Available at https://openknowledge.worldbank.org/handle/10986/29865 (accessed July 15, 2019).

Index

Printed in the United States
by Baker & Taylor Publisher Services